THE FEMALE BODY
IN MEDICINE AND LITERATURE

T0385541

The Female Body
in Medicine and Literature

Edited by
Andrew Mangham
and
Greta Depledge

LIVERPOOL UNIVERSITY PRESS

First published 2011 by
Liverpool University Press
4 Cambridge Street
Liverpool L69 7ZU

This paperback edition published 2012

British Library Cataloguing-in-Publication Data
A British Library CIP Record is available

ISBN 978-1-84631-852-8

Typeset by Carnegie Book Production, Lancaster
Printed and bound by CPI Group (UK) Ltd, Croydon, CR0 4YY

Contents

Acknowledgements

It is often the way with multi-authored works that original deadlines and completion dates disappear in the mists of time – this collection has been no exception. The editors would like to thank everyone involved with this project for their patience and commitment over the last few years.

We would especially like to thank Anthony Cond and Helen Tookey at Liverpool University Press for their good-natured help and invaluable support with the completion of this project. Many colleagues and friends have offered helpful and insightful comments during the process of bringing this collection together and the editors are particularly grateful to Katherine Inglis for her thoughts on aspects of this collection. We would also like to acknowledge the excellent feedback we received from the anonymous reader at Liverpool University Press.

We would also like to thank Hannah Simpson for demonstrating extraordinary meticulousness and generosity in helping with the formatting of this volume.

It is to our families that we owe the greatest debt of thanks. In the time it has taken to bring this collection to completion, loved ones have been lost and new ones joyfully gained. It is to them that we dedicate this book.

Notes on Contributors

Janice Allan is a Senior Lecturer in the School of English, Sociology, Politics and Contemporary History at the University of Salford, UK. She is the Editor of *Bleak House: A Sourcebook* (Routledge, 2004) and sits on the editorial board of *Clues: a Journal of Detection*. In recent years she has published various articles and chapters on Wilkie Collins, sensation fiction, and its critical reception. She is currently working on *The Sensation Novel Sourcebook* for Liverpool University Press.

Madeleine K. Davies is a Lecturer in the Department of English at the University of Reading, UK, where she specializes in women's writing and feminist theory. Her other research and teaching interests include Margaret Atwood, on whom she has published widely, Virginia Woolf, and ideologies. Madeleine K. Davies has also published extensively in the fields of media studies and modern drama, is the author of *Peter Shaffer: Theatre and Drama*, the Editor of *British Television Drama: Past, Present and Future*, and has published numerous essays in the field of formative, 'one off' television events. She is currently working on a monograph exploring the uses and abuses of feminist theory in academic research and pedagogic practice.

Greta Depledge is an Associate Tutor for the Open University and for the Faculty of Lifelong Learning at Birkbeck College, London. She is a co-founder (with Jane Jordan) of the Victorian Popular Fiction Association. Her main research interests are the nineteenth-century novelist Florence Marryat, the relationship between medicine and literature in the nineteenth century, and crime fiction of the nineteenth and twentieth centuries. She has edited several Florence Marryat novels for Victorian Secrets Publishing House, was an invited speaker at the Reading Festival of Crime Writing (2008 and 2009), and is currently working on a monograph on animal and human vivisection in nineteenth-century literature and culture.

Laurie Garrison is Senior Lecturer in English at the University of Lincoln. She has published on various aspects of Victorian popular and material culture, including a monograph titled *Science, Sexuality and Sensation*

Novels: Pleasures of the Senses (Palgrave, 2010). Current projects include scholarly editions of print texts related to the panorama as well as previously unpublished plays in the Lord Chamberlain's collection.

Joanna Grant is Collegiate Professor and Wandering Scholar for the University of Maryland University College. She has worked in the field since the summer of 2010, teaching in Japan and Kuwait. Her first book, *Modernism's Middle East: Journeys to Barbary*, was published in 2008. She has published numerous critical articles and creative works.

Lori Schroeder Haslem is a Professor of English at Knox College in Illinois, USA. Her publications include several scholarly articles on representations of the female body in plays by Shakespeare, Jonson, and Webster in journals such as *Shakespeare Studies, Modern Philology, The Upstart Crow, English Language Notes* and MLA's *Profession*. She has also published numerous book reviews in *Theater Journal, Renaissance Quarterly* and other publications. More recently she has been researching popular and legal accounts of child victims and witnesses of crime in early modern England alongside the representations of such children in selected Shakespeare plays.

Dominic Janes is a lecturer in the Department of History of Art, Birkbeck College, London. He is a historian of culture, ideas, and the arts who is interested in exploring literary texts and images. He specializes in the study of Christianity in modern Britain and is particularly interested in exploring its connections with the ideas and cultures of antiquity, science, and other religions. His most recent book is *Victorian Reformation: the Fight over Idolatry in the Church of England, 1840–60* (Oxford University Press, 2009).

Emma L. Jones received her PhD from the University of London in 2007 for her thesis 'Abortion in England, 1861–1967'. Since 2006 she has been a Research Associate at the Centre for the History of Science, Technology and Medicine and Wellcome Unit for the History of Medicine at the University of Manchester, UK. She works on the history of abortion, family planning, the NHS, public health, and women's medicine. She is currently engaged in a Wellcome Trust-funded project examining the history of premenstrual syndrome in twentieth-century Britain. Her essay in this volume was completed as part of an ESRC Postdoctoral Fellowship (Award Reference: PTA–026–27–1810).

Karín Lesnik-Oberstein is a Reader in Critical Theory in the Department of English and American Literature at the University of Reading, UK, and the Director of the Department's Centre for International Research in Childhood: Literature, Culture, Media (CIRCL). Her research is in the area of multi- and interdisciplinary critical theory, particularly as it relates to issues of identity. Besides her extensive work on childhood, her previous publications specifically on gender include (as Editor and a contributor) *The Last Taboo: Women and Body Hair* (Manchester University Press, 2006) and the monograph *On Having an Own Child: Reproductive Technologies and the Cultural Construction of Childhood* (London: Karnac Books, 2008).

Pam Lieske is an Associate Professor of English at Kent State University at Trumbull, USA. In addition to teaching various writing and literature courses, she holds research interests in women's literature, eighteenth-century British literature, and the history of science and medicine. Her article on the history of British obstetrical machines, which appears in this anthology, is an outgrowth of her recent project: editing a twelve-volume set of primary facsimile texts on eighteenth-century midwifery and childbirth entitled *Eighteenth-Century British Midwifery* (Pickering and Chatto, 2007–2009).

Andrew Mangham is a lecturer in the Department of English and American Literature at the University of Reading, UK. He specializes in interdisciplinary literary criticism, especially the intersections between medicine, crime and popular fiction in the nineteenth century. His publications include *Violent Women and Sensation Fiction* (2007) and *Wilkie Collins: Interdisciplinary Essays* (2007). He is currently at work on a book on Dickens and anatomical medicine.

Emma L. E. Rees is Deputy Head of English and Senior Lecturer at the University of Chester, UK. Research and teaching interests include gender representation, Shakespeare and early modern studies, and film. Her book *Margaret Cavendish* was published in 2004, and she is currently working on a monograph entitled *Can't: Uncovering the Postmodern Vagina*, which examines how female anatomy is simultaneously displayed and silenced in filmic and literary texts. She has contributed essays to several recent books, including a chapter on Shakespeare and gender for *Rhetorics of Bodily Disease and Health in Medieval and Early Modern England*; a section on Shakespeare and the Renaissance for *Studying Literature*; and a chapter, co-authored with Richard E. Wilson, on Freudian fetishism, in *Led Zeppelin and Philosophy*.

Sheena Sommers is a doctoral candidate at the University of Toronto in the Department of History. She is a recipient of the Master's Graduate Scholarship and Doctoral Scholarship awarded by The Social Science and Humanities Research Council of Canada. Her research interests include the history of the body and medicine and colonialism in the late eighteenth and early nineteenth century.

Susan C. Staub is a professor of English at Appalachian State University in the mountains of North Carolina, USA, where she teaches early modern literature. She has published on various aspects of Renaissance prose, poetry, and culture. Her recent scholarship includes *Nature's Cruel Stepdames*, a study of depictions of murderous women in seventeenth-century news pamphlets, and several essays on motherhood and on gynaecology in the period. Her current project is a book-length study of the cultural significance of the strange story of Anne Greene, of which her essay in this volume is a part.

Carolyn D. Williams is a Senior Lecturer in the Department of English and American Literature at the University of Reading, UK, and a committee member of the Reading University Early Modern Research Centre and the London-based Women's Studies Group, 1500–1837.

1

Introduction

ANDREW MANGHAM

and

GRETA DEPLEDGE

This collection draws on two research contexts that are distinct in their disciplinary character yet linked inexorably in the development of British culture: literature and the history of medicine. Like many of the historicist and interdisciplinary studies that have emerged in recent years, this volume aims to draw on the strengths of two forms of knowledge and their attendant methodological practices in order to provide a thoughtful and productive consideration of the 'treatment' of the female body between, approximately, 1600 and 2000. The positioning of women vis-à-vis the man of science is a subject that enters a busy and exciting field of study: feminist approaches to literature and historical considerations of medicine have, for quite some time now, retained an unyielding focus on the female body.[1] Yet although there have been some excellent discussions of the links between *psychiatric* treatments of women and literature,[2] there remains no single work, to date, that fully explores the impact of women's surgery, gynaecology, and obstetrics on literary production. Nor has there been, conversely, a sustained consideration of how literary trends and styles have shaped the course of gynaecology and other branches of women's medicine. Working at the interface of medical history from another direction (that which acknowledges literature as a key player in the formation of our current understandings of the female body), this volume seeks to augment the existing body of work by stressing the ways in which the science draws upon, modifies, and learns from the 'metaphors, myths, and narrative patterns'[3] of popular literature.

Historical considerations of the development of women's medicine have tended to use literary models sparsely; and when used at all, they have been briefly and inadequately acknowledged as evidence of how a particular development in medicine became *so* pervasive that literary figures exploited it as a means of making their novels marketable and topical.[4] We do not suggest that in many cases this is untrue, but we do aim to underscore the need to accept how the complex intersections between medicine and literature have been of great benefit to the former as well as the latter. Gillian Beer famously observed that the inspired relationship between science and literature has involved intellectual traffic that is 'two-way'.[5] Literature has not only been inspired by medicine but it has also, in turn, *inspired* medicine: in the age of clinics and print technologies Jane Wood observes, 'medicine and literature [have] looked to each other for elucidation and inspiration'.[6]

An emphasis on language and its interpretive qualities is central to any work that crosses the boundaries of medical history and literary criticism. By bringing fresh analysis to both medical and fictional texts in this collection we elucidate alternative readings to well-known literary texts and explore the literary merit and influence of medical treatises in order to provide a more fulsome understanding of women's medicine in the period covered. Arguably it is Dora's case history, as presented by Freud, which best illustrates the literary two-way traffic between literature and medical reportage. The case study of Dora has been subjected to extensive analysis, with many contemporary critics commenting on its potential as a literary work.[7] Freud insists on the medical credibility of this case history: 'I must now turn to consider a further complication to which I should certainly give no space if I were a man of letters engaged upon the creation of a mental state like this for a short story, instead of being a medical man engaged upon its dissection [...] in the world of reality which I am trying to depict here'.[8] That Freud introduces a literary parallel in his case history is most interesting. It is not unreasonable to suggest that, as with much of Freud's oeuvre, fiction influences the writing up of this case history – a case history which in turn influenced the treatment of many patients by legions of Freud's professional followers. He acknowledges, in the prefatory remarks which accompany this case, that he did not take written notes during consultations with Dora 'for fear of shaking the patient's confidence' and that this case history was 'committed to writing from memory', which indicates that a certain literary licence was taken in the transcription of events as Freud remembered them.[9] Indeed, to assist in the interpretation of one incident reported by Dora, Freud writes 'I have formed in my own mind the following reconstruction of the scene'.[10] The influence of literary models seems intrinsic to medical case history.

In a letter to Wilhelm Fliess of 25 January 1900, Freud wrote that he had produced a case history that he wished to publish: 'it is the most subtle thing I have yet written and will produce an even more horrifying effect than usual'.[11] These words could have been penned by a sensation writer talking of a latest novel produced to astonish and shock his or her reading public. However, Freud was referring to an ostensibly scientific case history that he wished to see published in a professional journal, to be read by his peers. Therefore, he bestows on his factual work an adjective that would seem more at home in a review of the latest potboiler. It seems unlikely that fellow psychoanalysts would turn to their professional journals with the expectation of being 'horrified'. This confession of a sensational aspect to his work indicates that Freud was very aware of his 'literary' potential. Even when vouching for the veracity of what he had written Freud undermined his alleged truth: 'my recollection of the case was still fresh and was heightened by my interest in its publication'.[12] Clearly this statement raises as many questions as it solves. If Freud committed this case history to writing because of his desire to publish, both literary endeavour and poetic licence have to be considered when attempting to analyse his analysis. Therefore, it is prudent to take an open-minded, interdisciplinary approach to interpreting some medical treatises.

We must also, always, consider the intended audience for any work of literary production and, while intended audience and *actual* audience can vary for both medical treatises and works of 'fiction', it is important to remember that the medical establishment has been a fairly self-enclosed world. Medical journals and textbooks usually have a medical readership as the target audience. This raises the question of how medical texts, discussed throughout this collection, accrued authority. Ultimately, the aim is for respect and appreciation among peers; authority within society comes as a result of the steadily increasing status of the medical profession throughout history and the ascendancy of the medical profession is given a very clear chronology through the essays included here. The medical writing is, primarily, a discourse between men and, secondarily, a discourse about women. While many may have been read by the lay-reading public and by literary men and women of letters, the sense of competition within the profession, which is displayed in medical writing, indicates that the assumed readership is most likely to have been other medical professionals. To go back to Freud, he wrote in his case history of Dora that 'publication of the case in a purely scientific and technical periodical should, further, afford a guarantee against unauthorized readers'.[13]

We note how, so often, it is women writers who challenge medical authority with their works of fiction. However, in his extensive work on hysteria Mark S. Micale states that, particularly in French fiction, *Madame Bovary* influenced French physicians. He argues that this was because 'of the power of Flaubert's characterisation [and ...] because of the presence of medical personalities in the novel',[14] making the text compulsive reading for physicians who would desire to see how they were portrayed in contemporary fiction. However, Micale believes that any acknowledgement of a literary influence was not forthcoming because of the medical profession's need to enhance the notion of their speciality as 'based on research in pathology and physiology',[15] not in writing fiction. The sense of power that comes with scientific training, providing medical authority, is implicit in much of the medical writing of the time. To acknowledge literary influence would be to undermine the prestige of the profession. We may well see clear evidence of the two-way traffic, but was it acknowledged by contemporaries?

An article in *The Lancet* in 1888 shows that the profession was aware of its depiction in works of fiction in the late nineteenth century. The article praises Dickens, 'who delighted to paint, not average humanities, but oddities, whether amiable or ridiculous, [...] the ludicrous side of medical life', and reveres George Eliot's portrayal of Lydgate in *Middlemarch*, 'a professional portrait of which we may be justly proud'.[16] The writer acknowledges that:

> it is most true that the books we read influence our mental and moral nature as powerfully, though as insensibly, as the air we breathe affects our bodies; and hence the fiction of the day not only reflects, but to no inconsiderable extent moulds, current thought and opinion. It is not, then, a matter of indifference to us that our professional methods, aims and work should be honestly depicted, and not maliciously caricatured, in the pages of a modern novel.[17]

In an article which ostensibly worries that the public may become misinformed on medicine and distrustful of its practitioners due to misrepresentation in fiction, the message is that, inevitably, we are all influenced by what we read. While the writer feigns an air of detachment, it is clear that the medical profession is as susceptible to influence through literature as the lay-reading public. Therefore, perhaps unwittingly, this article provides an implicit justification of Micale's argument, echoed throughout this collection, that the medical profession was influenced by contemporary literature. The piece suggests that the lay reading public are likely to believe that caricatures of the medical profession are true reflections of what they might encounter. Therefore, might not a medical man call to mind the behaviour of a troublesome female character and her maladies in a recently read novel when faced with a patient displaying a baffling plethora of symptoms? It could be that fear of misrepresentation and damage to professional standing kept the medical profession up to date with fictional narratives, thoughts, and suggestions.

The brief nods towards literary appropriations of scientific ideas that are found in historical studies of medicine fail to acknowledge how ideas are transformed, twisted, and manipulated in order to find a place within the literary narrative. Considering the shifts, slippages, and 'creative misprision'[18] that occurs as ideas spread from medical to literary texts is a very important part of reading the complex theoretical history of the female body. In employing the theoretical tools used in literary criticism as well as history, we hope to be better qualified at identifying and exploring the prejudices, ideologies, and fault lines running through the specialized understandings of women.

The history of the female body is a story, we argue, that no single discipline can understand entirely. Instead, it is a complex nexus of intersections and conflicts that can only begin to be referenced by a series of voices, with distinct individualistic aims, methodological approaches, and disciplinary trainings. The essay collection format is ideally suited to perform this enterprise because it provides a platform for a range of distinct voices to comment on a single topic.[19] In his 1969 book *The Archaeology of Knowledge*, Michel Foucault writes about the occurrence of real events and the ways in which history, as a discipline, processes them. His ideas are applicable to the occurrence of a historical *development*, including medical and literary 'treatments' of the female body, and sum up the rationale of *The Female Body in Medicine and Literature*:

> But if we isolate, in relation to the language and to thought, the occurrence of the statement/event, it is not in order to spread over everything a dust of facts. It is in order to be sure that this occurrence is not linked with synthesizing operations of a purely psychological kind (the intention of the author, the form of his mind, the rigour of his thought, the themes that obsess him, the project that traverses his existence and gives it meaning) and to be able to grasp other forms of regularity, other types of relations. Relations between statements (even if the author is unaware of them; even if the statements do not have the same author; even if the authors were unaware of each others' existence); relations between groups of statements thus established (even if these groups do not concern the same, or even adjacent, fields; even if they do not possess the same formal level; even if they are not the locus of assignable changes); relations between statements and groups of statement and events of a quite different kind (technical, economic, social, political). To reveal in all its purity the space in which discursive events are deployed is not to undertake to re-establish it as an isolation that nothing could overcome; it is not to close it upon itself; it is to leave oneself free to describe the interplay of relations within it and outside it.[20]

Ours is a book that, like any other, can only begin to unfold the complexities of its chosen subject. We are not claiming to be comprehensive or 'even' in tone (we would be wary of any collection of essays that *did* claim to be so). Instead, we attempt to challenge the institutionalized methods of observing the female body, in history, as a homogeneous and unified story by presenting a collective voice that is *necessarily* uneven, incomplete, and varied. The history of the female body is a massive, bewildering, and complex narrative which we can only make a start at narrating here; yet the way in which we go about it, by revealing the story's meaning to be an intricate system of relationships and contradictions, is a significant step towards appreciating the 'immense density of systematicities' and 'tight group[ing] of multiple relations' that characterize the female body in medicine and literature.[21]

In much of the writing that considers the female body in these fields, perhaps especially in the nineteenth century, there seems to be a somewhat pessimistic assumption that the woman is in thrall to the medical profession her whole life. In an address to the Cambridge Ladies' Discussion Society in 1891, Frances Power Cobbe talked about her concern that women were particularly vulnerable at the hands of the medical profession, saying: 'We, women, above all are born to be their Patients. We are ushered into the world by them. We are vaccinated as Patients, become mothers as Patients, are perpetually being 'treated' and coddled as Patients, and, of course, at last we die as Patients'.[22]

Without doubt Frances Power Cobbe was notoriously damning of the medical profession. However, bondage in biology was, and is, a fact of life for women and is acknowledged by Ornella Moscucci, who states that 'the science of gynaecology was far more than the investigation and treatment of the ailments which affected women's reproductive organs: it was a comprehensive inquiry into the physiological, mental, social and moral peculiarities that were deemed to result from a woman's biological role'.[23] However, to understand the significance of surgical procedures and approaches to the female body we need to move beyond the view of nineteenth-century patriarchy, which has been far too reductive, obscuring as it does the clinical remit of the procedures, operations, and developments that have been made throughout history. We are looking to go beyond the monolithic readings of many feminist histories which flatten out the multiple resistances of women.

Many of the doctors who specialized in medicine for women felt themselves to be pioneers of medical advancement. However flawed their advances may have been, the ambition to succeed where others had failed is evident. In many ways a sense of heroism that helped to generate a competitive environment is seen in the medical writing discussed. While masculine competitiveness and rivalry may be no nobler than 'sadism', 'patriarchy', or 'dominance', it is important that we broaden our understanding into a more comprehensive analysis of the material available if we are to achieve an understanding of the full significance of the female body as construct.

Arguably, developments in the treatment of women reached a vanguard in the nineteenth century and this period receives significant attention in this collection. Roy Porter wrote of the emerging speciality of surgery, particularly at that time, that: 'The body's interior seemed an Africa in microcosm, that dark continent being opened up, mapped and transformed.

Fame and fortune awaited the surgical pioneer who first laid the knife to some hitherto untouched part – perhaps he would be immortalised by an eponymous operation'.[24] Barbara Harrison has argued that theories surrounding the health and treatment of women in the nineteenth century 'require[d] a consideration of doctors' own professional insecurity'.[25] One way to set aside these insecurities would be to carve a name for oneself with a pioneering surgical endeavour. Diane Scully reads both control and opportunism into nineteenth-century women's medicine: 'Gynaecologists used surgery to enforce values and control women, and, too, many were ambitious, competitive men who sought professional prominence and wealth by manipulation and excavation of the female pelvis'.[26] And, while both these writers refer to medicine in the nineteenth century, their interpretations can also be applied to the wider period covered by this volume. We would suggest that a very mixed bag of motivations drove the medical advances and understandings of the female body in the work examined here, yet an appreciation of the genuine desire to alleviate and cure should be placed among any assessment of female medicine.

We begin, then, with an essay by Carolyn D. Williams, '"Difficulties, at present in no Degree clear'd up": The Controversial Mother, 1600–1800', which discusses knowledge of maternal influences on birth and generation within a broad range of texts and case histories. Williams questions whether beliefs regarding the mother's biological 'impressions' on newborn children can be compared to knowledge of paternal influences via the potency of his 'seed'. Such configurations can be linked, according to this argument, to increasing, professionalized attempts to assert man's central position in obstetric medicine. The generative process, she concludes, 'is too important, and too multifaceted, to be monopolized' by any single claim to expertise. Williams sets the tone for many of the essays that follow. She is interested in the contest between men and women for control over the lying-in chamber – a fight that would eventually be won, it seems, by men's formidable arsenal of theories, methods, and instruments.

Lori Schroeder Haslem's essay which follows, 'Monstrous Issues: The Uterus as Riddle in Early Modern Medical Texts', argues what is the central tenet of this collection: that female bodies, like riddles, occupy 'a complex position within the various cultures and at various historical moments'. The riddle, like the female body, has baffled, challenged, and exasperated scientists, writers, and thinkers. As Haslem argues, we get from these medical texts a sense of the female body as an uncontainable force – a reading that is reproduced in many of the other essays included here.

It seems, as Haslem so clearly teases out, that the female body was – and arguably still is – something to be feared. Haslem's exploration of the coexisting moods of medical knowledge, myths, and superstition highlights an attitude which permeates, in subtly different ways, much of the writing surrounding women in this volume. Throughout history we see how women were kept in ignorance about the workings of their bodies, and this recurring attitude is typified in Haslem's essay when she discusses riddles that deal with fears over how a child could be conceived. It is also pertinent, we would suggest, how these early modern riddles link to myths and superstitions that have been used, through generations, to keep young girls chaste and fearful of unwanted pregnancy.

As is discussed above, while recognizing the importance of the language used in recorded medical material, this book remains conscious of the potential 'literary' perspective of the medical treatises referred to herein. The use of language by these earlier physicians is as important to this study as is the medical practice and writing which we explore extensively.

The common perception of woman as a complex and volatile entity inevitably helped to create an impression of authority for those whose life's work was the treatment of the female population. It seems inevitable that a physician's stature would be enhanced if he could show that he had conquered a particularly troublesome problem. However, as Ruth Harris has established, there was a fine line between doctors proving their authority because of their superior medical knowledge and those 'trying to enhance their own status as the privileged confidant'.[27] We concur that doctors were as dependent on their female patients as the patients were on them. What this collection makes clear is that, throughout the period covered, doctors, physicians, the medical 'elite', needed women to be a working problem, which, if solved, would aggrandize their subsequent careers. It is important, therefore, to explore how culturally pervasive the prejudices and preconceptions of the medical profession were across a wide literary field.

Indeed, despite its wish to access new and open-minded ways of thinking about literature, interdisciplinary literary theory, which is currently fashionable in Western scholarship, runs the risk of being limited in its corpus and sites of interpretation if it does not do more to incorporate populist and ephemeral narrative modes when selecting its source materials. The incorporation of popular forms of narrative is important in topics like the one driving this volume because people of any given period are more liable to encounter science and literature in forms that are most accessible to them and are likely, therefore, to make judgements about the value and weight of scientific knowledge based on these discourses. Hence, an individual is more likely to read about the female body through newspaper reports and pamphlets than through the medium of medical textbooks or philosophical treatises. While this volume draws on the intellectual precedents of interdisciplinary literary work on canonical writers and scientists, it also develops a more dynamic methodology and addresses a broader written archive in order to give due attention to the mutually informing nature of literature and medicine. Through an analysis of Anne Greene's remarkable story, told in the pamphlet *Newes from the Dead* (1651), for instance, Susan C. Staub notices fascinating signals that seventeenth-century physicians sought to usurp women's authority and expertise over the treatment of their bodies by forming elite and exclusive networks based on training and privilege. Staub's essay, entitled 'Surveilling the Secrets of the Female Body: The Contest for Reproductive Authority in the Popular Press of the Seventeenth Century', concludes that 'in its detailed account of the treatment of Anne's body and its reactions to doctors' varied ministrations, 'the pamphlet becomes a homosocial celebration of masculine power and male expertise'.

In the fourth essay in this collection, '"Made in Imitation of Real Women and Children": Obstetrical Machines in Eighteenth-Century Britain', Pam Lieske sets about challenging scholarly assumptions that the use of obstetrical machines and models exposed male practitioners of the Enlightenment to be little more than quacks and showmen. She claims, by means of contrast, that these sophisticated anatomical models were a vital part of the history of gynaecological and obstetrical medicine and that 'further inquiry into these issues, with a focus on class and gender, seems in order'. Lieske's analysis exposes the danger that Foucault identified as 'synthesizing operations of a purely psychological kind (the intention of the author, the form of his mind, the rigour of his thought, the themes that obsess him, the project that traverses his existence and gives it meaning)'.

Throughout this collection the very complex nature of the relationship between the female patient and the male practitioner – male midwife or doctor – is central. Questions are raised about need and dependence in the doctor/patient relationship. While the patient's need or reliance on the expertise and knowledge of the physician is well established, we also see how the dependence of the doctor on his patients counterbalances (in a complicated way) what has previously been regarded by medical historians as a very one-sided, oppressive relationship. As Sheena Sommers makes clear in her essay, the 'man-midwife came to represent yet another element of conspicuous consumption', as women began to choose male practitioners over female midwives.

In the years immediately following the feminist movement of the late twentieth century, many studies have concentrated on the sensual, the shocking, the humiliating, the unjust, and the ridiculous as a means of constructing a history of women's medicine as a story of universal misogyny. Although institutionalized notions of women as inherently different, inferior, and pathological have unquestionably come into play at every stage in the historical record of woman's relationship with the medical arts, Pam Lieske's essay, in particular, demonstrates how we should be wary of simplifying that record in order to suit the radical methodologies we have grown used to.

Sheena Sommers' essay, entitled 'Transcending the Sexed Body: Reason, Sympathy, and "Thinking Machines" in the Debates over Male Midwifery', explores how women were being removed slowly from the birthing room. Sommers discusses Enlightenment ideas of natural law, sexual difference, and reason, which provide a complex analysis of ideas surrounding gender difference. The professionalization of the male midwife, as discussed in Sommers' essay, is also representative of the larger picture of the professionalization of physicians throughout the period covered by this collection. As Sommers argues, 'the knowledge which obstetrical studies entailed had therefore as much to do with the medical professional's self-presentations as it did with any specific truths about female anatomy'.

In his essay entitled 'Emma Martin and the Manhandled Womb in Early Victorian England', Dominic Janes discusses, by focusing on the life and works of Emma Martin, the importance of gendered, symbolic imagery in nineteenth-century, medico-religious treatments of the female body. Martin, Janes observes, attempted to

> wrench debates on religion away from arcane preoccupations of denominational differences centred on phallocentric social politics and [...] insist[ed] on the importance of women's bodies. [...] Martin was arguing that textual obsessions with male desire and disgust were obscuring an essential bodily truth: that the essence of regeneration lay not in an act of priapic exuberance (the end result of a fetishistic manipulation of body parts by men) but in the wondrous female gestation of a newborn child.

The successful gestation of a child is central to the 'science' explored in Joanna Grant's essay '"Those Parts Peculiar to Her Organization": Some Observations on the History of Pelvimetry, a Nearly Forgotten Obstetric Sub-speciality'. The regulation of the female body, or, rather, the attempt to regulate it, was essential to the somewhat curious obstetric practice of pelvimetry. The use of scientific instruments that would provide scientific data on the structure of the female pelvis further removed the management of childbearing away from the seemingly increasingly old-fashioned culture of female midwifery. Grant argues that the science of pelvimetry reduces women to a sum of their parts and, as a result, they are viewed largely through the dimensions of their pelvis and their potential for delivering a child safely, indicating an 'overarching obsession with efficiency' in the medical profession. The regulation of women's bodies, whether in part or as a whole, is a theme that emerges repeatedly in this collection.

In one of two essays on the act of female onanism in the mid-Victorian period, Emma L. E. Rees contributes 'Narrating the Victorian Vagina:

Charlotte Brontë and the Masturbating Woman'. She considers the links between Brontë's *Villette* (1855) and the attempts of the nineteenth-century medical profession to regulate the female body through discourses and registers of shame. 'The secrecy and shame surrounding women's bodies', it is noted, 'was not so much *de*mythologised by doctors like [Alfred] Poulet and [Charles] Meigs, but was rather reemphasized and reinvigorated by their endeavours to project their morally unpolluted vision of what it meant to be a woman'. Such attempts to bolster traditional views of women as passively and morally obligated inspired Brontë's portraits of rebellious, feeling, and sexualized women like the actress Vashti.

The nineteenth-century fascination with masturbation is explored further in Laurie Garrison's essay '"She read on more eagerly, almost breathlessly": Mary Elizabeth Braddon's Challenge to Medical Depictions of Female Masturbation in *The Doctor's Wife*', where masturbation and sexual titillation are aligned with reading, female self-indulgence, and vice. Garrison provides, through analyses of the under-studied Braddon text, a case for reading the novel as a 'cultural refiguring of addiction'. The intertextual reading of *The Doctor's Wife* and medical treatises on masturbation show how Braddon depicts female desire and erotic fantasies in a way that would have been unacceptable in medical treatises, despite the seeming need of the medical professions to pathologize aberrant female behaviour. Garrison highlights the somewhat prudish use of language used by writers of medical 'fact' and juxtaposes it with the poetic descriptions provided by Braddon. The latter gives full utterance to the feelings, emotions, and sensations of the reading woman. The complexities and contradictions that surround the idea of the female masturbator in medical texts are teased out in this essay, which argues that the 'interaction between the reader and the supposedly scholarly author was part of a larger trend of exchange between readers and texts that played on readers' and writers' desires in a variety of ways'.

Female desire, real or perceived, and the dangers of this are further explored by a thorough and meticulous reading of the Robinson vs. Robinson and Lane divorce case of 1858 in 'Mrs Robinson's "Day-book of Iniquity": Reading Bodies of/and Evidence in the Context of the 1858 Medical Reform Act' by Janice M. Allan. This essay discusses how the pathologization of female behaviour was seemingly endemic in the nineteenth century and considers the reportage on Mrs Robinson's 'extraordinary delusions' in the daily papers. Allan highlights the vulnerability of Mrs Robinson and, by default, all 'transgressive' women when placed at the mercy of medical figures, legal professionals, the press, and its moralizing readers. This medicalization of behaviour shows how women were made 'safe' if they could be diagnosed, labelled, and treated. What this case illustrates is how, by this point in the nineteenth century, there was a prevailing assumption 'that all women were, from puberty through menopause, ruled and governed by a uterine economy'.

Without doubt many of the gynaecological and obstetric practices through our period (roughly 1600–2000) were felt by many women to be barbaric invasions of their bodies. What this collection explores is not only how medical practice on the female body developed and evolved over the period but also how this developing practice enabled society and medicine to pathologize the female body and classify certain aspects of female behaviour as 'troublesome'. This medicalization of perceived aberrant conduct, which challenged gender norms, led to a belief that it was necessary to establish moral control of women. As Allan argues, the 'unstable' female body was believed to be in need of 'expert interpretations and superintendence'. It seems, then, that moral governance is a priority in texts ostensibly concerned with the physiology of women's bodies. However, this collection builds on previous arguments by proposing that we require a more thorough interdisciplinary study in which far-reaching understandings of the complex nature of the patient/male practitioner relationship are sought. What becomes clear as this book progresses is that women did muster some, albeit sometimes tenuous, control over their bodies and desires. What it is also important to acknowledge is that medical practices were propelled by professional rivalries in the race towards groundbreaking medical advances. The desire to exert power and control was not simply about mastering women, but also involved gaining prestige over professional colleagues, and this is prevalent in much of the writing we examine.

In her reading of Daphne du Maurier's *Rebecca* (1938), Madeleine Davies argues that the author satirizes the desire for moral control over women by suggesting that the double punishment of Rebecca – not only a diseased, 'abnormal' womb but also that same womb becoming the target of Maxim's bullet – is an 'ironic over-fulfilment of just deserts'. And while this gynocentric, double punishment for her eponymous 'heroine' might be ironic, the lifelong punishment of wandering aimlessly around Europe for Maxim and the narrator is not. Davies explores issues of aberrant sexuality – both male and female – but argues that while gynocentric (dis)ease is still central to ideas of patriarchal punishment, du Maurier takes a subversive look at how sexual desire in women has been vilified by giving Rebecca the upper hand – she cheats a slow, painful death and arguably leaves Maxim in torment. The novel is thus a 'narrative stab at the heart of the rule of law'.

Through her sensitive combing of case studies and legislature from the twentieth century in 'Representations of Illegal Abortionists in England, 1900–1967', Emma Jones reconstructs the cultural significance of the illegal abortionist. As is visible in both novels and films, illegal terminations hold a powerful position in our collective consciousness. This is because, Jones argues, attempts to regulate the act of abortion between 1900 and 1967 speak directly to concomitant concerns over sanitation, women's rights, and population numbers. Jones' 'varied sources provide several interweaving and competing realities of the illegal abortionist that together make up the social and cultural history of this issue; and it is a history that continues to be retold'. The 2004 filming of *Vera Drake*, in particular, signifies how 'even today, when abortion can be practised legally up to the twenty-fourth week of pregnancy with medical approval, [...] the illegal abortionist continues to hold a place in the popular imagination'.

With this collection we have posed questions about the role and power of the female patient. In 1896 the journal *Shafts* wrote that: 'Women, necessarily, have more power over the medical world than men can ever have'.[28] Arguably, a fear of the potentially incurable nature of certain women's diseases, the power and life-giving potential of the female body, lent women a certain, sometimes negative, power, positioning them antagonistically vis-à-vis the medical profession. Women, their bodies, and their (dis)ease, have proved a challenge: while facilitating medical practitioners aiming to advance their reputations, female patients have just as often found themselves in a self-defeating position. To posit them as uncomplicatedly 'powerful' is, therefore, too simplistic.

Much of the writing about the female body in literature and medicine might be seen, retrospectively, as misguided – anatomically, morally, and ethically. But we cannot deny that the desire to know, manage, and understand the female body encompasses a genuine desire to alleviate some of the most debilitating conditions experienced by women. By exploring a wide literary field we are able to give a more cohesive voice to the disparate encounters that the female body experiences, and highlight the pervasive cultural impact these encounters have on the meaning of sex and reproduction.

However, the socio-political aspects of what medicine has been responsible for with reference to the female body throughout history is likely to be a long-debated issue. What this collection shows is how powerful this branch of medicine has proved to be for the production of writing across a range of intellectual disciplines.

NOTES

1. It would be impossible to provide an exhaustive list here, but see, for example, Ann Dally, *Women Under the Knife: A History of Surgery* (London: Hutchinson Radius, 1991); Audrey Eccles, *Obstetrics and Gynaecology in Tudor and Stuart England* (London and Canberra: Croom Helm, 1982); Lisa Forman Cody, *Birthing the Nation: Sex, Science, and the Conception of Eighteenth-Century Britons* (Oxford: Oxford University Press, 2005); Helen King, *Hippocrates' Woman: Reading the Female Body in Ancient Greece* (London and New York: Routledge, 1998); Ornella

Moscucci, *The Science of Woman: Gynaecology and Gender in England, 1800–1929* (Cambridge, UK: Cambridge University Press, 1990); Elaine Showalter, *The Female Malady: Women, Madness and English Culture, 1830–1980* (London: Virago Press, 1987); Adrian Wilson, *The Making of Man-Midwifery: Childbirth in England 1660–1770* (London: UCL Press, 1995).

2. See Sally Shuttleworth, 'Demonic Mothers: Ideologies of Bourgeois Motherhood in the Mid-Victorian Era', in Linda M. Shires (ed.), *Rewriting the Victorians: Theory, History and the Politics of Gender* (London: Routledge, 1993), pp. 31–51; Sally Shuttleworth, *Charlotte Brontë and Victorian Psychology* (Cambridge, UK: Cambridge University Press, 1996); Helen Small, *Love's Madness: Medicine, The Novel, and Female Insanity, 1800–1865* (Oxford: Oxford University Press, 1996); Jane Wood, *Passion and Pathology in Victorian Fiction* (Oxford: Oxford University Press, 2001); and Andrew Mangham, *Violent Women and Sensation Fiction: Crime, Medicine and Victorian Popular Culture* (Basingstoke, UK: Palgrave Macmillan, 2007).

3. Gillian Beer, *Darwin's Plots: Evolutionary Narrative in Darwin, George Eliot and Nineteenth-Century Fiction* (1983; London: Routledge, 2000), p. 5.

4. An example of this is provided in Showalter's *The Female Malady*. Otherwise a powerful and groundbreaking study, the monograph's use of texts such as Florence Nightingale's *Cassandra* (1852) and Charlotte Perkins Gilman's *The Yellow Wallpaper* (1892) views the literary text as additional support in its historical reconstruction of women's psychiatric care. In this form of linking the two disciplines, the literary text becomes two-dimensional, a historical document, and not (which is really the case) a powerful forum for discussing and *questioning* the assumptions of clinical science.

5. Beer, *Darwin's Plots*, p. 5.

6. Jane Wood, *Passion and Pathology in Victorian Fiction* (Oxford: Oxford University Press, 2001), p. 1.

7. Steven Marcus, 'Freud and Dora: Story, History, Case History', in Charles Bernheimer and Claire Kahane (eds.), *In Dora's Case: Freud – Hysteria – Feminism* (New York: Columbia University Press, 1985), pp. 56–91 (p. 57); and Maria Ramas, 'Freud's Dora, Dora's Hysteria', in *In Dora's Case*, pp. 149–80 (p. 150), both remark on the literary aspects of this particular case history. See also Nina Auerbach, *Woman and the Demon. The Life of a Victorian Myth* (Cambridge, MA, and London: Harvard University Press, 1982), pp. 27–31.

8. Sigmund Freud, *Case Histories I* (1905, repr. trans.by Alix Strachey and James Strachey, ed. James Strachey et al. (London: Penguin Books, 1990), p. 94.

9. Freud, *Case Histories I*, p. 38.

10. Freud, *Case Histories I*, p. 60.

11. Freud, *Case Histories I*, p. 32.

12. Freud, *Case Histories I*, p. 38.

13. Freud, *Case Histories I*, p. 37.

14. Mark. S. Micale, *Approaching Hysteria. Disease and Its Interpretations* (Princeton, NJ: Princeton University Press, 1995), p. 233.

15. Micale, *Approaching Hysteria*, p. 234.

16. Anon, *The Lancet*, 7 April 1888: 685–86 (685).

17. Anon, *The Lancet*, 7 April 1888: 685–86 (686).

18. Beer, *Darwin's Plots*, p. 5.

19. Interdisciplinary essay collections on the female body, though not specifically on the medical treatment of the female body, include Mary Jacobus, Evelyn Fox Keller and Sally Shuttleworth (eds.), *Body/Politics: Women and the Discourses of Science* (London: Routledge, 1990); Marina Benjamin (ed.), *A Question of Identity: Women, Science,* and *Literature* (NJ: Rutgers University Press, 1993); and Susan C. Greenfield and Carol Barash (eds.), *Inventing Maternity: Politics, Science, and Literature 1650–1865* (Lexington, KY: The University of Kentucky Press, 1999).
20. Michel Foucault, *The Archaeology of Knowledge*, trans. A. M. Sheridan Smith (1969; London and New York: Routledge, 2002), pp. 31–32.
21. Foucault, *The Archaeology of Knowledge*, p. 85.
22. Frances Power Cobbe, '"Health and Holiness" An Address read to the Cambridge Ladies' Discussion Society, November 6th, 1891' (London: George Bell & Sons, 1891), pp. 7–8.
23. Ornella Moscucci, 'Hermaphroditism and Sex Difference: The Construction of Gender in Victorian England', in Marina Benjamin (ed.), *Science and Sensibility: Gender and Scientific Enquiry 1780–1945* (Oxford: Basil Blackwell, 1991), pp. 174–99 (p. 191).
24. Roy Porter, *The Greatest Benefit to Mankind. A Medical History of Humanity From Antiquity to the Present* (London: Harper Collins Publishers, 1997), p. 599.
25. Barbara Harrison, 'Women and Health', in June Purvis (ed.), *Women's History: Britain, 1850–1945* (London: UCL Press Ltd, 1995), pp. 157–92 (p. 176).
26. Diana Scully, Men *Who Control Women's Health. The Miseducation of Obstetrician-Gynaecologists* (Boston, MA: Houghton Mifflin Co., 1980), p. 55.
27. Ruth Harris, *Murders and Madness: Medicine, Law, and Society in the Fin de Siècle* (Oxford: Clarendon Press, 1989), p. 191.
28. W. W, 'Should Vivisection Be Permitted?', *Shafts* 5 (1896): 60.

2

'Difficulties, at present in no Degree clear'd up': The Controversial Mother, 1600–1800

CAROLYN D. WILLIAMS

Early modern interest in conception, pregnancy and labour extended far beyond medical specialists: Audrey Eccles' study of the literature in the period 1540–1740 shows that 'The public was evidently fascinated by the subject'.[1] Lisa Forman Cody continues the story through the eighteenth century, noting that 'tales of the body and birth, both normal and strange' are plentiful 'across genres, disciplines and locations'.[2] Discourses associated with various professions interacted vigorously in discussions of two controversial issues: the child's inheritance from mother and father at conception, and the power of the mother's imagination to affect the child in her womb. Matters became even more heated when pregnancy reached its end: not only were there interdisciplinary debates about the best means of bringing the mother's labour to a successful conclusion, and how much of the work was being done by the baby, but the pressure of changing practices upon professional boundaries occasioned complex negotiations, and sometimes fierce rivalries, between physicians, apothecaries, surgeons, and midwives both male and female.[3] Furthermore, in the competitive atmosphere of the period, some practitioners felt it necessary to conceal their most effectual equipment, and occasionally incurred reproaches, not for being unprofessional, since the word was not yet being used in an appropriate sense, but for failing to be proper gentlemen, which meant much the same thing. Meanwhile, the whole area was patrolled by poets, novelists and satirists, whose response illuminated ethical and emotional concerns, some of which are still relevant to the place of science within society. In the course of these conflicts, female reproductive bodies, human and animal, were not only objects of professional attention but also the means of interrogating concepts and practices central to everything we define as 'professional' today.

Was the female body really reproductive, or just a production line for items of exclusively male manufacture?[4] For those who enjoyed the benefits of a classical education, there were different options. In the *Generation of Animals*, Aristotle asserts that the male provides seed, the female only a growth medium and a site for its development. The idea that both sexes contribute seed to the child appears in the corpus of works ascribed to Hippocrates.[5] It was later elaborated by Galen. Yet the two-seed theory failed to value both parents' contributions equally. Galen, for example, compared the effect of semen on the blood in the female's womb to the actions of a great sculptor fashioning wonderful statues from his materials.[6]

Not even this generous concession to the father's importance was enough to prevent debate. One upholder of Aristotelian views on generation was Alexander Ross, Doctor of Divinity, who in 1652 used the axioms of scholastic logic in his attempt to prove that the woman provides only nourishment to the child: 'If the females seed bee active, and the males too, it will follow, that two efficients numerically different, and having no subordination to each other, do produce one effect, which is absurd'.[7] If this were the case, the female would be 'perfecter than the male, as having more principles of generation, to wit, the seed, the blood, and the place or matrix', a proposition so self-evidently nonsensical that there was no need to dispute it.[8] This sterile word-mongering was rapidly becoming outdated: most educated observers would soon come to the conclusion that scholastic logic was absurd. (Its use by low comedians in Shakespeare's plays suggests that uneducated people had always suspected this.) Meanwhile, a third theory on generation had appeared in the *Exercitationes de Generatione Animalium* (1651) by the physician William Harvey, who also displayed great respect for the conventions of scholastic logic in the presentation of his ideas, but derived his data from investigation of organisms. His dictum *'ex ovo omnia'*, inscribed on the title page, summarized his belief that all animal life emerged from eggs in the mother's body. Studies along these lines gave rise to the theory later known as 'ovarism' or 'ovism': the idea that children derive their bodies entirely from their mothers. This assertion of the female's reproductive role, however, did little or nothing to advance the status of motherhood. In fact, it encouraged a retreat from the Galenic two-seed position to the Aristotelian idea that the mother contributed only matter, while the father provided form and spirit. Harvey believed there was no contact between sperm and ovum, but that a woman was *'impregnated by the conception of a generall immaterial idea'*, which elevated the father's role to a lofty spiritual plane.[9] If Harvey, unlike his contemporary Ross, is revered for increasing our understanding of generation, it is largely due to his conviction that, while the path to truth still leads through the School of Logic, it could take a detour through the dissecting room and the laboratory.

More sensitive optical equipment revealed a fourth possibility. In 1677, the Dutchman Anthony van Leeuwenhoek, a successful linen draper with a flair for grinding lenses, discovered living creatures in spermatic fluid.[10] Those who believed they played a key role in generation, and might even be potential embryos, dubbed them *animalculi* (little animals); those found in human sperm were called *homunculi* (little men). The idea gained currency far beyond the boundaries of medical science. In 1742 Edward Young, clergyman and poet, evoked animalculism when seeking an apt simile for the human soul's state within the living body:

> *Life's* Theater as yet is shut, and Death,
> Strong Death alone can heave the massy bar,
> This gross impediment of Clay remove,
> And make us Embryos of Existence free.
> From *real* life, but little more remote
> Is *He*, not yet a candidate for Light,
> The *future* Embryo, slumbering in his Sire.[11]

Participants in the controversy often appealed to religion. An extreme form of ovism was promoted by Père Nicolas de Malebranche in his *De la Recherche de la Vérité* (1674): he said that 'the Females of the Original Creatures were, for ought we know, created together, with all those of the same *Species* which have been, or shall be, begotten or procreated whilst the World stands'.[12] Under this dispensation, the woman's body became a hatchery, her ovaries filled with sons who were reproductive dead ends, and daughters with descendants stacked like matryoshka dolls. The more impossible it seemed, the more impressively it demonstrated God's infinite power. The physician Robert James objected to animalculism for the opposite reason: his Deity's most salient characteristic was economy of effort. Leeuwenhoek himself had admitted, 'It may be queried, If one *Animalcule* of Seed be sufficient to produce a *Foetus*, why are there so many Thousands in one drop of it?'[13] His answer envisaged the spermatozoa as dauntless mariners sailing a vast ocean: 'the Womb being so large in Comparison of so small a Creature, and there being so few *Vessels* and places fit to feed it, and bring it up to a *Foetus*, there cannot be too great a number of Adventurers, when there is so great a likelyhood to miscarry'.[14] James, calculating that only one out of three thousand million animalcules would survive, rejects the necessity for such tragically extravagant waste. Abandoning naval for military imagery, he portrays the animalculists' idea of the womb as a battlefield or firing range, inhabited by living projectiles: 'we must suppose, that Providence aims very ill, if oblig'd to load her Engine so enormously, in order to be able to hit the Mark propos'd'.[15] Ultimately, he finds himself unable to say what the womb is really like: instead, he wisely concludes that the subject of generation raises 'Difficulties, at present in no Degree clear'd up'.[16]

Some disputants found their difficulties cleared up by specific passages in the scriptures. The Bible abounds with references to all aspects of reproduction, but offers no explicit statement on the nature of generation. Readers had to take account of tangential, often contradictory, remarks. The pious physician Thomas Browne (1605–1682) condemns the statement that 'the female sex have no generative emission' as a literally diabolical lie.[17] He points out that in *Genesis* 3:15, God tells the serpent that the seed of the woman will bruise his head. Christians interpreted this as a promise that Jesus would be born of the Virgin Mary: how could this happen if women had no seed? But Mary was not necessarily a precedent for other women. The Scottish Episcopalian clergyman George Garden attempted in 1691 to reconcile animalculism with the doctrine of the Virgin Birth by depicting Mary as the miraculous exception that proves the rule, 'all the rest of Mankind being thus most properly and truly the Seed of the Man'.[18]

Devotees of animalculism found their proof text in Paul's *Epistle to the Hebrews*. Examination of this text and its history casts light on the opportunistic way in which theories about generation can be formed under the pressure of the need to compose a convincing argument about something else. Paul was trying to convert the Jews to Christianity by persuading them that Jesus was the Messiah, the priest and king foretold in the Old Testament. As he wrestled with the minutiae of Judaic law, he faced two problems: no Jew had ever combined the roles of priest and king; Jesus was descended from Judah, whereas all Jewish priests came from the house of Levi (*Hebrews* 7:14). Even if Mary had been descended from the house of Levi, she could 'not be the mother of a priest since she had been first married to one not of priestly stock'.[19] Paul needed a different model of priesthood for Jesus, and found it in the Old Testament. In *Hebrews* 6:20 he calls Jesus a priest 'after the order of Melchisedec'.[20] The phrase comes from Psalms 110:4, interpreted here as a Messianic prophecy. Melchizedek appears briefly in *Genesis*: a priest and king who met Abraham on his way back from a great victory, and blessed him (14:18); Abraham rewarded him with a tenth of his spoils, just as, in later years, Jews would pay tithes to their priests. According to the biblical narrative, there was no question of Melchizedek being a Levite; he was not even a Jew, and Levi, Abraham's great-grandson, was still unbegotten. But a reference to the reproductive process bridges the generation gap, while demonstrating Melchizedek's superiority: he was such a great priest that Levi, whose descendants received tithes from all other Jews, actually paid tithes to *him*: 'And as I may so say, Levi also who receiveth tithes, payed tithes in Abraham. For hee was yet in the loines of his Father when Melchisedec met him' (Hebrews 7:9–10). If this passage had been originally intended as a statement about male and female reproductive functions, it would probably have mentioned Sarah, Abraham's wife, just to dismiss any claim that she might have had a genetic stake in his offspring. Yet it was to become very useful in inspiring, or perhaps confirming, theories about the importance of fatherhood.

One reference to this text, which must have been brought to the attention of many well-trained children in dissenting families, appears in a dialogue on original sin in *An Explanation of the Shorter Catechism* (1675) by nonconformist minister Thomas Lye. The scheme of this work, like others of the same kind, was to suggest that certain questions should be proposed by a parent or other responsible person, and that the child should learn to answer 'Yes' or 'No' at the appropriate times:

> Were not all the posterity of *Adam* then unborn when *Adam* first sinned? yes. And yet were they in him before they were born? yes. How do you mean, virtually? That is, they were in his loins, as *Levi* is said to pay tythes in *Abraham* when he was only in his loins, *Heb.*7:10. So *Adam's* Posterity sinned in him, because they were in his loins? yes.[21]

Thus a conscientious catechist would undermine belief in maternal inheritance.

Joyce Irwin argues that using scripture as evidence for scientific theories 'reveals both scientific naïveté and exaggerated confidence in the literal text of the Bible'.[22] However, in an age when Christians were regularly taught that the 'Holy Scriptures' were 'immediately inspired and indited by the Holy Ghost', many scholars might have considered it dangerously naïve to publish an open challenge to their literal sense.[23] There were, of course, others who were never conscious of any clash between their researches and their religious convictions. In this spirit, *Hebrews* was cited by Dutch physician Jan Swammerdam, one of the founders of modern biology, who wished to demonstrate the orderliness of God's creation, and argued in that all so-called generation was only 'the continuation, as it were, of the generation already performed'.[24] The physician John Cook, in his 1730 declaration for animalculism, attacks the theological interpreters such as Lye on the grounds that they do not follow the literal sense of the Bible closely enough:

> If *Isaac, Jacob*, and the whole Tribe of *Levi*, were once in the Loins of *Abraham*, we need not to doubt, but that we were all in like manner once wholly in *Adam*; and consequently, are all propagated from him, not virtually, according to the old Cant, but literally and actually, according to the aforesaid Theory.[25]

Melchizedek reappears in another argument whose thrust, like that in *Hebrews*, was legal rather than scientific. The lawyer James Boswell reminisced about his attempt to persuade his father to disinherit all his female relations. He explains to the reader that, in his youth, he 'had a zealous partiality for heirs male, however remote, which I maintained by arguments which appeared to me to have considerable weight': his language suggests that he subsequently changed his mind.[26] He cites 'the opinion of some distinguished naturalists, that our species is transmitted through males only, the females being all along no more than a *nidus*, or nurse, as Mother Earth is to plants of every sort', a notion which 'seems to be confirmed' by *Hebrews* 7:10.[27] Boswell laid his case before his friend and mentor Samuel Johnson, a deeply religious layman, who advised him to consult Lord Hailes on the grounds that he was 'both a Christian and a Lawyer'.[28] Despite his own lifelong interest in medicine, Johnson did not suggest that any physicians should be brought into the affair: presumably, he considered it was none of their business.[29] *Hebrews* had failed to carry instant conviction; Johnson might have been remembering apparently contradictory texts, or he may just have been considering, as many educated readers seemed to do, that the Bible and natural philosophy did not always relate to each other in ways that human beings could understand. Boswell makes no further reference to the matter.

The most celebrated cultural artefact to emerge from the debate was the novel *Tristram Shandy* (1759–67), by the clergyman Laurence Sterne, which ridiculed animalculism by a strategy popular among eighteenth-century ironists: he wrote repeated, voluminous and enthusiastic accounts of the theory, putting them in the mouth of an obsessive fool.[30] Like Paul and Boswell, Walter Shandy erects a legal argument on the mother's presumed lack of seed; in this case he is trying to convince Parson Yorick that the father has greater authority over his children than the mother:

> She is under authority herself, said my father: – and besides, continued my father, nodding his head and laying his finger upon the side of his nose, as he assigned his reason, – *she is not the principal agent*, Yorick. – In what? Quoth my uncle *Toby*, stopping his pipe. – Though by all means, added my father (not attending to my uncle *Toby*) '*The son ought to pay her respect*', as you may read, *Yorick*, at large in the first book of the Institutes of *Justinian*, at the eleventh title and the tenth section. – I can read it as well, replied *Yorick*, in the Catechism.[31]

Yorick, who is in many ways Sterne's alter ego, guiding the reader's responses, appears as unimpressed by the doctrine of animalculism as by Shandy's legal reference. It seems unlikely that the loins of Abraham would figure prominently in his explication of the catechism.

A more urgent question (because it had more obvious practical implications) concerned the effect of the mother's thoughts on the unborn child.[32] If sudden frights or unsatisfied cravings deformed the foetus, care should be taken to protect mothers from unpleasantness and indulge their whims. A great deal of anxiety, and expense, would be spared if it could be proved that there was no connection between the mother's mind and the child's body. Disputes over the natural processes involved drew on medical and theological evidence, while attempts to capitalize on traditional beliefs brought the law into play.

The crucial biblical text in this case concerned Abraham's grandson Jacob, who made his sheep and goats look at striped rods while they were mating, in order to produce striped and spotted offspring in a flock from which all such animals had been removed (*Genesis* 30:39). No respectable writer could afford to ignore this passage. For opponents of the imagination theory, one strategy was to emulate the anonymous correspondent of *The Gentleman's Magazine* who reminds readers that Jacob's story concerned only 'the very moment of conception': after that, nothing passing through the mother's mind could affect her child.[33] The physician James Augustus Blondel, as skilled in Hebrew and theology as he was in medicine, took an even harder line, denying the mother's influence on the unborn child at any stage. In a book which condemned the imagination theory as a '*Vulgar Error*', he pitted his own learning against the combined skills of the scholars who produced the Authorized Version of the Bible: 'There's good Reason to suspect the Exactness of the Translation, and that the Divines in King *James*'s Time were guided more by their Prejudices, than by the Original'.[34] His basic thesis is that Jacob's flocks did not derive their colour from their mothers' imaginations, but from their fathers' physical characteristics. The rods were used to manipulate the females' sexual preferences. He fancifully declares that, 'As the Scripture does not tell us in what manner the Rods were placed, we may lawfully suppose, that they made afar off a rough Representation of a speckled Ram, or He-goat'.[35] He then suggests a less elaborate process: 'as the Ews, in that hot Country, could have no Water, except they drank it, where the party-coloured Rods were placed, that Colour became very pleasant to them, and naturally determined their Inclination towards the speckled Rams'.[36] Unfortunately, Blondel contradicted some statements previously published by the physician Daniel Turner (1667–1741), who, adopting a time-honoured procedure in academic disputes, retaliated by attacking every aspect of Blondel's book, including his biblical exegesis. He points out Blondel's inconsistencies and notes a serious flaw in his reading of the story: remembering the plain colouring of Jacob's flocks, he demands, '*How came the Rams to be ring-straked?*'[37] Turner performs less well when dealing with physiological matters. Failing to respond to Blondel's insistence that the offspring's colouring was influenced by paternal inheritance rather than maternal experience, he merely asks, 'if the *Ewes* conceived these ring-straked Cattle by looking on the *speckled Rams*, is it not the same, in respect to their *Imagination*, as if they had beheld the *speckled Rods?*'[38]

While medical gentlemen attempted to acquire or defend high professional status by their learned arguments on maternal imagination, members of the lower orders tried to profit from the theory more directly. In 1726, a woman named Mary Toft or Tofts, the wife of a journeyman clothier who lived in Godalming, near Guildford in Surrey, attempted to exploit imagination theory by a succession of monstrous births: she claimed to have suffered from an unsatisfied craving for rabbit during pregnancy, and as a result of this gave birth to fragments of rabbit bodies, one of which turned out to be a portion of cat. In fact, there is no evidence that she gained anything from her enterprise, but it was not for want of trying.[39] Many people, including famous medical men, went to see her performances at Godalming; some believed the births were genuine. Eventually, she was taken to London on 29 December by a party of investigators who included the physician Sir Richard Manningham: according to his diary of the affair, 'we brought *Mary Toft* to London with us, and lodg'd her at Mr. *Lacy*'s Bagnio in *Leicester Fields*: I sat up with her all that Night'.[40] Constant surveillance produced the result Manningham had expected: the amazing births ceased. Toft was finally exposed when '*Thomas Howard*, Porter to Mr. *Lacy*'s *Bagnio*, made an Information against Mary Toft, before Sir *Thomas Clarges*, Bart. One of His Majesty's Justices of Peace, concerning a Rabbet she had clandestinely procured by his Assistance'.[41] At this point, Manningham wryly observes that the law succeeded where medical science had failed: 'Sir *Thomas* threaten'd her severely, and began to appear the most properest Physician in her Case, and his Remedies took Place, and seem'd to promise a perfect Cure; for we heard no more of her former Labour-like Pains'.[42] Manningham himself began to act more like an interrogator, even a torturer, than a physician, threatening 'to try a very painful Experiment upon her' if she did not admit that the births were a fraud.[43] This crossing of professional frontiers typifies the confusions arising from the unanswerable questions posed by mothers of 'monsters'. In the face of these problems, biblical texts could mean anything, while experienced practitioners of law and medicine struggled to establish the relationship between pregnancy and crime.

A more common strategy was adopted by maimed and deformed beggars, who used their unsightliness to extort money. At this point, too, the law might be invoked, as it was on 4 September 1731, when 'Sir John Gonson, and other Justices of Westminster, order'd the High-Constables, &c. to apprehended [*sic*] several Vagrants with stump Hands, sore Arms, Legs and Faces, who insolently presented themselves before pregnant Gentlewomen at Church Doors'.[44] These vagrants invoked a deep and persistent fear: over thirty years later, the distinguished surgeon Samuel Sharp mentioned a story that 'a lady advanced five or six months in her pregnancy, has been so terrified, by a beggar's thrusting suddenly the stump of an amputated arm into her coach, that the child, of which she was afterwards brought to bed, was born with the stump of an arm, resembling that of the beggar'.[45]

Sharp produced strong evidence to disprove the story, including the baby's unwounded skin, and the failure of the missing limb to appear in the birth canal. Sadly, no argument against the malign force of maternal imagination, however reasonable it might appear today, could carry complete conviction in the face of distressing experience.

More interdisciplinary controversies surrounded the subject of birth. In the first place, there was doubt about the baby's contribution to the process. Even Alexander Ross, who had employed scholastic logic to argue that mothers were not related to their children, was prepared to concede that a baby's birth was normally a cooperative effort, achieved partly by its own struggles, and 'partly by the contraction of the matrix'.[46] The idea that a baby was capable of adjusting its own position underlies a letter sent by an anonymous correspondent to *The Gentleman's Magazine*, saying that if a paste of laurel leaves and olive oil were spread on the navel of a woman in labour, 'in whatever unnatural or irregular position the child may be, it will immediately turn and present itself readily, and in the best and most happy manner'.[47] A few months later, an anxious reader wrote in to point out a probable error: no doubt was expressed about the baby's ability to perform the necessary gyrations, but there was a strong likelihood that a Latin source had been mistranslated. 'I suspect, that instead of *laurel*, we should read *bay-leaves*', since laurel is poisonous, whereas bay has been recommended 'as of service to women in labour', and the word has been often mistranslated by readers of Virgil's *Georgics*.[48] This brief correspondence seems surreal, yet quaintly endearing. After all, rubbing herbal remedies onto the belly of a woman in labour was no more likely to do harm than good.

Yet uncertainty about this aspect of labour could be a matter of life and death for the mother of an illegitimate child. She might fall foul of the law by which mothers of dead bastards were presumed guilty of infanticide unless proved innocent. One of the books which a magistrate might consult in doubtful cases was *The Country Justice*, written by Michael Dalton. He would learn that

> in every such case, the said Mother so offending, shall suffer Death as in case of Murder, except she can prove that the Child was born dead, 21 *Jac. Cap. 27.*
>
> Now the Mother's proof that her Child was born dead, must be by Witnesses: And therefore, if the Mother will call for no help at the time of her Labour, but secretly be delivered, and then the Child be found dead, it is a strong presumption against her, that she murdered it; and

the rather, for it is a received opinion, That if the Child were dead in her Body, she could not then be delivered without the help of some others. Which opinion, notwithstanding some worshipful and grave Matrons have denied, and that of their own knowledge.[49]

A woman in this plight might well die from ignorance.[50]

Most pregnant women would, of course, seek help, but whose? In the eighteenth century, increasing numbers of male practitioners were employed. This development still engenders high feeling; as Cody observes, 'No topic raises more ire or encomia among historians of medicine, midwifery, gender, and the family than that of the place of medical men in the lying-in chamber, with scholars even disputing how commonly men attended child-births before the mid-eighteenth century'.[51]

The usual situation, as described by Adrian Wilson, is that from the seventeenth century until the early eighteenth century, 'The normal birth of a living child, comprising the vast majority of deliveries, was the province of the midwife; the surgeon's task was the delivery of a dead child in the tiny minority of difficult births'.[52] There were exceptions, but the physician and man-midwife Percivall Willughby records a sadly typical incident from his own practice, which occurred in 1632. He was called to a patient who had already lost a lot of blood: 'Shee was very faint, yet, in her weaknes, the child had entered through a great part of the Bones, and would come no farther by nature's enforcement, nor was shee any more releeved by her midwife'.[53] The only way to save her would be to fasten a hook, or 'crochet', in the baby's head, and draw it out: a process that would severely injure and probably kill it, if it was still alive. Willughby hesitated, since he was not sure the baby was dead, but the patient's husband made his wife's survival the highest priority, and the patient consented to the operation, so he extracted the child. The mother died five hours later, from her previous blood loss. The only faint consolation was that the baby had died before extraction.[54] During the following century, however, instead of being harbingers of doom rushed in at the last minute, male practitioners became more closely integrated into the lives and birthing plans of the women wealthy enough to afford their services, and they were employed in the expectation of the safe delivery of a living baby.[55] David Harley observes that, by the end of the eighteenth century, 'it is possible that in some parts of England about half of all deliveries were attended by men'.[56] Even this statement makes it clear that the majority of English deliveries were still all-female affairs. Nevertheless, the midwife's position was becoming increasingly insecure.

There is no single obvious reason for this important social change. Midwives tended to be respected members of the community, with high levels of skill, experience, and training.[57] The term 'professed midwife' can carry strong connotations of approval: for example, it appears in an account of a widow 'of a spotless and unblameable life and conversation; of singular use to her neighbours: for she is a professed midwife, happy and successful in that undertaking'.[58] Elizabeth Nihell proudly describes herself as a 'Professed Midwife' on the title page of two published works from 1760.[59] The man-midwife might be equipped with forceps or other apparatus for adjusting a baby's position or pulling it out alive from the mother's body; midwives and their supporters would retort by claiming that these instruments were dangerous, unnecessary and inferior to 'the hands of women, who ought therefore to be preferred to the man, and to be restored to their antient and rightful possession'.[60] Besides, women were not really bereft of instruments. Jane Sharp instructed midwives to deliver hydrocephalic babies, whose heads were enlarged by excessive amounts of fluid, by making incisions in the skull to drain out the water, and to cut up and remove piecemeal the skulls or entire bodies of dead babies if all other means to deliver them failed.[61] Sarah Stone used Sharp's method for dealing with hydrocephalus, and took it for granted that midwives would have hooks, though she advocated great care in their use.[62] Whatever the midwives' methods, historians have found evidence suggesting that they were good at their job: a high percentage of births concluded with mother and child doing well. Cody argues compellingly that the 'professional ascent of the eighteenth-century man-midwife' was a response to changing social and political pressures rather than to clinical necessity.[63]

The male practitioners' social aspirations precipitated a conflict between two forms of what we today would call 'professional' activity: working for payment versus the disinterested practice of a discipline. A man-midwife with an eye to the main chance would preserve his monopoly of any particularly effective instrument by concealing it from everybody, including the mother for whose benefit it was deployed. He took advantage of his patient's modesty, keeping his head and arms covered by a sheet, 'working blind, with only his sense of touch to guide him'.[64] The most successful, and secretive, man-midwives were the Chamberlens, a family of surgeons and physicians who had arrived in England in the early seventeenth century. Eventually, after the deaths of Hugh Chamberlen the younger in 1728 and his cousin Middleton Walker in 1732, no male descendant survived to carry on the family business, and various new forms of obstetric apparatus, including forceps, fillets (strips of firm cloth), and the vectis (rather like a shoehorn) began to appear in the hands of obstetrical and medical practitioners.[65]

The attitude of Hugh Chamberlen the elder appears clearly in a passage that seems about to reveal a major obstetric breakthrough, but ends in a combination of secrecy and self-advertisement. After mentioning the prevalent use of hooks in difficult labours, he adds,

my Father, Brothers, and my Self, (though none else in *Europe* that I know)
have by Gods blessing, and our industry, attained to, and long practised
a way to deliver a Woman in this case without any prejudice to her or her
Infant; though all others, (being reduced, for want of such an expedient,
to imploy the common way) do, and must endanger, if not destroy one or
both, by means of the Crochets.[66]

Chamberlen explains why he has not given details:

there being my Father and two Brothers living, that practise this Art, I
cannot esteeme it my own to dispose of, nor publish it without injury to
them; and think I have not been unserviceable to my Country, although
I do but inform them that the forementioned three persons of our family
and my self, can serve them in these extremities with greater safety than
others.[67]

This approach, despite Chamberlen's claims that he is actuated by filial and
fraternal loyalty, is not immediately attractive to present-day readers. He is
particularly easy to dislike because his methods were not useless curiosities
of medical history: they would, in some cases, have worked. Yet this kind
of secretiveness was not restricted to the Chamberlens, or even to man-
midwives. Sarah Stone mentions that she has a method for saving women
who have suffered severe haemorrhage, then adds: 'It is a secret I would
willingly have made known, for the benefit of my Sisters in the Profession;
but, having a Daughter that has practiced the same Art these ten years,
with as good success as my self, I shall leave it in her power to make it
known'.[68]
   It would be anachronistic to reproach them too severely for trying to
secure a comfortable living for their families, in an age far less affluent than
our own, when patents were not so efficiently managed. The task of providing
proper remuneration for inventors and manufacturers of remedies while
meeting the medical needs of patients remains difficult and controversial.
   Nevertheless, the Chamberlens, and other obstetric practitioners who
refused to reveal their lifesaving instruments and techniques, were reproached
by contemporaries who aspired to become professionals in a different sense.
The physician and man-midwife William Smellie declared in 1762:

I have heard a gentleman of eminence in one of the branches of medicine
affirm, that he never knew one person of our profession, who did not
pretend to be in possession of some secret or another: From whence he
concluded, that we were altogether a body of empirics. Such reflections
ought to make a suitable impression upon the minds of the honest and
ingenuous, prompt them to lay aside all such pitiful, selfish considerations,
and, for the future, act with openness and candour; which cannot fail of

redounding to the honour of the profession, and the good of society, as well as their own advantage.[69]

He gave wide publicity to the design and deployment of obstetric instruments and urged the importance of further research in the design of forceps and other devices to help women in labour, but insisted that the results should be shared: 'I hope every gentleman will despise and avoid the character of a selfish secret-monger'.[70]

Ironically, the spread of knowledge did not banish secrecy from the birthing chamber. Formerly hidden to prevent rivals finding out anything about them, instruments were now concealed to avoid frightening patients who had heard of the damage they could do in the wrong hands. Smellie says that, 'as women are commonly frightened at the very name of an instrument, it is advisable to conceal them as much as possible, until the character of the operator is fully established'.[71] They were not just hidden from view: in order to muffle the telltale sounds and sensations of metal, Smellie covered his forceps with leather.[72] Readers concerned with hygiene might be somewhat reassured by his observation that the blades 'ought to be new covered with stripes of washed leather after they shall have been used, especially in delivering a woman suspected of having an infectious distemper'.[73] There were also times when Smellie himself failed to maintain his elitist stance of disinterested generosity. Bonnie Blackwell argues that he 'made it his life's work to democratize access to the forceps, because access to the instrument meant more male practitioners and an end to the female monopoly on midwifery', but adds that he failed to publish the plans of a mechanical model of a mother and baby, whose exclusive use gave him 'a monopoly on educating future obstetricians'.[74] Like others before and since, he was professional in more than one sense.

As experiments and observations increased the amount of knowledge about female reproduction, questions were raised about the subject's utility, and the means used to acquire it. Abstruse investigations also raised religious scruples: perhaps these processes were obscure for a reason, and should be regarded as sacred mysteries not intended for human investigation. The affair of the virgin rabbits was one such instance, setting professional author against professional scientist.

On 2 February 1797, a paper by John Haighton, surgeon, demonstrator in anatomy, and lecturer on physiology and midwifery, was read to the Royal Society: it recorded dissections and vivisections of female rabbits in various stages of the breeding cycle:

> Having procured a full grown virgin rabbit, which had betrayed signs of disposition for the male, I made an incision into the posterior part of each flank, exactly upon the part where the tubes are situated. By means of my

finger and a bent probe, I drew out a very small portion of the middle of the tube, and cut out about 1/8 of an inch. The two ends were returned into their former situation, and the wound closed by what surgeons call the quill suture. The same operation was performed on the opposite side, and in a few days both wounds were healed.

As soon as this rabbit appeared in health, it was admitted to the male, but the venereal appetite seemed to be entirely lost.[75]

This experiment, and others like it, were brought to the notice of the satirist Thomas James Mathias, a learned man whose footnotes are more interesting than his poetry. In his verse, he says, rather enigmatically, 'I spurn'd unfeeling science, cruel tales/ Of virgin rabbets, and of headless snails'.[76] Yet he annotates his abhorrence with impassioned clarity:

> I allude in general to all needless, and cruel experiments upon animals. [...] Surely to sit calmly and watch with an impure, and inhuman, and unhallowed curiosity the progress of the desires, and the extinction of the natural passions in devoted animals after such mutilations and experiments, is a practice useless, wicked, foolish, degrading, and barbarous. There is no justification to be offered. The mystery itself is not to be disclosed to men. But we will know every thing; I wish we would recollect that we must account for our knowledge. [...] WHY HAS THE SOCIETY A COUNCIL? THE COUNCIL should be a literary and philosophical *Grand Jury*.[77]

Mathias might appear short-sighted, as he denies the value of the investigations that would, ultimately, clear up all the difficulties discussed in this chapter, and lead to more effective treatment of pregnant women. But his insistence that what we would think of as 'science' should be controlled by laymen, including practitioners of the 'arts', has much in common with the aims of ethical committees today. It also chimes in with the chorus of competing discourses that echoed around the mothers' mysteriously fertile bodies: however 'profession' is defined, childbirth is too important, and too multifaceted, to be monopolized by any one of them.

NOTES

1. Audrey Eccles, *Obstetrics and Gynaecology in Tudor and Stuart England* (London and Canberra: Croom Helm, 1982), p. 7.
2. Lisa Forman Cody, *Birthing the Nation: Sex, Science, and the Conception of Eighteenth-Century Britons* (Oxford: Oxford University Press, 2005), p. 7.
3. See Adrian Wilson, *The Making of Man-Midwifery: Childbirth in England 1660–1770* (London: UCL Press, 1995), p. 201.
4. Two pioneering general studies of early modern ideas on generation are R. C. Punnett, 'Ovists and Animalculists', *The American Naturalist*, 62 (1928): 481–507, and Francis J. Cole, *Early Theories of Sexual Generation* (Oxford: Clarendon, 1930). For debates

between preformationists (who believed the foetus existed in the father's sperm or the mother's egg) and those who believed in epigenesis (the development of the child as a combination of egg and sperm), see Shirley A. Roe, *Matter, Life, and Generation: Eighteenth-Century Embryology and the Haller-Wolff Debate* (Cambridge, UK: Cambridge University Press, 1981).

5. See Aristotle, *De Generatione Animalium*, ed. and trans. A. L. Peck (c. 330 BC; London: William Heinemann; Cambridge, MA: Harvard University Press, 1943), 729b, pp. 112–15. See Hippocrates, *On Generation*, 6, 7, 8, in *Oeuvres Complètes d'Hippocrate*, ed. E. Littré, 10 vols. (c. 3rd century BC; Amsterdam: Adolf M. Hakkert, 1961–62), vol. 7, pp. 478–83.

6. Galen, *On the Natural Faculties*, trans. Arthur John Brock (AD 170; London: William Heinemann; New York: G. P. Putnam's Sons, 1916), pp. 130–33.

7. Alexander Ross, *Arcana Microcosmi* (1651; London: John Clark, 1652), p. 28.

8. Ross, *Arcana Microcosmi*, p. 29.

9. William Harvey, *Anatomical Exercitations, Concerning the Generation of Living Creatures* (London: Octavian Pulleyn, 1653), p. 546. For the original Latin see William Harvey, *Exercitationes de Generatione Animalium* (London: Octavian Pulleyn, 1651), p. 296.

10. Anthony van Leeuwenhoek, Letter to 'D. D. Vicecomiti Brouncker [...] Nov. 1677', *Philosophical Transactions*, 12.142 (1679): 1040–43.

11. Edward Young, *The Complaint: Or, Night-Thoughts on Life, Death and Immortality* (London: R. Dodsley, 1742), p. 8.

12. Nicolas de Malebranche, *Treatise Concerning the Search after Truth*, trans. T. Taylor (1694; London: T. Bennet et al., 1700), p. 14.

13. Anthony van Leeuwenhoek, 'An abstract of a Letter [...] to Sir C. W.', *Philosophical Transactions*, 13. 145 (1683): 74–81 (76).

14. Leeuwenhoek, 'An abstract of a Letter', p. 76.

15. Robert James, *A Medicinal Dictionary*, 3 vols. (London: J. Roberts, 1743–45), sub 'Generatio'.

16. James, *A Medicinal Dictionary*, sub 'Generatio'.

17. Thomas Browne, *Pseudodoxia Epidemica*, ed. Robin R. Robbins, 2 vols. (1646; Oxford: Clarendon, 1981), Vol. 1, p. 71.

18. George Garden, 'A Discourse Concerning the Modern Theory of Generation, by Dr George Garden, of Aberdeen, being part of a Letter to Dr. William Musgrave, L.L.D. Reg. Soc. S. and by him communicated to the Royal Society', *Philosophical Transactions*, 17.192 (1691): 474–83 (478).

19. Fred J. Horton Jr., *The Melchizedek Tradition: A Critical Examination of the Sources to the fifth Century A.D. and in the Epistle to the Hebrews* (Cambridge, UK: Cambridge University Press, 1978), p. 163, n.

20. All biblical quotations are taken from *The Holy Bible, Containing the Old Testament, and the New: Newly Translated out of the Original Tongues: and with the Former Translations Diligently compared and Revised, by his Majestie's Speciall Commandement* (1611; London: Robert Barker, 1614).

21. Thomas Lye, *An Explanation of the Shorter Catechism, Compos'd by the Assembly of Divines at Westminster* (1673; London: Thomas Parkhurst, 1702), p. 28.

22. Joyce Irwin, 'Embryology and the Incarnation: A Sixteenth-Century Debate', *The Sixteenth Century Journal*, 9.3 (1978): 93–104 (98).

23. Thomas Lye, *An Explanation*, p. 6.

24. Jan Swammerdam, *The Book of Nature; or, The History of Insects*, trans. John Hill as *Biblia Naturae* (1737; London: C. D. Seyffert, 1758), p. 16.

25. John Cook, *An Anatomical and Mechanical Essay on the Whole Animal Economy*, 2 vols. (London: W. Meadows, 1730), Vol. 1, p. 29.

26. James Boswell, *Boswell's Life of Johnson*, ed. George Birkbeck Hill, 6 vols. (1791; Oxford: Clarendon, 1887), Vol. 2, p. 414.

27. Boswell, *Life of Johnson*, p. 414, n.

28. Boswell, *Life of Johnson*, p. 415.

29. See William Kurtz Wimsatt, Jr., *Philosophic Words: A Study of Style and Meaning in the Rambler and Dictionary of Samuel Johnson* (New Haven, CT: Yale University Press, 1948), and John Wiltshire, *Samuel Johnson in the Medical World: The Doctor and the Patient* (Cambridge, New York, and Melbourne: Cambridge University Press, 1991).

30. A classic introduction to *Tristram Shandy*'s reproductive context is Louis A. Landa, 'The Shandean Homunculus: The Background of Sterne's "Little Gentleman"', in *Restoration and Eighteenth-Century Literature: Essays in Honor of Alan Dugald McKillop*, ed. Carroll Gordon (Chicago, Ill, and London: University of Chicago Press, 1963), pp. 49–68.

31. Laurence Sterne, *The Life and Opinions of Tristram Shandy, Gentleman*, 3 vols., ed. Melvyn New, Joan New, Richard A. Davies and W. G. Day (1759–67; Gainesville, FL: University Presses of Florida, 1978–84), Vol. 1, p. 468. Yorick alludes to the fifth commandment, 'Honour thy father and thy mother, that thy dayes may bee prolonged in the land which the Lord thy God giveth thee' (Exodus 20:12).

32. See David Todd, *Imagining Monsters: Miscreations of the Self in Eighteenth-Century England* (Chicago, Ill: University of Chicago Press, 1995).

33. *The Gentleman's Magazine*, 34 (December 1764): 563.

34. James Augustus Blondel, *The Strength of Imagination in Pregnant Women Examin'd: And the Opinion that Marks and Deformities in Children Arrive from Thence, Demonstrated to be a Vulgar Error* (London: J. Peele, 1727), p. 34.

35. Blondel, *The Strength of Imagination*, p. 35.

36. Blondel, *The Strength of Imagination*, p. 36.

37. Daniel Turner, *A Discourse Concerning Gleets* [...] *To which is added, A Defence of the 12th Chapter of a Treatise De Morbis Cutaneis* (London: John Clarke, 1729), pp. 128–29.

38. Turner, *A Discourse Concerning Gleets*, p. 128.

39. For Toft's confessions, see Cody, *Birthing the Nation*, pp. 123–37. See also Lewis Wall, 'The Strange Case of Mary Toft (Who Was Delivered of Sixteen Rabbits and a Tabby Cat in 1726)', *Medical Heritage*, 1:3 (May/June 1985): 199–212.

40. Sir Richard Manningham, *An Exact Diary of What was Observ'd during a close Attendance upon Mary Tofts, the Pretended Rabbet-Breeder of Godalming in Surrey, From Monday Nov. 28, to Wednesday Dec. 7 Following. Together with An Account of her Confession of the Fraud* (London: J. Roberts, 1726), p. 19.

41. Manningham, *An Exact Diary*, p. 25.

42. Manningham, *An Exact Diary*, p. 31.

43. Manningham, *An Exact Diary*, p. 32.

44. Anon., *The Gentleman's Magazine*, 1 (September 1721): 401.

45. [Samuel Sharp], 'A Letter from an eminent Physician to a married Lady', *The Gentleman's Magazine*, 43 (October 1764): 455–57 (456). For Sharp's authorship of

this article, which appears anonymously, see *The Gentleman's Magazine*, 55 (January 1785): 62.

46. Alexander Ross, *Arcana Microcosmi*, p. 52.

47. Anon., 'To procure an easy Delivery to Women with Child', *The Gentleman's Magazine*, 23 (October 1753): 451.

48. Anon., *The Gentleman's Magazine*, 24 (January 1754): 23.

49. Michael Dalton, *The Country Justice* (1618; London: Richard and Edward Atkyns, 1717), p. 393. For women's ability to give birth to dead babies unaided, see Jane Sharp, *The Midwives Book* (London: Simon Miller, 1671), p. 190.

50. For a discussion of this topic in broader contexts see Garthine Walker, *Crime, Gender and Social Order in Early Modern England* (Cambridge, UK: Cambridge University Press, 2003).

51. Cody, *Birthing the Nation*, p. 41.

52. Wilson, *The Making of Man-Midwifery*, p. 53. See also Ornella Moscucci, *The Science of Woman: Gynaecology and Gender in England, 1800–1929* (Cambridge, UK: Cambridge University Press, 1990), p. 46.

53. Percivall Willughby, *Observations in Midwifery. As Also The country Midwifes Opusculum or Vade Mecum*, ed. Henry Blenkinsop (1630–85; Warwick: H. T. Cooke and Son, 1863), p. 192.

54. Willughby, *Observations in Midwifery*, p. 192.

55. See Adrian Wilson, 'William Hunter and the Varieties of Man-Midwifery', in *William Hunter and the Eighteenth-Century Medical World*, ed. W. F. Bynum and Roy Porter (Cambridge, UK: Cambridge University Press, 1985), pp. 343–69.

56. David Harley, 'Provincial midwives in England: Lancashire and Cheshire, 1660–1760', in *The Art of Midwifery: Early Modern Midwives in Europe*, ed. Hilary Marland (London and New York: Routledge, 1993), pp. 27–43 (p. 43). See also Moscucci, *The Science of Woman*, pp. 50–57.

57. See Wilson, *The Making of Man-Midwifery*, pp. 36, 32; and David Harley, 'Provincial midwives in England', in *The Art of Midwifery*, ed. Marland, pp. 31, 35.

58. James Caulfield, *Portraits, Memoirs, and Characters of Remarkable Persons, from the Reign of Edward the Third, to the Revolution*, 2 vols. (London: J. Caulfield and Isaac Herbert; J. Caulfield and Messrs. Harding, 1794–95), Vol. 1, p. 21. Reprint of *A Brief Narrative of A Strange and Wonderful Old Woman, who hath A Pair of Horns, Growing upon her Head* (London: T. J., 1679).

59. See Elizabeth Nihell, *A Treatise on the Art of Midwifery* (London: A. Morley, 1760), and Elizabeth Nihell, *An Answer to the Author of the Critical Review, For March, 1760, Upon the Article of Mrs. Nihell's Treatise on the Art of Midwifery* (London: A. Morley, 1760).

60. Nihell, *A Treatise on the Art of Midwifery*, p. 57.

61. See Sharp, *The Midwives Book*, pp. 193–94.

62. See Sarah Stone, *A Complete Practice of Midwifery* (London: T. Cooper, 1737), pp. 18, 22, 155; Sharp, *The Midwives Book*, p. 194.

63. Cody, *Birthing the Nation*, p. 197.

64. Walter Radcliffe, *The Secret Instrument* (London: William Heinemann, 1947), p. 30.

65. See Wilson, *The Making of Man-Midwifery*, pp. 56–57.

66. Hugh Chamberlen, 'The Translator to the Reader', in François Mauriceau, *The Diseases of Women with Child, and in Child-Bed*, trans. Hugh Chamberlen (1668;

London: R. Clavel, W. Cooper, Benj. Billingsly, W. Cadman, 1672), a2R (italics reversed).

67. Chamberlen, 'The Translator to the Reader', a2V (italics reversed).

68. Stone, *A Complete Practice of Midwifery*, p. 148.

69. William Smellie, *A Treatise on the Theory and Practice of Midwifery*, 3 vols. (1752; London: D. Wilson and T. Durham, 1762), Vol. 1, p. lxxi.

70. Smellie, *A Treatise on the Theory and Practice of Midwifery*, p. 257.

71. Smellie, *A Treatise on the Theory and Practice of Midwifery*, p. 265.

72. See Wilson, *The Making of Man-Midwifery*, p. 129.

73. Smellie, *A Treatise on the Theory and Practice of Midwifery*, p. 289.

74. Bonnie Blackwell, '*Tristram Shandy* and the Theater of the Mechanical Mother', *ELH*, 68. 1 (2001): 81–133 (93).

75. John Haighton, M.D., 'An Experimental Inquiry concerning Animal Impregnation', communicated by Maxwell Garthshore, *Philosophical Transactions*, 87 (1797): 159–96 (173).

76. Thomas James Mathias, *The Pursuits of Literature: A Satirical Poem in Dialogue. With Notes. Part the Fourth and Last* (1794; London: T. Becket, 1797), p. 84.

77. Mathias, *The Pursuits of Literature*, pp. 84–85.

3

Monstrous Issues:
The Uterus as Riddle
in Early Modern Medical Texts

LORI SCHROEDER HASLEM

The female reproductive system has, from very early on, been cast as the riddle of all riddles, as an entity calling for confounding and astounding descriptions that only the riddle is uniquely constructed to convey. To bear and to be born, these strike one as originary elemental riddles somehow in defiance of Aristotle's dictum that nothing can come from nothing. One of the earliest and possibly best-known recorded riddles about the mysterious uterus appeared for centuries in a Latin primer: 'My mother bore me, and soon was born of me'. The solution presented is water and ice, which in a sense 'give birth' to one another by moving through the processes of freezing and melting. Perhaps equally old is the one about clouds, presented riddlingly as that which 'becomes pregnant without conceiving'.[1] While these ancient riddles figure procreation in elemental terms, anthropologists have also long considered the cultural bases and implications of such procreation riddles, observing just how the social rituals of riddling work, for instance, to entrench incest taboos.[2] And from yet another perspective, just why procreation should be repeatedly encoded in the form of the riddle might be explained by human psychology, for as Freud observed, the central riddle of childhood is 'where do babies come from?'[3]

It is a mistake to think transhistorically of the riddle, to think of it as a durable rhetorical or linguistic form akin to anagrams and palindromes and serving mainly as a distraction or light entertainment. Riddles, like other linguistic forms, occupy a complex position within various cultures and at various historical moments. Recent critical works have done much to persuade us that historically grounded studies of linguistic forms such as puns and riddles and of rhetorical practices such as dilation and equivocation are crucial to our understanding of the interactions between early modern culture and literature.[4] And early modern literary accounts in

England are particularly thick with descriptions of the seemingly mysterious and miraculous workings – one might indeed say the riddle – of sexuality, especially female sexuality.

As for the riddle's place within 'serious' literature, critics and poets from the late sixteenth and early seventeenth century seem at odds. For some, riddles are nearly synonymous with condemnable affectation and obscurity in formal writing. 'Whatever looseth the grace, and clearenesse', writes Ben Jonson, 'converts into a Riddle; the obscurity is mark'd, but not the valew'.[5] And when writing to one's 'betters', both 'riotous' prose and 'Riddles of wit' are especially to be avoided.[6] On the other hand, during this period there is also significant evidence, including work by Sir Thomas More and Hoby's 1561 translation of *The Courtier*, that all sorts of 'merry jests' and even 'effective puns' were most certainly regarded as a reflection of real wit.[7] Moreover, because wonder is a concept and experience so central to seventeenth-century poetry, poets such as John Donne use the riddle to challenge the reader into puzzling out what seem to be astounding descriptions.[8] Similarly invested in the ethos of wonder, a number of Shakespearean romantic comedies make use of the riddle, specifically the riddle posed by a female character about some aspect of her sexual identity, as a means for achieving romantic closure. With the solving of such riddles, there is usually an implied 'solving' of a perceived ambiguity of or anxiety about the female.[9] Within early modern English culture, the riddle was indeed a popular form of entertainment, but riddling could also carry a deeper sense of the miraculous and the mystical than it does today.[10]

Engaging in riddle work in this period was also thought to serve the practical purpose of assessing one's intellectual abilities.[11] The title page of the 1617 *Booke of meery riddles*, so popular in its day, announces a twofold purpose, one to 'make pleasant pastime' but the other to provide a 'behooveful' test for a young man or child 'to know whether he be quick-witted or no'.[12] Early modern writers on rhetorical forms such as George Puttenham and Henry Peacham were sometimes concerned about the cultural implications of the popular bawdy riddles of their day, cautioning those who would be entertained by them to keep their wits sharp and to be vigilant against the 'naughtie' and 'undecent' thoughts that such riddles were apt to stir in the listener.[13] Old English riddles still in circulation frequently turned on double entendres involving sexual arousal, intercourse, and procreation, dating back at least to the *Exeter Book* (probably translated from Latin around the eleventh century), which contains seven so-called obscene riddles. There is, for example, one about that which 'grow[s] very tall, erect in a bed', is 'hairy underneath' and sometimes 'rob[bed] of [its] head' by beautiful girls who later cry at remembering the encounter (solution: onion). And the one about an object that 'grows / in the corner, rises and expands, throws up a crust',

Fig. 1: Figure of Dorothy, pregnant
with so many children that she must brace
her womb with a hoop (Ambroise Paré,
On Monsters and Marvels).

a 'boneless wonder' that becomes a 'swollen thing' a proud wife covers with
a cloth (solution: dough).[14] A true wit will see through the easy, obscene
answer to the more complex, supposedly more thoughtful solution.

Many of the more current riddles of the sixteenth and seventeenth
centuries were similarly bawdy. There is, for instance, the one about the
rough, bristly, red thing that 'never a Lady in this land but will be content
to take … in her hand' (solution: eglantine berry).[15] Or that which is
long and narrow and can be held in one's hand but will not lie in a great
chest (solution: a long spear). But increasingly the popular riddles of these
centuries turn on images of unnatural procreation,[16] for example a mother
who produces an impossible number of offspring, or an infant whose human
form is strangely altered, bestial, or otherwise abhorrent. The riddles of
unnatural procreation often depend upon notions of the female sexual body
as a potentially independent or nearly uncontainable force. Thus virgins or
girls may become 'pregnant' after running, playing, or dancing (solution:
spindles grow larger as they are wrapped with thread). One mother's body
produced ten thousand children, all of which have since died (solution:
a tree, its fruit, and its leaves).[17] The riddle might even centre on the act
of birthing as peculiar or even monstrous, as in the following: '[U]nto
the exchange [I] went some knacks for to buy, within a cloister there was
panting a monster certainly: foot & hands it had full eight, & four eyes clear
of sight: four ears whereby to hear, & two bodies exceeding clear'.[18] One is
prompted to visualize a monster, only to be soothed with the solution that
this is but a natural (though ominously public) scene of a mother birthing a
child. Importantly, such riddles offer a conceptually perverse image not of
the interpreter of the riddle but of the delivering mother herself.

Fig. 2: Figure of 'monster' born with four
arms and four legs (Ambroise Paré,
On Monsters and Marvels).

Indeed, alongside the proliferation of early modern sex and procreation riddles – and curiously connected to them – is the proliferation throughout Europe of a popular literature about monsters.[19] Some of the popular medical texts of this period present explicitly visual material that plays to notions about the possibly monstrous issue of the uterus. Many such illustrations appear in Ambroise Paré's 1573 *On Monsters and Marvels*, a book – like several others – that testifies to the enormous popular interest in unusual, miraculous, and monstrous births reported as documentable fact by early modern physicians. In fact, two of the illustrations found in Paré might even be said to offer visual solutions to two of the popular riddles about female reproduction just cited. 'Dorothy' (Fig. 1), said to have delivered a total of 22 babies during two confinements, is the monstrous solution initially evoked by the riddle about the prolific tree, while Paré's illustration of an infant 'deformed' with extra sets of limbs (Fig. 2) provides the image initially called up by the riddle of the monster born in the marketplace.

Each of these riddles has two viable and vying answers within the popular imagination, the one unnatural and monstrous, the other natural and benign (a tree dropping its leaves, a typical birthing).

Alongside texts and public shows featuring such monstrous creatures came theories on the causes of them, theories that shifted in a significant way during the early modern period. In the Middle Ages, and dating back to much earlier times, fear of monstrous offspring was rooted in the belief that such occurrences were signs from God and often directly attributable to moral failings in the parents of said monsters.[20] A mother's depraved imaginings of a monkey, a horse, or other animals, thought to directly affect her womb, might also bring about animalistic features in her baby. In fact, the imagination was believed to hold such sway over the uterus that it was said a baby could even resemble an adulterous woman's husband so long as she envisaged him while conceiving the child with another man,[21] a notion that might well have fomented already intense male fears of cuckoldry. There was, in short, an established tradition of mistrusting the imagination's potentially monstrous effects on the uterus and its contents.[22] Taboo sexual activity might also produce monstrous offspring. Bestiality was but one such deviance believed to cause monstrous births. Parents who ignored a priest's injunction against copulating on a Sunday night might produce a 'crippled, epileptic, or leprous' child. And the appearance of a uterine mola might signal a divinely instituted punishment of sterility, or a sign of witchcraft in the mother whose uterus produced such a thing.[23]

In the sixteenth century, however, the belief in God's role in creating such monsters as a direct sign or punishment began to give way to a somewhat different outlook. French social historian Jacques Gélis explains: 'The time of the monster as a sign or enigma had gone by. Monsters were now to be accounted for purely by the interplay of physical forces. [...] The monster became more and more a medical object, and should be spoken of "properly, as a physician would"'.[24]

So at the very time that the popular riddle became more frequently focused on *unnatural* procreation, the medical texts themselves were also more focused on the *natural* production of offspring, including offspring deformed for purportedly scientific reasons. Physicians such as Paré and midwives such as Jane Sharp, for instance, point to an 'excess of seed' as the main clinical cause for an infant born with extra limbs.[25]

In her recent work on the ascendancy of gynaecology as a medical specialty, Monica Green documents the sixteenth century as a time in which major works in the field of gynaecology and obstetrics proliferated across Europe, a testament to the project of medicalizing gynaecology and obstetrics.[26] However, while much in these texts does indeed attend to the anatomical facts of the female reproductive system, there are nevertheless sections in them that draw heavily from, and are in some sense overlaid with, longstanding popular suspicions and fears about aberrant female sexuality. Take, for instance, the 'true story' about one woman whose hymen was impenetrable by her husband and had to be surgically cut. Strangely, the story goes, she was already advanced in pregnancy even at the time of her surgery, purportedly impregnated by the seed of a man who had bathed in the same water she had.[27] Such a story is not so far from those riddles that depicted virgins (spindles) as capable of becoming pregnant from running or dancing too much. Bathing, it seems, could have been included in that list of reproductive activities. Similarly, next to one gynaecological text's otherwise very clinical set of instructions on delivering an infant appears the gloss 'Meanes to know whether the child be a monster or no'.[28] While approaching obstetrics clinically is clearly a goal of such texts, at such points there is also a subtext that warns against

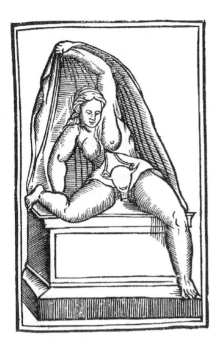 

Figs. 3 and 4: Female figures lifting the veil to display reproductive organs (from Berengarius, *Isagoge Breves* (1522)).

forgetting earlier taboos and superstitions. In fact, I argue that the popular riddles and the gynaecological texts of this period reveal a shared anxiety about the female reproductive body and that both discourses – seemingly engaging somewhat different audiences – attempt to grapple with this anxiety in a similar way: by showing that which is spooky, aberrant, or otherwise monstrous to be natural, normal, and intellectually explicable to those who are quick-witted and willing to see. At the same time, neither the riddles nor the gynaecological texts are fully successful in erasing the images of the aberrant or monstrous that they seek to resolve.

While in the medieval period descriptions of the imagined human uterus and of actual dissections of female pigs' uteruses draw attention to the 'tunic' or 'chemise' of the womb that can be drawn (almost like a curtain) to reveal the chambers or cells within,[29] in the sixteenth and seventeenth centuries actual female uteruses were publicly revealed in the popular 'anatomy theatres'.[30] Accordingly, the gynaecological texts of this period often present the female reproductive body as a mystery that is finally to be understood, unveiled. Both the written texts and the illustrations often liken the anatomizing of reproductive organs to the casting off of one or several coats or veils before the viewer's gaze (figs. 3 and 4).[31]

Given the potentially erotic nature of such a pose and of the subject matter more generally, it is perhaps not surprising that many of the writers of gynaecological texts express concern about those who might disregard the seriousness of the medical project, seeking out these texts instead for indecent purposes.[32] *The birth of mankynde* (1545) suggests that envious and malicious midwives are the ones promoting such fears, telling their acquaintances that these texts are but 'a slander to women and that every boy and knave had of these books, reading them as openly as the tales of Robin Hood'.[33] Trying to work around the problem of revealing what decorum perhaps requires should remain concealed, the 1612 translator of Guillemeau's *Child-Birth, or The Happy Deliverie of Women* begins by conceding that some might accuse him of making 'common a commodity which the learned would have had private to themselves', while others might find him 'offensive to Women in divulging that which they would not have come to open light, and which beside cannot be expressed in such modest terms as are fit for the virginity of pen and paper and the white sheets of their childbed'. To counter such accusations of bawdiness, this text announces the paradoxical goal of being as 'private and retired...in expressing all the passages in this kind as possible'.[34] The author endeavors to make matters clear while remaining modestly obscure. Helkiah Crooke announces similarly at the outset of his seventeenth-century anatomy, *Microscosmographia*, that he hopes to escape charges of lewdness by using 'honest words and circumlocutions to mollify the harshness of his argument'.[35] More the exception than the rule is Nicholas Culpeper, who states forthrightly near the beginning of his 1651 *Directory for Midwives* – a text that many argued played to prurient interests – that no apology is necessary for revealing the workings of female anatomy and that women themselves would be apt to thank him for 'telling them something they knew not before'.[36]

There are some fairly clear, though broad, reasons for early modern ambivalence about showing the workings of the female body, which had long been portrayed in literary, religious, and cultural texts alike as both powerful and inscrutable, miraculous and threatening. Some of these inherited texts – especially the religious and literary texts – were given to casting maternal workings as mystical and pregnancy as an almost magical spinning of something out of nothing.[37] Typologically, the riddling mystery of ideal female sexuality is figured in the Virgin Mary, a 'maid' who according to Vives is herself a kind of riddle – 'both mother, spouse, and daughter to that god' whom she 'gettest and art gotten [by] and [is] married unto'. The maternal body of a good and chaste Christian mother could be miraculous in its way too, though a body whose mystery must be closely guarded and hidden, a body that 'none can open but he hath the key of David, that is thy spouse'.[38]

Again, early modern texts – especially those rooted in the ancient medical texts – also treat the womb as a force whose likes, dislikes, and powers were threateningly susceptible to the influence both of the imagination and the moon.[39] Nicholas Culpeper emphasizes – with the ancients – that the womb is suspiciously unstable, even paradoxical, and others repeat the old idea that the uterus itself is almost an animal in its own right, aggressively sucking in semen when it becomes available, thus constructing female sexual desire as strongly driven and threatening.[40] Moreover, the Aristotelian notion of the female body as an aberration of nature – a failed version of the *male* body – persisted, to such a degree that the early modern Helkiah Crooke felt compelled to comment at some length on this view of the female as 'the first monster in nature'.[41] Early modern writers and readers of medical texts apparently wanted to know this 'monster', but the widespread uneasiness about publishing potentially obscene, illustrated texts on female anatomy reveals that the curious were also ambivalent about fixing their eyes fully upon it.

There is, then, an intriguing parallel between the ambivalent strains that I have just outlined from the gynaecological texts – ambivalence between lifting and not lifting the veil to learn about female reproductive processes, as well as ambivalence about what such knowledge would bring – and the ambivalent attitudes revealed in, and by, popular riddles. In both, the 'secret' of female anatomy is presented as an image (whether conceptual or visual) that loses its potentially monstrous, even its potentially threatening, meaning if only it can be opened, shown, known, visualized, and/or somehow fixed. In both cases, the thrust is to remove ambivalence about the object of the female body by achieving mastery over it. And to achieve such mastery, both sets of texts employ a similar process of first obscuring, mystifying, and/or demonizing the conceptualization of the reproductive female and then revealing it as something more knowable and 'natural' than is at first presented.

Why in particular do riddles reflect some of the same impulses as early modern medical explanations, descriptions, and illustrations of the female body? The answer, I believe, lies with recognizing that both the verbal and the visual images of female anatomy in the medical texts are presented in a way remarkably similar to how the riddle form itself works. To see this parallel, one can usefully consider three features of the riddle (though not mutually exclusive features) that make it especially fit for conveying and constructing a number of complex early modern cultural ambivalences about the workings of the female body.

First, the riddle almost always involves a visual image, and – importantly – it is an image that is both obscured and revealed by the riddle's own language. Northrop Frye observed that the riddle mediates between the visual and the conceptual in the human mind, just as the charm mediates between the aural and the conceptual.[42] Thus, the riddle about the monster in the marketplace first offers an obscured and culturally demonized picture and then – with its seemingly obvious, simple solution – alters the image to present a suggestively more naturalistic and rationally understood explanation. But in the course of altering the image, the riddle inscribes the scene of childbirth as a monstrous image at the same time as it seemingly undoes that inscription. The association of birthing with monstrosity, suggested both by the very public display of the act in the marketplace and by the seemingly extraneous number of limbs on view, cannot be completely undone by the proposed solution. Such a riddle as this privileges one answer over another while still allowing psychological room for the original impression: a kind of palimpsest remains, images of maternal monstrosity remaining visible beneath images of the natural. As Iago says to an Othello who would like to undo the 'monstrous' scenes of sexuality he has been brought to imagine, 'What you know, you know'.[43]

Descriptions of the female sexual body in the early modern gynaecological texts operate similarly, purportedly overlaying existing popular views of female anatomy with a new and epistemologically correct view. These texts undertake to explain (both with words and visuals) the female reproductive organs to men long discouraged from attending births lest they see too much of those parts of women that they were never meant to see. Yet while many of the individual writers claim that their texts erase all obscene visualizations of the female body, the texts themselves often pull in the opposite direction, revealing and playing to a desire to *see* the workings of the female sexual body. As though presenting the solution to an enigma or riddle, then, the medical texts work to create the sense that one can suddenly 'see' (or at least can conceptualize seeing) what one could not 'see' before and may not or should not be able to see first hand. Some early modern European texts such as those by Vesalius, Spigelius, and Estienne (whose anatomies provide illustrations of the human body based on actual human dissections) especially elucidate this problematic pull between the urges to see and not to see. In such illustrations, a female nude typically displays a modesty that the male nude does not, but she covers up early in the text as precursor to being fully displayed later.[44] Thus, as one critic observes, the emphasis on her modesty is ironic since it will be in 'enormous contrast to the relentless "immodesty" the female body will be made to display in the anatomy itself'.[45]

As the uterus was put on display, whether literally so in the anatomy theatres or reproduced in the medical texts, it 'had to be mastered', says Jonathan Sawday 'in a complex process of representation'. Those attending anatomy theatres who felt compelled either to show or to gaze upon the female uterus displayed there, Sawday argues, also felt a compulsion to suppress, to erase, perhaps to return to the uninitiated state they occupied before viewing the displayed uterus. As such, the early modern period teems with images intended somehow to master the female sex organs, allowing them to be something both 'fetishistically adored' and 'violently suppressed'.[46] I contend that this impulse to suppress after having seen is similar to that displayed by those early modern rhetoricians worried about the effects of the bawdy riddle, which gained its power by enticing the riddlee into visualizing an obscene solution only to ask him/her to undo that bawdy solution by overlaying a more decent and even perhaps more logical solution. Such an erasure cannot, of course, fully occur. The riddle about the woman giving birth in the marketplace, once solved, will always retain something of the monstrous. Nevertheless, the medical texts – like riddles in general – also suggest that perhaps a kind of mastery over seemingly obscene visualizations of female anatomy can be gained by ascribing a non-obscene meaning to them. As the bawdy riddle has its 'correct', non-bawdy solution, so the public dissections of female anatomy (often carried out after cruel and hurried executions) carry a seemingly non-perverse meaning and wholly epistemological purpose when presented as illustrations in the medical texts, such pictorials working to suppress the sense that there is something obscene either in the female anatomy itself or in fixing one's gaze upon it.

Even those texts that do not include actual illustrations of sex organs highlight the scientific importance of being able to visualize the anatomical features of male and female sex organs alike. Because wombs were less often on actual display for doctors and midwives to observe, writers of the gynaecological texts often take care to enumerate the number of times they have witnessed a surgery or a public anatomy that displayed a uterus before their very eyes. In his Prologue, Thomas Raynald explains that the figures included in his text 'may be as exactly and clearly perceived as though ye were present at the cutting open of Anatomy of a dead woman'.[47] Similarly establishing their credentials, Helkiah Crooke and Jane Sharp describe a number of 'corrupted' or 'cancred [sic]' uteri that they witnessed being 'drawn forth' from women, each writer testifying to the whole and healthy life that such women afterwards enjoyed.[48] The eyes of these writers substitute for the eyes of the readers of these texts, who might themselves benefit from seeing a uterus on display. Such readers are therefore called upon to exercise their best visualization skills as they read what is outlined for them by the first-hand witnesses. As Helkiah Crooke explains, 'And that you may somewhat satisfy your self, of [the womb's] figure, place, and situation, you may see the underwritten figures immediately following; to the seeing of which let not him come which is not ingenuous and expert in lines, and shadow, or in picture, which doth much help physicians'.[49]

Crooke goes on to delineate several 'figures' of the womb, or matrix as it is more often called in these texts, with great care and detail. He emphasizes here the responsibility, not of the subject on display, nor of the presenter of said figures, but of the reader. As the reader of *The Booke of meery riddles* is warned that he is about to engage in a test of his wit, so the reader of Crooke's text must understand that his wit and intellect are being tested as he attempts to reconstruct the anatomical figures that he must in part draw with his own mind's eye.

A second feature of the riddle that aligns it conceptually with the early gynaecological texts is the crucial emphasis on gaining knowledge and, through knowledge, power. Anthropologically, riddling is often associated with rituals that impart real or symbolic knowledge that in turn initiates one into a group, often into sexual and/or social adulthood.[50] In literature, a riddler whose riddle is solved usually relinquishes power, sometimes dramatically so, as when the Sphinx throws herself from the citadel once Oedipus solves her riddle. So, too, the medical texts, taken as a whole, heighten the sense of what can be gained by *knowing* a body – that is, in intellectual and medical terms – but especially by knowing the female body. The Prologue to *The birth of mankynde* observes that 'there is no man, whatsoever he be, that shall become an absolute and perfect physician unless he have absolute and perfect knowledge of all the inwards and outwards of man's and woman's body' and concludes that all 'crafty invention and diverse manners in the ministrations in the noble science of Physic proceedeth and spring from the profound knowledge of Anatomy'.[51] The knowledge that comes with seeing the answer, with perceiving the truth of the human anatomy, is the key to a powerful ability to 'minister' to the body. Such an outlook is in keeping with the broader empirical, Baconian project of the seventeenth century. Indeed, Bacon even borrows the language of the physician in articulating his epistemological stance towards previously hidden or superstitiously understood features of nature. 'For I am building in the human understanding a true model of the world, such as it is in fact', says Bacon in *Novum Organum* (1620), 'not such as man's own reason would have it to be; a thing which cannot be done without a very diligent dissection of the anatomy of the world'.[52]

Part of the Baconian project was to bring to light what intellectuals increasingly regarded as superstitious views towards monsters and prodigies.[53] Thus while the popular imagination in this century still held notions about the potentially monstrous answers to the mysteries and riddles of female anatomy and the uterus in particular, the natural philosophers of this period sought, in the words of one scholar, not to 'construct the monstrous as a category [but rather to] seek to erase it altogether. The fabulous, the marvelous, and the monstrous become the matter of a serious and sober "science" only as they are subjected to explanation, stripped of the wonder that makes them fabulous, marvelous, and monstrous'.[54] Accordingly, the epistemological project of the early part of the seventeenth century shares with riddling – especially riddling about procreation – a basic attempt to demystify, to medicalize, and to explain rationally the processes of female reproduction and the uterus in particular, to move deliberately away from providing the formerly constructed 'monstrous' solutions to the riddle of female anatomy.[55]

A third intriguing likeness between the approach to female anatomy of the medical texts and the riddles is their shared emphasis on the very condition and moment of either knowing or not knowing, seemingly allowing for no grey area in between. In its most basic form a riddle either means nothing (a signifier without a sign) when it is unsolved or it means something (though not necessarily a stable 'something') when it is solved. In one of its particular forms, too, the quibblingly bawdy riddle already mentioned, there is an either-or choice about meaning: one solution being construed as negative, bawdy, perhaps even monstrous and the other as positive, non-bawdy, and natural. Such a dichotomous outlook on sexuality – and especially on female sexuality – is frequently found in both the religious and medical texts of the day. One 1590 English sermon reminds women that they are apt to bear monsters unless God intervenes directly: 'It is from his mercy that you conceive, that you fulfill your time, that you are delivered of children, not of monsters'.[56] And other English preachers – among them John Donne – were given to equating the sinful human condition with the manner in which all were born from the mother's 'filthy, vile, and contaminated womb'. Conversely, though, many other sermons in the period hail the utter naturalness of the God-ordained reproductive process as practised by husband and wife.[57] Thus, the female sexual body is natural, chaste, God-given, and redemptive if read or inscribed in one way, or monstrous, threatening, and of the Devil if read or inscribed in another way. Similarly, while the medical writers often take pains to emphasize the potential hideousness of any issue coming from the animal-like, environmentally sensitive, and easily influenced womb, they also frequently note that there is absolutely nothing lewd, loathsome, or hideous about maternal workings. Almost as with the familiar Gestaltist rabbit-duck visual, such writings urge one to see the female sexual body in one way or the other but not in both ways at the same time.

Similarly, even while tending to work towards demystifying the processes of the female sexual body in the vein of Baconian scientific study, the gynaecological writings at times vacillate between a newfound sense of confidence in knowing and a retreat to the hitherto mysterious and superstitious. Ambroise Paré, the French physician said by some scholars to have made the most significant progress in naturalizing those born as 'monsters', typically explains their deformities in terms of the parents' contribution of too much or too little 'seed' or some other such physiological imbalance, rather than attributing their existence to some superstitious, God-directed punishment.[58] But even Paré is unwilling to commit entirely to natural explanations for such monstrous births, listing also among their causes both the glory of and the wrath of God.[59] Similarly, Jane Sharp, devoting several pages to explaining how and why the 'Mole and Monsters, distorted, imperfect, ill qualified Children are begotten', at first turns mainly to physiological causes. The cause of such aberrations, she says with confidence, is 'womens carnally knowing their Husbands when their Terms are purging forth'. But Sharp goes on to relate a story about a woman who purged two serpents from her womb several months after having given birth and then adds almost as an afterthought the older view that 'Imagination ofttimes also produceth Monstrous births, when women look too much on strange objects'.[60] And even while she cautions women to avoid sexual intercourse while they are menstruating, she seems unable to close the topic without harking back to the older view of monstrous births reflecting God's will. 'Let such as fear God, or love themselves, or their posterity', she warns, remember that 'yet God can punish the world with such grievous punishments, and that justly for our sins'.[61] Like Paré, she enumerates both natural and God-ordained reasons for monsters alongside one another. Presenting the causes of monstrous births both ways, Sharp's insights on how to avoid them operate equivocally, riddlingly, with a more superstitious, mysterious meaning just under the surface of the rational, supposedly more clinical explanation.

Considering the sex and procreation riddles of the sixteenth and seventeenth centuries alongside the gynaecological texts of the same period affords us a fascinating look at a historical moment of ambivalence and anxiety, a moment of medical optimism and inquiry that was tinged with old beliefs and superstitions. It is a moment when gynaecology was moving from a practical matter attended to by lower-class women to an art learned by aspiring male physicians. At the centre of this shift was the quest for knowledge that could once and for all clear up the riddling complexities of sex and procreation. It was knowledge, too, that for ages had been culturally and psychologically regarded as unique, in contrast with other forms of knowledge that learned men might seek in the form of philosophy or letters. 'It is not hard words that perform the work [of midwifery], as if none understood the Art that cannot understand Greek', Sharp sniffs. 'Words are but the shell, that we ofttimes break our Teeth with [...] to come at the kernel, I mean our brains to know what is the meaning of them'.[62] This slipperiness of language, this inability to be sure that one truly knows even what is set forth in words, Sharp implies, is the lot of any man who would study gynaecology and obstetrics, the kernel knowledge perhaps residing somewhere beyond his intellectual grasp. Such slipperiness and lack of sure linguistic meaning was a phenomenon already familiar from riddles of old and they were still current in early modern popular thought. In the gynaecological texts we find telling traces of those early popular riddles, in which female reproductive activity so frequently threatened to slide from the medical and the rational into the irrational, the mysterious, the obscene, and the monstrous.

NOTES

1. Eleanor Cook, 'Riddles of Procreation', *Connotations*, 8.3 (1998–99): 271–72.
2. See, for instance, Roger Abrahams, who draws on Levi-Strauss in *Between the Living and the Dead* (Helsinki: Folklore Fellows Communications, 1980), pp. 20–22, 225. See also Thomas A. Burns, 'Riddling: Occasion to Act', *Journal of American Folklore*, 89 (April–June 1976): 139–65; and Thomas V. Peterson, 'Initiation Rite as Riddle', *Journal of Ritual Studies*, 1.1 (1987): 73–84.
3. Sigmund Freud, *Three Essays on the Theory of Sexuality*, revised edition (Basic Books, 2000), p. 61.
4. Valerie Wayne and Catherine Belsey, *The Matter of Difference; Materialist Feminist Criticism of Shakespeare* (Ithaca, NY: Cornell University Press, 1991); Patricia Parker, *Shakespeare from the Margins* (Chicago, Ill: University of Chicago Press, 1996); Mary Bly, *Queer Virgins and Virgin Queans on the Early Modern Stage* (Oxford: Oxford University Press, 2000); Steven Mullaney, *The Place of the Stage: License, Play, and Power in Renaissance England* (Ann Arbor, MI: University of Michigan Press, 1995).
5. Ben Jonson, 'Timber: or, Discoveries', in *Literary Criticism of Seventeenth-Century England*, ed. Edward W. Tayler (New York: Knopf, 1967), p. 122.
6. Jonson, 'Timber', in *Literary Criticism*, ed. Edward W. Tayler, p. 128.
7. William Crane, Wit and Rhetoric in the Renaissance: The Formal Basis of Elizabethan Prose Style (NY: Columbia University Press, 1937), p. 20.
8. James Biester, *Lyric Wonder: Rhetoric and Wit in Renaissance English Poetry* (Ithaca, NY: Cornell University Press, 1997), p. 14.
9. T. G. Bishop, *Shakespeare and the Theatre of Wonder* (Cambridge, UK: Cambridge University Press, 1996); Lori Schroeder Haslem, 'Riddles, Female Space, and Closure in *All's Well That Ends Well*', *English Language Notes*, 38.4 (June 2001): 19–33.
10. On sacred versus literary uses of the riddle see Roger D. Abrahams, 'The Literary Study of the Riddle', in *Texas Studies in Literature*, 14.1 (1972): 177–97.
11. Biester, *Lyric Wonder*, p. 15.
12. *The Booke of meery riddles: together with proper questions and witty proverbs... To Know if he be Quick-Witted, or No* (1617; London: Printed for John Stafford and W.G., 1660; Ann Arbor, MI: University Microfilms International, 1985).
13. George Puttenham, 'The Arte of Poesie', in *The English Experience*, 342 (New York: Da Capo, 1971), pp. 155–57; also on Puttenham, see Haslem, 'Riddles, Female

Space and Closure', pp. 25–26; on Peacham, see Cook, 'Riddles of Procreation', p. 272.

14. *Anglo-Saxon Riddles of the Exeter Book*, trans. Paull F. Baum (Durham, NC: Duke University Press, 1963).

15. From *The Booke of meery riddles.*

16. Cook, 'Riddles of Procreation', pp. 273–74.

17. From *The Booke of meery riddles.*

18. All the riddles cited are indexed in Archer Taylor, *English Riddles from Oral Tradition* (Berkeley, CA: University of California Press, 1951); the riddle of the monster in the marketplace is taken from *Holme Riddles*, 134 (cited as such in Taylor).

19. Ambroise Paré, *On Monsters and Marvels*, trans. and ed. Janis L. Pallister (Chicago, Ill: University of Chicago Press, 1982); see also Lorraine Daston and Katharine Park, *Wonders and the Order of Nature, 1150–1750* (New York: Zone Books, 1998), pp. 173–214.

20. Jacques Gélis, *History of Childbirth: Fertility, Pregnancy and Birth in Early Modern Europe*, trans. Rosemary Morris (Boston, MA: Northeastern University Press, 1991), pp. 255–69; Lorraine Daston, 'Marvelous Facts and Miraculous Evidence in Early Modern Europe', in *Critical Inquiry*, 18.1 (Autumn 1991): 93–124.

21. John Sadler, *The Sicke Womans Private Looking-Glasse*, quoted in Paré, *On Monsters and Marvels*, Appendix 3, p. 175; Paré himself, though skeptical, cites several renowned ancients (Heliodorus, Damascene, Hippocrates) who recorded the phenomenon of a woman giving birth to a child resembling the picture of a man she looked upon during conception (sometimes a man of a different race), pp. 39–41.

22. Many of the early modern gynaecological texts take for granted this ancient link between the imagination and the womb, and some further correlate the female imagination with particular sinfulness or evil capable also of deforming an infant. See Gail Kern Paster, *The Body Embarrassed: Drama and the Disciplines of Shame in Early Modern England* (Ithaca, NY: Cornell University Press, 1983), pp. 163–82; and Mary E. Fissell, *Vernacular Bodies: The Politics of Reproduction in Early Modern England* (Oxford: Oxford University Press, 2007), pp. 53–89.

23. Gélis, *History of Childbirth*, pp. 258–59, 264; Helen King, *Midwifery, Obstetrics and the Rise of Gynaecology: The Uses of a Sixteenth-Century Compendium* (Hants, UK: Ashgate, 2007), pp. 59–64.

24. Gélis, *History of Childbirth*, p. 267.

25. Paré, *On Monsters and Marvels*, especially pp. 3–23; Jane Sharp, *The Midwives Book: Or the Whole Art of Midwifry Discovered*, ed. Elaine Hobby (New York and Oxford: Oxford University Press, 1999), pp. 91–92.

26. Monica H. Green, *Making Women's Medicine Masculine: The Rise of Male Authority in Pre-Modern Gynaecology* (Oxford: Oxford University Press, 2008), p. 275.

27. Jacques Guillemeau, *Child-birth, or The Happy Deliverie of Women* (London: Hatfield, 1612), pp. 108–09.

28. Guillemeau, *Child-birth*, p. 174. While the meaning of the term 'monster' was also sliding into something more clinical (being used here in a section on how to determine whether twins are conjoined or separate during delivery), the use of the word here is nevertheless loaded with its historical meaning.

29. Danielle Jacquart and Claude Thomasset, *Sexuality and Medicine in the Middle*

Ages, trans. Matthew Adamson (Princeton, NJ: Princeton University Press, 1988), pp. 26–27.

30. Jonathan Sawday, *The Body Emblazoned: Dissection and the Human Body in Renaissance Culture* (London: Routledge, 1995).

31. See illustrations by Berengarius that follow. Paré comments that 'women have as much hidden within the body as men have exposed outside' (*On Monsters and Marvels*, p. 32). Sharp (*The Midwives Book*) regularly refers to the 'coats' (by which she sometimes means skin and sometimes means membranes that cover the sex organs); another popular gynaecological text anatomizes the body by describing in turn each 'investiture or clothing of the body' (Eucharius Roesslin, *The birth of mankynde, otherwise named the woman's book*, trans. Thomas Raynald [Center for Research Libraries, electronic text, 1545], p. 18).

32. David Cressy, *Birth, Marriage, and Death: Ritual, Religion, and the Life-Cycle in Tudor and Stuart England* (Oxford: Oxford University Press, 1997), pp. 39–41.

33. Roesslin, *The birth of mankynde*, p. 15.

34. Guillemeau, *Child-birth*, pp. 2–3.

35. Quoted in Cressy, *Birth, Marriage, and Death*, p. 40.

36. Quoted in Kate Aughterson (ed.), *Renaissance Woman: A Sourcebook: Constructions of Femininity in England* (London: Routledge, 1995), p. 57.

37. For the ancient, mythological roots of this notion of womb as web and women as spinners of the human fabric, see Erich Neumann, *The Great Mother: An Analysis of the Archetype*, trans. Ralph Manheim (Princeton, NJ: Princeton University Press, 1972), pp. 227–31.

38. Juan Luis Vives, 'Instruction of a Christian Woman', *Daughters, Wives, and Widows: Writings by Men about Women and Marriage in England, 1550–1640*, ed. Joan Larsen Klein (Urbana and Chicago, Ill: University of Illinois Press, 1992), p. 104; Mary Fissell, *Vernacular Bodies: The Politics of Reproduction in Early Modern England* (Oxford and New York: Oxford University Press, 2004), p. 53, argues that this positive, miraculous view of the uterus began to wane when, increasingly, Protestant women were no longer taught to identify their wombs with that of the Virgin Mary.

39. On this concept, see Ian Maclean, *The Renaissance Notion of Woman: A Study in the Fortunes of Scholasticism and Medical Science in European Intellectual Life* (Cambridge, UK: Cambridge University Press, 1980); Aubrey Eccles, *Obstetrics and Gynaecology in Tudor and Stuart England* (Kent, OH: Kent State University Press, 1982); Paster, *The Body Embarrassed*, p. 175

40. On the womb as unstable and paradoxical, see Paster, *The Body Embarrassed*, p. 174; on the womb as animal, see Gélis, *History of Childbirth*, pp. 59–61.

41. Quoted in Aughterson, *Renaissance Woman*, p. 55; on this view more generally, see Maclean, *Renaissance Notion of Woman*, pp. 30–32.

42. Northrop Frye, 'Charms and Riddles', in *Spiritus Mundi: Essays on Literature, Myth, and Society* (Bloomington, IN: University of Indiana Press, 1976), p. 124.

43. William Shakespeare, *Othello, the Moor of Venice*, 5.2.303, *The Riverside Shakespeare*, ed. G. Blakemore Evans et al. (Boston, Mass.: Houghton Mifflin, 1974).

44. See Sawday, *The Body Emblazoned*, pp. 183–229 (with illustrations).

45. Howard Marchitello, 'Vesalius' *Fabrica* and Shakespeare's *Othello*: Anatomy, Gender, and the Narrative Production of Meaning', *Criticism* 35.4 (Fall 1993): 541.

46. Sawday, *The Body Emblazoned*, pp. 222–23.

47. Roesslin, *The birth of mankynde*, p. 7.
48. Helkiah Crooke, *Microcosmographia: a description of the body of man… out of all the best authors of anatomy* (1615; Ann Arbor, MI: UMI, 1970), p. 108; Sharp, *Midwives Book*, p. 36.
49. Crooke, *Microcosmographia*, p. 107.
50. Burns. 'Riddling: Occasion to Act'; Peterson, 'Initiation Rite as Riddle'.
51. Roesslin, *The birth of mankynde*, pp. 7–8.
52. Francis Bacon, *Francis Bacon: A Selection of His Works*, ed. Sidney Warhaft (Indianapolis, IN: Bobbs-Merrill, 1984), p. 370.
53. Katharine Park and Lorraine Daston, 'The Study of Monsters in Sixteenth- and Seventeenth-Century France and England', *Past and Present*, 92 (August 1981): 20–54; Daston, 'Marvelous Facts and Miraculous Evidence in Early Modern Europe'; Arnold I. Davidson, 'The Horror of Monsters', in *The Boundaries of Humanity: Humans, Animals, Machines*, ed. James J. Sheehan and Morton Sosna (Berkeley, CA: University of California Press, 1991), pp. 36–67.
54. Robert Stillman, 'The Universal Philosophy of Politics and Monsters of Metaphor', *The New Philosophy and Universal Languages in Seventeenth-Century England: Bacon, Hobbes, and Wilkins* (Cranbury, NJ: Associated University Presses, 1995), p. 128.
55. Haslem, 'Riddles, Female Space, and Closure', p. 22.
56. Christopher Hooke, 'The childbirth', quoted in Aughterson, *Renaissance Woman*, p. 123.
57. Cressy, *Birth, Marriage, and Death*, pp. 18–20.
58. Jean Cérard is credited with this observation (Gélis, *History of Childbirth*, p. 267).
59. Paré, *On Monsters and Marvels*, p. 3.
60. Sharp, *Midwives Book*, pp. 86, 88.
61. Sharp, *Midwives Book*, p. 91.
62. Sharp, *Midwives Book*, pp. 12–13.

4

Surveilling the Secrets of the Female Body: The Contest for Reproductive Authority in the Popular Press of the Seventeenth Century

SUSAN C. STAUB

In its 12–19 December issue of 1650, Marchamont Nedham's parliamentarian newsbook, *Mercurius Politicus*, recounted the startling story of Anne Greene, a 22-year old Oxford woman convicted and hanged for the murder of her newborn son, but discovered still to be alive as she was prepared for a public anatomy lecture:

> Being cut down, she was put into a Coffin, and brought to the house where the body was appointed to be dissected before the company of Physicians, and other ingenuous Gentleman, who have a weekly meeting at Mr. *Clarks* the Apothecary, about naturall enquiries and experiments [...]. When they opened the Coffin to prepare the body for dissection, they perceived some small ratling in her throat [...] Dr. *Petty*, with Mr. *Clerk* of *Magdalen* Colledg, and Mr. *Willis* of *Christ Church*, fell speedily to use means to bring her to life. They opened a vein, layed her in a warm bed, procured a woman to goe into bed with her, and continued the use of divers other remedies respecting her senslesnesse, head, throat, and breast, so that it pleased God within 14 hours she spake, and the next day talk'd and coughed very heartily, and is now in great hope of recovery.

Characterizing the event as 'a remarkable act of providence', insisting on Greene's innocence of the crime for which she was executed, and warning that 'such a contrary verdict from heaven' should 'strike terror to the consciences of those who have been any way faulty in this businesse', the account also offered forensic evidence that should have resulted in Greene's acquittal – the estimated gestation period ('near the fourth moneth of her time'), Greene's lack of awareness that she was pregnant, and the unformed state of the foetus ('not above a span long, and of whether sexe scarce distinguished'). Three weeks later, the newsbook took up the story again by investigating Greene's memories of the ordeal she suffered from her time on the gallows through to her recovery.[1] Around the same time, another account of this event appeared, in *'A Wonder of Wonders, Being a faithful Narrative and true Relation, of one Anne Green'* (1651), followed later in the year by *'A Declaration from Oxford, of Anne Greene'* (1651), and two separate editions of *'Newes from the Dead or a True and Exact Narration of the miraculous deliverance of Anne Greene'* (1651). Greene's story continued to be told throughout the seventeenth and eighteenth centuries.[2]

Greene's resurrection was just the kind of subject about which the popular press clamoured. There were dozens of street pamphlets published in the seventeenth century detailing various unnatural or wondrous events – the appearance of a blazing star or the birth of a two-headed baby, for instance – as well as accounts of heinous murders and other violent crimes.[3] Child murder was a frequent topic. Although there were many instances of infanticide recorded in court documents during the period and several in the popular press, Greene's story was unique because it was retold many times, each rendition with varying emphases and agendas. As a near-death experience that also affirmed divine justice, it is not hard to imagine why this narrative might have captured the imagination; at a time of great cultural upheaval, it offered comforting assurance of a providential order that superseded earthly statutes when necessary. Despite its sensational characteristics, however, the event and the narratives recounting it had broader social significance – legal, theological, political, domestic, and scientific.[4]

The most unusual and complex of these accounts is *'Newes from the Dead'*, a pamphlet attributed to Richard Watkins by the *Short Title Catalogue* but obviously shaped by the first-hand account of anatomist William Petty's role in Greene's recovery.[5] As a popular pamphlet the text is an anomaly because of its analytical and scientific tone. It is at once a scientific explanation of an extraordinary event and, concomitantly, a rather voyeuristic examination of female bodily functions. This version of the story is of particular interest for the history of medicine because in its detailed assessment of Greene's body and its reaction to the doctors' care, it takes on characteristics of a medical case history and, at the same time, vividly illustrates the intersection of the two types of knowledge vying for authority over the female body in the period: the intuitive, 'amateur' knowledge of midwives and matrons and the 'professional', scientific knowledge of male physicians. Laura Gowing also discusses this case as one that 'seems to pit amateur women against professional men', but Gowing concludes that Greene's revival can 'be read as a victory of women's tactile knowledge against male scientific investigation'.

While I see ambivalence towards midwifery and intuitive female knowledge in this story, I read it as ultimately confirming male superiority.[6] As such, *'Newes from the Dead'* plays out in its pages the contest for control of the reproductive body that raged throughout the seventeenth century. While scholars have documented in some detail the shift taking place in medical thought and in attitudes towards women's bodies and reproduction in this time period, this essay seeks to examine more fully how this specific case participates in changing ideological constructions of the female body. My interest, then, is in the way this particular narrative of Greene's story illustrates fundamental changes taking place in the fields of childbirth and medicine, and in attitudes towards female bodies. Furthermore, in this text we see the convergence of medical, legal, and popular discourses working together to transform the reproductive body into something public, potentially knowable and, therefore, controllable. I argue that this text captures a transitional cultural moment in the reinterpretation of female bodies.

Scholars have long recognized the growing role of male physicians and their encroachment into the female-centred world of reproduction and childbirth in the seventeenth century. Patricia Crawford argues that there was a change in the transmission of sexual knowledge in the sixteenth and seventeenth centuries, a privileging of textual and anatomical forms of knowledge over women's orally shared, practical knowledge.[7] The shift to anatomical knowledge was marked by a preoccupation with 'ocular inspection', in the words of William Harvey, an impulse that sought to turn the power of the scientific gaze onto the previously closed or hidden secrets of the female body. At the same time, this exposure of the body sought to control its rebellious nature, at least metaphorically.[8]

The scientific secularization of the female body that dissection and anatomy helped create was enhanced by several laws passed during the period shortly before Greene's execution. Of particular importance is the notorious infanticide law of 1624, 'An Acte to Prevent the Destroying and Murthering of Bastard Children', which made concealing the death of an illegitimate infant a felony punishable by hanging. I include the full text of the statute here because its rhetoric of suspicion and moral judgement ('lewd', 'shame', 'secret', 'alledge', 'hardly to be proved', 'great mischief') is quite striking:

> Whereas many *lewd* Women that have been delivered of *Bastard* children, to avoid their shame and to escape punishment, do secretly bury or conceal the death of their children, and after, if the child be found dead, the said women do alledge, that the said child was born dead; whereas it falleth out sometimes (although hardly is it to be proved) that the said child or children were murthered by the said women, their *lewd* mothers, or by

their assent or procurement: For the preventing therefore of this great mischief, be it enacted by the authority of the present parliament, ... That if any woman be delivered of any issue of her body, male or female, which being born alive, should by the laws of this realm be a *bastard*, and that she endeavour privately, either by drowning or secret burying thereof, or any other way, either by her self or the procuring of others, so to conceal the death thereof, as that it may not come to light, whether it were born alive or not, but be concealed: in every such case the said mother so offending shall suffer death as in the case of murther, except such mother can make proof by one witness at the least, that the child (whose death was by her so intended to be concealed) was born dead.[9]

It was under this statute that Greene was condemned. Through most of the sixteenth century, infanticide had largely been a private matter, or at most, a transgression regulated by church courts. But after the passage of this law (as well as several other 'poor' laws in the late sixteenth century) infanticide became a unique type of homicide. It was redefined as a crime committed only by unmarried women, and the concealment of pregnancy and/or death of a baby became the primary evidence of guilt. Reversing the normal rules of evidence, the statute presumed the mother's guilt in the death of an infant unless she could prove otherwise. Although the law made concealment of the death of a bastard child the indictable crime, hiding the pregnancy was viewed as substantiating evidence that the mother intended to do away with her infant. A woman who hid her pregnancy, and whose baby died in childbirth, was judged guilty of murder unless she had a witness to the birth or could show she had prepared for it.[10] Secrecy was thus the crime – secrecy about illicit sex, secrecy about pregnancy, and secrecy about childbirth.

As a grisly side benefit, the policing of female sexuality evident in the 1624 statute provided a source of female corpses for male anatomists. Although some scholars see a discrepancy between the severity of the 1624 law and the leniency with which it was enforced, it seems clear that the number of women indicted and executed for infanticide increased in the years immediately following the statute. In some scholars' estimates more women were executed for infanticide than for the more notorious crime of witchcraft.[11] Exact numbers are difficult to discern. In his examination of Essex court records from 1601 to 1665, for example, Keith Wrightson found 60 cases of infanticide, with only 8 of those indictments occurring before 1625. In the 25 years following the passage of the infanticide statute, Wrightson notes 31 prosecutions. While these numbers are relatively small and localized, they nonetheless suggest a marked increase in the number of women tried and subsequently executed for infanticide after 1624.[12]

Despite the apparent increase in the numbers of women executed, women as a whole were executed with far less frequency than men in early modern England, and women's bodies would have been less available for study than men's. Before 1660, it is difficult to trace the actual identity – and hence gender – of those dissected in public anatomies from extant records. But given the relative scarcity of women executed in comparison to men – most place this number at around 10 per cent – it seems reasonable to conclude that the numbers of female bodies available for anatomy lessons were comparable. Examining parish records between 1600 and 1735, Kate Cregan places the number of identifiably female bodies anatomized at 4 per cent in comparison to 40 per cent identifiable as male and estimates that roughly 4.7 women were anatomized per decade during this same time period.[13] Noting the apparent contradiction in the fact that most specific accounts of anatomization from the period involve women, Jonathan Sawday concludes that such stories survive only when 'something extraordinary seems to have occurred'. He further conjectures, 'if the scaffold afforded male bodies for the anatomists with some degree of regularity, female bodies were an altogether rarer commodity', a rarity, he concludes, that must have whet 'the appetites of the anatomists', particularly for a corpse of a woman of childbearing age.[14]

Ironically, the publicly shamed, sexually aberrant bodies of illegitimately pregnant women became the primary models for the reproductive body, the 'exemplars for the transmission of anatomical knowledge about female reproduction, knowledge that was applied *in extremis* in [the doctors'] intervention into difficult or arrested births. They become both the particular for the universal of social "evil" (uncontrolled fertility) and social "good" (legitimate maternity)'.[15] Ordinarily, women in the early modern period were governed by strict rules of modesty and privacy, but these rules were suspended for the woman accused of infanticide. Her initial sexual shame opens her body to the scrutiny of her society, and that body could be exposed in various ways: first in the court room and on the scaffold, and later by the doctors who dissected her in a public anatomy. (Greene's body will also be displayed after her 'resurrection' to the curious throngs who paid her father money for the privilege of viewing her. '*Newes from the Dead*' (p. 6) describes the aftermath: 'in the same Room where her Body was to have been dissected for the satisfaction of a few, she became a greater wonder, being reviv'd, to the satisfaction of multitudes that flocked thither daily to see her'). As is self-evident, then, even in the anatomy theatre, the obsession with the female body was not merely scientific. As Sawday explains:

> To open the female body was not just to embark upon a voyage of scientific discovery, but it was also to trace the lineaments of the rebellious nature

of womankind [...]. If the Renaissance anatomy theatre, in its modes of ritual and representation, offered the suggestion of redemption to the male cadaver, what it offered the female was the reverse: a demonstration of Eve's sin, a reinforcement of those structures of patriarchal control which, so the argument ran, were necessary to avoid a repetition of the first act of rebellion in the garden of Paradise.[16]

That Greene's story is not just a story of survival but of sexual transgression is especially clear in the case history Petty transcribed in his journal, which someone, perhaps not Petty himself, entitled, 'History of the Magdalen (or, The Raising of Anne Greene').[17] Magdalen here is used in the sense of a repentant female sinner, the allusion suggesting the cooperation of law, morality, and medicine in one woman's execution.

It is tempting to argue that the very fact that Greene was to be both hanged and publicly dissected shows the enormity of her transgression, but there is no real evidence that dissection was an additional penalty for infanticide in the period. Although public dissection was considered an extension of the initial punishment and a further degradation of the criminal body, the surgeons, not the sentencing judges, determined who was to be anatomized. A young woman of childbearing age like Greene offered the most scientific potential because of her reproductive capacity. The body thus became a commodity, and because it held such scientific value, 'the accumulated rituals and habits of centuries of religion and superstition were swept aside', as Peter Linebaugh notes.[18]

Although the passing of this law may at first seem to have little to do with the medicalization of childbirth, in its emphasis on seeing, on witnessing the reproductive body, the 1624 statute actually paved the way for the kind of increased specularization of the female body that anatomical dissection already demanded. Noting attempts to regulate midwives through licensing in 1616 and 1634, Kate Cregan sees a direct link between the infanticide law and the competition for control over pregnancy:

> It is important, then, that in the period when the act against infanticide was instituted – in terms that implicitly insisted upon the observation and examination of labouring women in general – that there was an avid contest over the professional monopoly to be performing the observation and examination. What more fortuitous law could be enacted than one that insisted upon the increased specularisation of birth?

In Cregan's estimation, this law actually helped bring about the professionalization of childbirth: 'the urge towards a monopoly market was implicit in the prosecution and the definition of infanticide in the seventeenth century [...] [It] helped to bolster the shift in power from female to male dominance of obstetric practices' because it emphasized the need for witnesses to childbirth

– the law made it imperative that 'women must be watched'.[19] The infanticide act thus encoded surveillance into legal statute.

Under ordinary circumstances, childbirth was the private domain of women – of the labouring mother, her midwife, and her female relatives and friends, or god-siblings. Male practitioners only assisted in the case of a difficult pregnancy, such as an obstructed foetus or one in which the mother or the baby were in danger. As interpreters of a privileged kind of knowledge, knowledge not just of pregnancy but also of virginity and paternity, early modern midwives occupied a unique social status. They overturned the normal distinctions of gender, class, and rank, and in their professional capacity often held authority over both men and women of a higher social position.[20] Offering expert testimony in cases of infanticide, child murder, and rape, they played a crucial role in the courts. As agents of the state charged with policing sexuality, they both protected patriarchy and were a threat to it. They were both the keepers and the revealers of secrets, sworn at once to uphold secrecy – 'You shall be secret, and not open any matter appertaining to your office in the presence of any men, unless necessity or great urgent cause do constrain you so to do' – and at the same time charged with upholding the public order – 'You shall not consent [...] that any woman be delivered secretly of that which goeth with, but in the presence of two or three lights ready'.[21] As one might expect, this privileged position made midwives the target of increased scrutiny and concern, particularly from those who recognized the larger significances – and the commercial potential – behind the management of reproduction.

The movement of professional men into the reproductive sphere occurred metaphorically in print long before it took place literally. As Laura Gowing explains it, the 'expanding role of male physicians' and 'the gradual eclipse of midwives by men was presaged' in the vernacular books on gynaecology that began appearing in the sixteenth century.[22] Although the first popular midwifery manual in England was published a full hundred years before Greene's execution, we see in these early texts some of the same assertions of male authority over the reproductive body that are evident in '*Newes from the Dead*'. The publication of midwifery and gynaecology manuals placed men into the private, female space of childbirth; the books served as literal substitutes for male practitioners and/or their knowledge as the writers imagine the midwife actually carrying them into the birthing chamber. Thomas Raynalde, for instance, envisages his text 'supply[ing] the roome and place of a goud mydwyfe'. And Jacob Rueff, author of *The Expert Midwife* (1637), replaces the woman's vision of her body with his own, likening the female reader to 'a blind man, which is deprived of the benefit of the light', and advising her to use his book as 'a Looking-glasse' in which she might see the female body reflected.[23] Caroline Bicks judges the looking glass image to be 'a particularly insidious kind of medical authority based on an invisible specular presence'.[24] Such texts, then, attempted to reconstruct the female body through tropes of male vision and knowledge. The number of these books increased throughout the seventeenth century, coming into full flower in the 1640s and 1650s.[25]

Perhaps the most important of these publications for my argument is Nicholas Culpeper's *Directory for Midwives* published in 1651, virtually concurrent with the stories circulating about Greene. Culpeper's text exhibits many of the same characteristics and attitudes towards intuitive female knowledge that we see in the pamphlet and, according to Fissell, marks a new way of looking at the reproductive body. It refocused attention onto the male reproductive body, which it typified as the 'norm' and discussed women's bodies dismissively and unashamedly.[26] Though at times Culpeper seems sympathetic in his attitude towards midwives, at others he attacks their authority directly. Taking on a didactic tone ('Let me instruct you', he says at the beginning of the book (p. 7)), Culpeper bemoans what he takes to be the willfulness of the physicians who have deliberately kept women ignorant: 'Through that ignorance you have been trained up in, you know not what belongs to these Veins', he posits at one point (p. 8). In another place, he chastises the doctors who have refused to allow women admittance into anatomies as 'high base' (p. 56). Depicting himself as an 'Eye-witness' (p. 5) and contrasting his own expertise with that of Galen and Vesalius, who, he says never saw a pregnant woman anatomized, but who 'our Anatomists follow [...] as little god-a-mighties' (p. 34), he insists: 'My self saw one Woman opened that died in Child-bed, not delivered, and that is more by one than most of our *Dons* have seen' (pp. 55–56). Without specific knowledge of anatomy, he asserts, midwives must humbly recognize their ignorance: 'All the Perfections that can be in a Woman, ought to be in a *Midwife*; the first step to which is, To know your ignorance in that part of Physick which is the Basis of your Art' (5v). By portraying midwifery as a branch of physic, Culpeper cleverly subjects it to male authority.[27] Simultaneously praising and discounting women's knowledge, Culpeper goes so far as to liken women's lack of insight about their bodies to someone groping for shoes in the dark and mistaking one shoe for the other.

Fissell characterizes *A Directory for Midwives* as 'a curious' and 'radical' book. Noting that it is addressed to women and dedicated to midwives, she argues that

> it attacks ways of knowing the body most often associated with women. [...] By anatomising the female body, Culpeper's book implicitly denies

that a female body might be the producer of knowledge itself. Only an anatomically trained person (which in mid-seventeenth-century England almost always meant a man) could make truths about the female body, truths that were hidden from view and inaccessible to the body that contained them.[28]

Further, as Fissell notes, Culpeper even takes over the very processes of generation himself in the imagery he uses to describe the writing and reading of his book. He portrays the writing process as a kind of birth: 'I conceived a few thoughts, and I hope to bring them to perfect birth' (3v). ('*Newes from the* Dead' also appropriates female reproductive tropes in its assessment of Petty and Willis's saving of Anne Greene as a 'miraculous *deliverance*'.)

Turning now to '*Newes from the Dead*', we see evidence of the same dismissive attitude towards female bodies and knowledge that was occurring culturally in medicine, law, and vernacular writings on midwifery. This text also exists on the nexus of debates about reproduction and its control. In his description of the physicians' cure of Greene, the pamphlet writer uses language of surveillance and control throughout: 'they perceive[ed]', 'they readily apprehended', 'they *wrenched* open her teeth', 'they *applied* plaster to her breasts and *ordered* an heating odoriferous Clyster to be cast up her body', 'the Physicians *took* from her right arm about nine ounces more of blood, and then *ordered* her a Julip' (pp. 2–3). The doctors manipulate every part of Anne's body, note her every reaction, and record everything she eats and drinks. The amount of detail is remarkable for a news pamphlet, its pseudo-scientific tone only thinly masking a prurient interest in the female body. The focus in the doctors' ministrations is overwhelmingly on the openings of that body – the mouth (the tongue and whether or not it is furry or numb gets particular attention), the bowels, and the genitals. ('*Newes from the* Dead' shows some discretion; Petty's account is much more explicit: 'She made some water this night, but had no stoole'; 'About 11 this day shee had an easy stoole, somewhat loose; eate severall tymes of her panada and barley water by little and little'; 'Her courses had come down fresh this morning. Her tongue not very dry, nor rough'; 'At night we saw her againe. She endeavoured to make water [but] could not'; 'Slept well, had a small stoole, made enough of reasonable good urine'.[29]) One of the most striking things about this pamphlet is that, like Culpeper's volume, it is not the least bit reticent about discussing the female body. While gynaecological manuals from the period had of necessity detailed the workings of the female reproductive organs, they did so cautiously and almost always with a concern that this exposure of female 'privities' 'would dishonour women and encourage men to "jest" about the female organs'.[30] This reticence was still operative in the 1650s; because of its explicit depiction of 'the organs of generation', Culpeper's *Directory for Midwives* was punningly dubbed 'Cul paper, paper fit to wipes one's breech withal' by one seventeenth-century critic.[31] Such contradictory impulses towards the female body – on the one hand, the insistence on exposure and on the other, a need for privacy – are everywhere present in this type of literature. While books on midwifery expose the reproductive body to scrutiny and surveillance while worrying about the dangers and propriety of revealing that body, '*Newes from the* Dead' exhibits no such ambivalence about publicly examining Greene's anatomy.

If the 'ideal' female body is enclosed and private as Peter Stallybrass contends,[32] it is clear that strict ideas of female modesty are suspended in this text, as they are for the female criminal on the scaffold and in the anatomy theatre. Of course, the female body was exposed in other ways in early modern culture: single women in particular were examined for signs of pregnancy on both official and unofficial occasions. The boundaries around the female body were hazily rendered, particularly those of working-class women, whose bodies were open to observation by employers, neighbours, and midwives. Although under the supervision of doctors, examinations of women were usually carried out by midwives or other women; immediately after death, male doctors were free to examine the corpse. In death the female body was no longer bound by the strictures of modesty. The miracle of Greene's survival opens her to the exposure of scientific inquiry, but she had already been made public by her crime because the female criminal on the scaffold disrupted the normative opposition of public/male space and private/female space. Her body, moreover, was exposed and made public by the pamphlet that chronicled how the doctors brought her back to life.

Although Petty and Willis were concerned with restoring Greene, almost all of the remedies described in the pamphlet were treatments for 'uterine fury' and/or the control of menstrual blood flow. Gynaecological texts from the period almost always posited a sympathy between the womb and other parts of the body. *The Woman's Doctour* (1652), for example, argues that 'the Matrix [that is, the womb] is the cause of all those diseases that happen to women':

> The Matrix hath a Sympathy with all the parts of the body; as with the Braine by the Nerves and Membranes of the parts about the spine, from which sometimes ariseth the paines, in the fore part, and the hinder part of the head, with the Heart also, both by the Spermatick, and the Epigastrick arteries, or those that lie about the abdomen at the bottome of the bellie, from hence cometh the paine of the heart, fainting and swounding fits, the passion of the Heart, anxietie of the minde, a dissolution of the spirits, insomuch as you cannot discerne, whether a woman breaths or not, or that she hath any pulse; it hath likewise a consent with the breasts; and from hence proceed those swellings, that hardness, and those terrible cancers

that afflict those tender parts, that a humour doth flow upwards, from the Matrix to the Breast, and downwards again, from the Breasts to the Matrix.[33]

Almost all women's illnesses were treated with remedies that sought either to increase or to decrease the flow of menstrual blood. (Curiously, Thomas Willis later rejected the so-called 'evil influence of the Womb' and blamed physicians for their proclivity to treat most diseases of women as such, treatments he characterized as 'a starting hole for ignorance'.[34]) Hilda Smith explains that women

> were bled, given herbs in either oral dosage or suppositories, or had suction cups or poultices applied, particularly to the breasts, to draw out evil vapors. Women's thighs were tightly bound to stop too heavy a flow or holes were cut in them to remove the evil humors or bile which coagulated and putrified the blood.[35]

Almost all of these remedies are used on Greene. If a physician wanted to decrease the flow of the blood, he sought to move it upwards towards the womb by bleeding the woman in her arms, as is done three times to Greene.[36] In 'ripe, young women who were plump and full of blood', bleeding was recommended from what was known as the 'hepatica' or liver vein in the right arm.[37] Apparently, because the liver was considered the seat of love and violent passion, bleeding the woman in this way sought to alleviate some of her sexual desires. The pamphlet describes Greene as 'strong' and 'fleshie' (p. 1), and twice she is bled from the right arm (once from the left). As Laurinda Dixon explains, the administering of clysters, or enemas (mentioned twice in the account of Greene's treatment) was thought to relieve uterine fits; clysters were 'applied rectally to purge corrupt humors and to irrigate the internal organs' and applied vaginally 'to cool and moisten the heated womb, or to lure the uterus back to its proper place by means of fragrant douches'. In her discussion of depictions of women and illness in pre-Enlightenment art, Dixon points out that illustrations of the administering of clysters 'conflate two standard cures for uterine disorders in a single image – clysters and, by innuendo, sexual intercourse'.[38] The links between the clyster and the phallus are made more obvious in Petty's diary where, he explains, 'wee used a candle end by way of a suppository'. Petty also uses this occasion to assert his superiority to his female assistant, complaining, '[t]he clyster, by the woman's unhandiness, was scarce halfe putt up'.[39] Even in the treatment that sought to preserve Greene's life, the assumption persists that her sexuality controls her other bodily functions, and that her body must, in turn, be controlled by the male doctors.

Once the doctors are certain of her life, they turn their attention to

Greene's legal situation, and here the physicians speculate about various reproductive functions – menstruation, childbirth, and the viability of the foetus. In this part of the pamphlet, as the narrative shifts from medical history to legal defence, the contest for control of the female body is most vividly illustrated. At Greene's trial, midwives and other women testified on her behalf, but for whatever reason their testimony fell on deaf ears.[40] Although the women are given some authority when their testimony is cited as evidence of Greene's innocence, the text suggests that their uncertain and conjectural knowledge must be confirmed by the more scientific knowledge of the male physicians before Greene can be pardoned. The phrasing used by the pamphlet writer illustrates the legitimizing power wielded by the physicians: 'The Midwife said also, that [the baby] had no haire, and that she did not beleive that ever it had life. Besides, her fellow-servants doe testifie, that she had certaine Issues for about a month before she miscarried, which were of the nature (Physitians say) as are not consistent with the vitality of a child' (p. 7). The parenthetical 'Physitians say' serves to subordinate the midwife's earlier testimony. While the text is not completely dismissive of the midwife and matrons, they clearly play an ancillary role to the doctors, who validate their assertions with scientific reasoning. The final definitive judgement comes from the doctors: the child was stillborn and not capable of being murdered; it was not 'above a span in length' and its 'sexe hardly to be distinguished'; it rather seemed a 'lumpe of flesh' than a 'well and duly formed Infant' (pp. 6–7).

In order to provide the most compelling evidence of her lack of culpability for the infant's death, the doctors effectively denied Greene any will or consciousness of her own. Articulating long-established arguments about the uncertainty of pregnancy and the distrust of women's natural knowledge of reproduction, the doctors contended that it was unlikely that Greene recognized that she was pregnant: she had

> continual Issues which lasted for a Moneth together: which long and great Evacuation might make her judge, that it was nothing else but a flux of those humors which for ten weekes before had been suppressed; and that the childe which then fell from her unawares, was nothing but a lump of the same matter coagulated. (p. 7)

Although midwifery manuals in the period speculated on the developing foetus, 'the signs to know it, and whether male or female, and of false conception', symptoms of pregnancy were notoriously ambiguous. The cessation of menstruation was not considered reliable evidence, as was the case here.[41] In this respect, Culpeper, too, is quite dismissive of women's bodily awareness, yet he intimates that some women are deliberately duplicitous: 'Some Women are so ignorant they do not know when they are conceived with Child, and others so coy they will not confess when they do know it' (p. 125). Although other accounts hedge on this point, 'Newes from the Dead' is quite direct in its insistence that Greene bears no responsibility for the death of the infant. One way that it accomplishes her certain innocence is by omitting the part of the story where she gives birth. Other accounts describe her straining at work when she suddenly falls ill and shortly thereafter delivers the child. She is clearly aware of what has happened and bemoans the fact that she now must 'live and die in shame and scorn'.[42] 'Newes from the Dead', on the other hand, simply states that the child 'fell from her unawares as she was in the house of office' (p. 6).

As for the pain she must have experienced, the doctors speculate that

> it must needs be different in such cases from that which accompanies the timely fruit of the womb: and by reason of those Issues coming from her, for so long continued a time before shee could not have those throwes and passions at the time of her abortion, as women in travel are subject unto. (p. 7)

Although it was widely held that the female body was unreliable and unreadable, the physicians seem confident in their assessments here. That Petty and Willis successfully intervened in the legal indictment by securing a pardon for Greene further enhances their authority in this text.[43]

From this point Greene and her body seem increasingly removed from the narrative; she becomes little more than the passive 'object of learned male solicitude', to borrow Katharine Park's words.[44] Eve Keller contends that the 'childbearing woman is decreasingly present as a subject' in popular midwives' books; the erasure of the woman occurs in this text as well.[45] Even as the pamphlet writer feels compelled to address what Greene experienced in the interim before she was 'brought back to life', he depicts her as 'benummed with fear' and like men 'buzz'd in the head with drink, or transposed with madness', insensible of everything that happened to her (p. 8). While we might expect the woman to play at least some role in her treatment and defence, she largely disappears by the end of the story. The ingenious and munificent physicians, now called 'Gentlemen', take centre stage. As he sums up his tale, the author 'reflects upon the generous attempt of those Gentlemen that freely undertook and so happily performed the Cure'. Anne Greene should 'account it her happiness to have fallen into such courteous and skilful hands' (p. 8). Thus the pamphlet encourages readers to view the doctors as interpreters of the reproductive body and miracle workers reviving the dead.

Although it is much more, this text seems to act as a propaganda piece, designed to increase the stature of Petty and Willis as physician-scientists and to advance the status of medicine in understanding and controlling the female body. Petty indicated as much himself, writing to a friend that 'my endeavours in this business have bettered my reputation'.[46] In this narration and in his journal, Petty fantasized about the god-like power of raising the dead. Although Willis reaped the benefits from *his* involvement in this case more slowly than Petty, spending several more years 'casting waters as a pisse-prophet', he too eventually made his name as a scientist and would be forever remembered for reviving Anne Greene.[47]

Not only is Anne Greene restored to life but the study and exposure of her body in *'Newes from the Dead' also* purges her of any transgressive sexuality. Her innocence established, she is now ready to step back into society as a 'proper' wife. But more importantly, in its detailed account of the treatment of Anne's body and its reactions to doctors' varied ministrations, the pamphlet becomes a homosocial celebration of masculine power and male expertise.[48] A compelling story that would continue to have resonance, *'Newes from the Dead'* successfully constructs a picture of physicians interceding in women's medical care and celebrates the achievements of professional medicine.

NOTES

1. *Mercurius Politicus*, 28 (12–19 December 1650): 468–69; and 32 (9–16 January 1651): 520–21. Joad Raymond includes these issues in *Making the News: An Anthology of Newsbooks of Revolutionary England, 1641–1660* (New York: St. Martin's Press, 1993), pp. 182–84.

2. There are references to Greene and her resurrection everywhere in the seventeenth and eighteenth centuries. See, for example, *Britannia Triumphalis: A Brief History of the Warres and Other State-Affairs of Great Britain* (London, 1654), pp. 82–84; Denis Petua, *History of the World* (London, 1659), p. 502; James Heath, *A Brief Chronicle of the Late Intestine War in the Three Kingdoms of England, Scotland & Ireland* (London, 1663), pp. 512–13; and Robert Plot, *The Natural History of Oxfordshire, Being an Essay toward the Natural History of England* (Oxford, 1677), pp. 197–99. Scott Mandelbrote presents an overview of the retellings of this event in 'William Petty and Anne Greene: Medical and Political Reform in Commonwealth Oxford', in Margaret Pelling (ed.), *The Practice of Reform in Health, Medicine and Science, 1500–2000* (Aldershot, UK: Ashgate, 2005), pp. 125–49. After a short assurance that the story is true, *Phoenix Britannicus: Being a Miscellaneous Collection of Scarce and Curious Tracts, Historical, Political, Biographical* (London, 1732), pp. 232–48, reprinted *'Newes from the Dead'* in its entirety. Even today, biographies of William Petty and Willis invariably note the importance of this event in the two men's professional lives. More recent fictionalizations are Douglas Angus, *The Green and the Burning* (London: Hale, 1958), Iain Pears, *An Instance of the Fingerpost* (London: Jonathan Cape, 1997), and the just published adolescent novel by Mary Hooper with the same title as the pamphlet discussed here, *Newes from the Dead* (London: Random House Children's Books, 2008).

3. I use the term 'street pamphlet' to refer to those hastily printed, cheap pamphlets published for a general readership. They tended to be occasional and brief (up to

60 pages), and were posted and sold in public places. Since they cost only a penny or twopence, we can assume that a wider range of readers could afford to buy them than could afford more elaborate literary texts. On the audience for these kinds of texts, see Tessa Watt, *Cheap Print and Popular Piety, 1550–1640* (New York: Cambridge University Press, 1991).

4. For a comparison of two of these accounts, '*A Wonder of Wonders*' and '*Newes from the Dead*', and their intervention in the critique of the 1624 'Acte to Prevent the Destroying and Murthering of Bastard Children', see my essay, 'The Popular Press and Providence: Explaining the Miraculous Recovery of Anne Greene' in Susan C. Staub, *Nature's Cruel Stepdames: Murderous Women in the Street Literature of Seventeenth Century England* (Pittsburgh, PA: Duquesne University Press, 2005), pp. 83–100.

5. [Richard Watkins], '*Newes from the Dead, or a True AND Exact Narration of the miraculous deliverance of Anne Greene*', Second Impression with Additions (Oxford, 1651), pp. 2–3. Subsequent references to this edition will appear in the body of the text. Petty's account is in the British Library, MS. Add. 72892, H75. The manuscript is published as 'History of the Magdalen (or The Raising of Anne Greene)', in The Marquis of Lansdowne (ed.), *The Petty Papers, Some Unpublished Writings of Sir William Petty*, 2 vols. (New York: Augustus M. Kelley, 1967), vol. 2, pp. 157–67. Carl Zimmer argues that Petty actually authorized the publication of '*Newes from the Dead*', and the repetition of Petty's phrasing in the pamphlet supports this argument (see Carl Zimmer, *The Soul Made Flesh: The Discovery of the Brain – and How It Changed the World* (New York: Free Press, 2004), pp. 109–10). Another of the popular accounts, '*A Wonder of Wonders*', although very different in tone and focus, includes Petty's name on the title page as witness.

6. Laura Gowing, *Common Bodies: Women, Touch and Power in Seventeenth-Century England* (New Haven, CT: Yale University Press, 2003), pp. 48–49.

7. Patricia Crawford, 'Sexual Knowledge in England, 1500–1750', in *Blood, Bodies and Families in Early Modern England* (Harlow, UK: Pearson Education Limited, 2004), pp. 54–78.

8. Patricia Parker, 'Fantasies of "Race" and "Gender": Africa, *Othello* and Bringing to Light', in Margo Hendricks and Patricia Parker (eds.), *Women, 'Race' and Writing in the Early Modern Period* (New York: Routledge, 1994), p. 87.

9. 21 James I, cap. 27. Danby Pickering (ed.), *Statutes at Large from Magna Charta to the End of the Eleventh Parliament of Great Britain, Anno 1761*, 8 vols. (Cambridge: Joseph Bentham, 1763), vol. 7, p. 298. This Act remained on the books until 1803. According to Hoffer and Hull, 'Bastard neonaticides constituted over 70 per cent of all murders of infants under nine years of age in the records. Concealment of pregnancy is mentioned in 55 per cent of these cases' (see Peter C. Hoffer and N. E. H. Hull, *Murdering Mothers: Infanticide in England and New England, 1558–1803* (New York: New York University Press, 1984), p. 18).

10. For further discussion of this statute, see Mark Jackson, 'Suspicious Infant Deaths: the Statute of 1624 and Medical Evidence at Coroners' Inquests', in Michael Clark and Catherine Crawford (eds.), *Legal Medicine in History* (Cambridge, UK: Cambridge University Press, 1994), pp. 65–69. In 'The Trial of Harriet Vooght: Continuity and Change in the History of Infanticide', Jackson illustrates that social anxiety about the sexual behaviour of unmarried women as reflected in the legal treatment of infanticide remains remarkably consistent through the

nineteenth century (see Mark Jackson (ed.), *Infanticide: Historical Perspectives on Child Murder and Concealment, 1550–2000* (Burlington, VT: Ashgate Publishing, 2002), pp. 1–17).

11. J. A. Sharpe, *Crime in Early Modern England, 1550–1750* (New York: Longman, 1999), p. 158.

12. Keith Wrightson, 'Infanticide in Earlier Seventeenth Century England', *Local Population Studies*, 15 (1975): 11–12.

13. Kate Cregan, *The Theatre of the Body: Staging Death and Embodying Life in Early-Modern London* (Turnhout, Belgium: Brepols Publishers, 2009), pp. 170–71.

14. Jonathan Sawday, *The Body Emblazoned: Dissection and the Human Body in Renaissance Culture* (New York: Routledge, 1995), pp. 220–21. Although Cregan agrees that the female body was a particular object of fascination, she disputes the idea that women's bodies were greatly prized in the anatomy theatre, arguing instead that women's bodies were available from other sources – death in childbirth, for one – and that barber-surgeons could choose which executed bodies they anatomized, but for some reason do not seem to have chosen female felons for their public anatomies. Since anatomical illustrations suggest a preoccupation with reproductive functions, we can imagine that interest in dissecting actual female bodies would be high. Cregan posits that female bodies may have been more available than records indicate. Post-mortem examinations and private anatomies may have provided other occasions for examination, but records of those activities are even more difficult to trace than the bodies of executed felons. Cregan, *Theatre of the Body*, pp. 171–72.

15. Kate Cregan, '[S]he Was Convicted and Condemned', *Social Semiotics*, 11.2 (2001): 125–37 (134).

16. Sawday, *The Body Emblazoned*, p. 224.

17. Scott Mandelbrote suggests that this title is a later addition, see 'William Petty and Anne Greene', in Margaret Pelling (ed.), *The Practice of Reform in Health, Medicine and Science*, p. 127, n.5.

18. Peter Linebaugh, 'The Tyburn Riot Against the Surgeons', in Douglas Hay *et al.* (eds.), *Albion's Fatal Tree: Crime and Society in Eighteenth Century England* (London: Allen Lane, 1975), p. 72.

19. Kate Cregan, '[S]he Was Convicted', pp. 133–34 and 129.

20. David Cressy, *Birth, Marriage, and Death: Ritual, Religion, and the Life-Cycle in Tudor and Stuart England* (New York: Oxford University Press, 1999), p. 60. See also, Caroline Bicks, *Midwiving Subjects in Shakespeare's England* (Burlington, VT: Ashgate, 2003).

21. Laura Gowing, *Common Bodies*, pp. 33–34. On the complex public role of midwives, see Lisa Forman Cody, 'The Politics of Reproduction: From Midwives' Alternative Public Sphere to the Public Spectacle of Man Midwifery', *Eighteenth Century Studies*, 32.4 (1999): 477–95.

22. Gowing, *Common Bodies*, p. 48.

23. Eucharius Roesslin, *The Birth of Mankynde*, trans. Thomas Raynald (London, 1545) and Jacob Rueff, *The Expert Midwife* (London, 1637), both quoted in Caroline Bicks, 'Stones Like Women's Paps: Revising Gender in Jane Sharp's *Midwives Book*', *Journal for Early Modern Cultural Studies*, 7.2 (2007): 4.

24. Bicks, 'Stones Like Women's Paps', p. 7.

25. Mary E. Fissell, 'The Marketplace of Print' in Mark S. R. Jenner and Patrick

Wallis (eds.), *Medicine and the Market in England and Its Colonies, c. 1450–1850* (New York: Palgrave Macmillan, 2007), pp. 108–32 (p. 113).

26. Mary E. Fissell, *Vernacular Bodies: The Politics of Reproduction in Early Modern England* (New York: Oxford University Press, 2004), p. 136. Nicholas Culpeper, *A Directory for Midwives* (London, 1651). Subsequent references to this edition will appear in the body of the text.

27. Fissell, *Vernacular Bodies*, pp. 148–49.

28. Fissell, *Vernacular Bodies*, p. 153.

29. Petty, 'History of the Magdalen', pp. 161–63.

30. Gowing, *Common Bodies*, pp. 29–30.

31. Cressy, *Birth, Marriage and Death*, p. 41.

32. As Stallybrass explains, the signs of the chaste woman are 'the enclosed body, the closed mouth, the locked house'. See 'Patriarchal Territories: The Body Enclosed', in Margaret W. Ferguson, Maureen Quilligan, and Nancy J. Vickers (eds.), *Rewriting the Renaissance: The Discourses of Sexual Difference in Early Modern Europe* (Chicago, Ill: University of Chicago Press, 1986), p. 127.

33. Nicholas Fontanus, *The Womans Doctour, or, an exact and distinct Explanation of all such Diseases as are peculiar to that Sex with Choise and Experimentall Remedies against the same* (London, 1652), quoted in Hilda Smith, 'Gynecology and Ideology in Seventeenth-Century England', in Berenice A. Carroll (ed.), *Liberating Women's History: Theoretical and Critical Essays* (Urbana, Ill: University of Illinois Press, 1976), pp. 100–01.

34. Smith, 'Gynecology and Ideology', in Berenice A. Carroll (ed.), *Liberating Women's History*, pp. 106–07.

35. Smith, 'Gynecology and Ideology', in Berenice A. Carroll (ed.), *Liberating Women's History*, p. 101.

36. Smith, 'Gynecology and Ideology', in Berenice A. Carroll (ed.), *Liberating Women's History*, p. 101.

37. Laurinda S. Dixon, *Perilous Chastity: Women and Illness in Pre-Enlightenment Art and Medicine* (Ithaca, NY: Cornell University Press, 1995), p. 153.

38. Dixon, *Perilous Chastity*, pp. 148–50.

39. Petty, 'History of the Magdalen', pp. 159, 161.

40. At least one of the accounts of Greene's case suggests that the court was corrupt, intimating that Greene's employer, the prominent Thomas Reade, had a hand in her conviction. Virtually all of the narratives from the period posit her innocence, at least of the crime of infanticide, though they vary in their assessment of her moral culpability. One account describes her hiding the foetus in a corner and covering it with dirt and rubbish. See William Burdet, *'A Wonder of Wonders'* (London, 1651).

41. Cressy, *Birth, Marriage and Death*, pp. 41–42.

42. Burdet, *'A Wonder of Wonders'*, p. 2.

43. The pardon here is unusual. According to Blackstone, 'it is clear that if, upon judgment to be hanged by the neck till he is dead, the criminal be not thoroughly killed, but revives, the sheriff must hang him again; for the former hanging was no execution of the sentence, and if a false tenderness were to be indulged in such cases, a multitude of collusions might ensue'. See Sir William Blackstone, *Ehrlich's Blackstone*, 2 vols., ed. J. W. Ehrlich (New York: Capricorn Books, 1959), vol. 2, p. 524.

44. Park is referring to Italian texts on 'the secrets of women', but her words seem to fit here as well. See Katharine Park, *Secrets of Women: Gender, Generation, and the Origins of Human Dissection* (New York: Zone Books, 2006), p. 96.

45. Eve Keller, 'The Subject of Touch: Medical Authority in Early Modern Midwifery', in Elizabeth D. Harvey (ed.), *Sensible Flesh: On Touch in Early Modern Culture* (Philadelphia, PA: University of Pennsylvania Press, 2003), p. 70.

46. Zimmer, *The Soul Made Flesh*, p. 109.

47. Zimmer, *The Soul Made Flesh*, p. 110.

48. The homosocial celebration of male power extends beyond the narrative in this text. Appended to the narrative are 24 pages of poetry written by the students at Oxford in reaction to this event. Where the narrative presents Anne as a scientific text to be examined and understood, in the poems she becomes a literary text. Earlier, her revival suggests scientific power and creativity; godlike, the scientists at the autopsy are credited with her resurrection. The poems, on the other hand, suggest another form of creativity and power as they resurrect her into art. And the poems also work to purify the female body: 'All's purg'd by Sacrifice:/ The Parent slain, doth not a Virgin Rise?' (12), says one, and another, 'Rare Innocence! a Wench re-woman'd!' (14), and 'The Mother dyed: may't not be said/ That the Survivor is a Maid?' (16, misnumbered 6).

5

'Made in Imitation of Real Women and Children': Obstetrical Machines in Eighteenth-Century Britain

PAM LIESKE

The collection and display of anatomical specimens was a particular area of interest during the Enlightenment. From 1739 until 1800 an estimated thirty-nine anatomy museums appeared in England.[1] Private individuals and anatomy teachers also kept their own collections and used specimens from human and comparative anatomy, as well as anatomical models and illustrations, for private display and for public teaching.[2] What is perhaps less well known is that many items found in collections centred on female reproduction. Growing interest in maternal bodies can be seen in two collections at opposite ends of the long eighteenth century. The first, depicted in Nehemiah Grew's catalogue of the Royal Society, *Musaeum Regalis Societatis* (1681), contained just three items centred on female reproduction. One was a preserved uterus, its vessels filled with wax, prepared by the Dutch physician and microbiologist Jan Swammerdam. Two other items are foetuses, one a foetal skeleton and the second a preserved foetus.[3] Some seventy years after Grew's catalogue first appeared in print, William Hunter began his 20-year study of the human gravid uterus, culminating in his obstetrical atlas, *The Anatomy of the Gravid Uterus Exhibited in Figures* (1774). Hunter died in 1783 and his massive and varied collection of art, literature, natural history, and medical teaching material was transferred to the University of Glasgow in 1807 and opened for public viewing. An early report of the collection indicates that one room contained 500 preparations and engravings of the gravid uterus, including a series of plaster casts of the pregnant uterus that correspond to illustrations of the gravid uterus found in Hunter's atlas.[4]

In the early eighteenth century, three-dimensional models of female reproductive anatomy could also be viewed by the general public. The Parisian anatomist and surgeon Guillaume Desnoues and the London-born anatomist Ambraham Chovet, who later taught anatomy in Philadelphia, both constructed, exhibited, and sold such models in London. A central figure in Desnoues' collection, which was exhibited in Paris and London between 1717 and 1729, was a wax model of a woman who died during labour with the baby's head pushing through the cervix.[5] Collaborating with the Italian waxwork modeller Gaetano Giuilo Zumbo, Desnoues produced a number of anatomical wax models and is known to have made at least one other figure of a woman giving birth.[6] A 1736 sale catalogue of his collection includes 37 lots, 11 of which consist of foetuses or other items of female reproduction.[7] The centrepiece of the collection was a full-term pregnant woman, the abdomen dissected but the uterus intact, with 'the little inhabitant endeavouring to quit his prison' its 'one hand [dangling] in the passage'.[8]

Like William Hunter and Desnoues, Abraham Chovet was no quack doctor. In the 1730s he demonstrated anatomy to the London Barber-Surgeons, and on 22 June 1732, he read and demonstrated two proposals for making anatomical waxworks to the Royal Society.[9] One of the proposed figures showed red liquid flowing through glass veins and arteries. It also had a heart that appeared to beat and lungs that moved air. Claiming that he had improved upon Desnoues' waxworks, Chovet almost certainly displayed his anatomical waxworks in his anatomy classes. One of his wax models was of a pregnant woman flayed alive, in which maternal-foetal blood was shown through coloured liquids. It was advertised for display in the 1730s, after which time Chovet sold his models to Benjamin Rackstrow, who also bought models from Desnoues.[10] Despite this transfer of ownership, the pregnant woman continued to be advertised in newspapers and pamphlets and remained a star attraction in Rackstrow's museum for the next several decades.[11] Rackstrow died in 1772, but the museum bearing his name lived on, as apparently did the pregnant woman. A 1784 catalogue of the museum's holdings contains numerous figures moulded from women who died in childbirth, one of which is a mother who died in the sixth month of her pregnancy. An animated and heavily dissected figure, it, too, depicted maternal-foetal circulation with coloured liquids flowing through glass vessels.[12]

The purpose of this essay is not to discuss waxwork models of female reproductive anatomy that were prepared by men of science and displayed to both popular and scientific audiences. Nor is it to examine the many anatomists and men-midwives who preserved dry or wet specimens, or made plaster of Paris replicas of female reproductive anatomy (such as pelvises, foetuses, uteri at different stages of gestation, cervices, fallopian tubes, and placentas). My aim is more specific: it is to examine the material represen-tation of maternity and childbirth as seen in the construction and use of obstetrical machines.[13] The preceding material should be read as context for my discussion, as it suggests the Enlightenment's fascination with the pregnant female body and provides a sense of what obstetrical machines were, and were not. Built by men-midwives and used widely throughout Britain and the continent, eighteenth-century obstetrical machines – also called phantoms, apparatuses, and occasionally manikins – are life-sized models of pregnant women and foetuses that are used for the hands-on training of midwives.[14]

Commonly consisting of a torso with the legs amputated above the knees – much like Hunter's later engravings of the human gravid uterus come to life – obstetrical machines are not the same as smaller wax anatomical models used for scientific display or public entertainment such as the 14½ inch long model of a pregnant woman that H. Wessels advertised for sale in 1755 to 'all men midwives, midwifes, students in midwifery and the curious'.[15] They are also not the same as ivory or bronze anatomical figures or dissectable life-size wax figure models which began to appear in the latter half of the eighteenth century. Often mechanized, with a frame of human bone, obstetrical machines were to be seen and, above all, to be used. While a foetus and pelvic cavity were common features in all machines, depending upon the credentials of the medical men who owned them and the ways in which they were used, the contents and technical sophistication of devices varied widely.[16] Some machines may have been little more than a female pelvis with a canvas bag inside, while others were extravagantly built, with contracting uteri, shifting fluid, and orifices that opened and closed in a manner reminiscent of the animated pregnant figure made by Chovet.

Scholarship in English on eighteenth-century British obstetrical machines is scarce, but that which exists falls into two distinct categories. The first are accounts written by historians of science and medicine, who typically conflate obstetrical machines with anatomical models, specimens, and illustrations, seeing them as just one of many items in a male midwife's arsenal of visual representations of female reproductive anatomy. Some mention that machines were used as pedagogical aids in the teaching of midwifery and even notice that machines were used for the hands-on teaching of midwifery, but discussion normally ends at this point. Even Adrian Wilson's masterful study of eighteenth-century British midwifery, which minutely documents how forceps knowledge was transmitted among individual practitioners, gives only passing acknowledgement of machines and neglects to mention that many practitioners learned how to use forceps and other instruments by practising on these devices.[17] In addition, while some accounts suggest that machines were widely used, little corroborating evidence, including the names and locations of practitioners and the dates machines were used, is provided. The end result is that obstetrical machines fall into a hazy void where their role in midwifery training is acknowledged, but details on what machines may have looked like and how they were used remain hidden.

Certain cultural and literary scholars account for the second category of scholarship. With well-intentioned but misplaced feminist sensibilities, they view obstetrical machines as a combination of misogynistic popular entertainment and bad science. These scholars ride the coat-tails of eighteenth-century, anti-male midwifery critics, such as William Douglas, Elizabeth Nihell, and Philip Thicknesse, and denigrate male midwifery through the childbirth practices of William Smellie, the seminal figure in eighteenth-century obstetrics.[18] Scottish in origin and void of the social graces and affluent clientele of William Hunter, with whom he is often compared, Smellie was a favourite target of ridicule by those opposed to male midwifery practice. He is known to have built and used a number of obstetrical machines, which he used to instruct more than nine hundred pupils over a ten-year period.[19]

Smellie's important place in the history of obstetrics is undisputed. He was the first to correctly understand the exact mechanics of labour and delivery and wrote a well-respected midwifery treatise (3 vols. 1752–64); the second and third volumes contain 531 meticulously described case histories. He also produced an important obstetric atlas that predated the one made by William Hunter by 20 years.[20] Scholars belonging to the second group dismiss these accomplishments to make hasty conclusions about Smellie's use of obstetrical machines and then suggest that his alleged faults are representative of all men midwives of the time. In these accounts, Smellie is presented as a showman – much like the man behind the curtain who brings the Wizard of Oz to life. Aiming to impress and astonish his student audience, he is said to pull levers connected to a glass uterus with a cavity filled with beer or Champagne and a leather child inside. After demonstrating labour and delivery 'in the theater of the mechanical mother', he then asks for volunteers to participate in this circus-like performance so that they, too, can learn the perennial evil of male midwifery practice: forceps delivery.[21]

These depictions of William Smellie's use of obstetrical machines, including his affinity for forceps delivery, are decidedly incorrect. Numerous midwives, besides Smellie, built and used obstetrical machines in their practice. A great number of them, including Smellie, held cautious views about the use of obstetrical instruments, taught midwifery to female students, and sincerely believed that student instruction on machines was a necessary precursor to practice on living bodies. In addition to documenting the widespread use of obstetrical machines in Britain, a major aim of this paper is to place obstetrical machines firmly back within the history of science and medicine, where they are not ignored or conflated with three-dimensional teaching aids or anatomical illustrations, nor dismissed as examples of 'bad science' or popular entertainment. While it is likely that some obstetrical machines were crudely rendered and used as a moneymaking gimmick by unscrupulous individuals, many other machines were carefully built by respectable men of science who considered their devices invaluable aids in their midwifery courses. Allowing student midwives the opportunity to visualize a pregnant and then labouring body and, above all, to gain hands-on experience in examining and treating certain conditions, obstetrical machines were considered a practical and humane way for students to gain the experience and knowledge they needed before they began to examine and care for real pregnant women. They also provided discursive space for dialogue about the scope and aim of medical training, the relationship between male doctors and female patients and, perhaps most importantly, the need for society and the medical community to value and care for pregnant women.

Before my focus shifts to British obstetrical machines, it is useful to mention the French national midwife Angélique Marguerit Le Boursier Du Coudray as she used machines in her teaching from 1760 to 1783 and distributed hundreds of them to rural midwives throughout France. One example, found at the Musée Flaubert in Rouen, still exists.[22] It represents the lower torso of a pregnant woman, the legs ending mid-thigh, with a full-term, extractable foetal doll. Accompanying the machine are various detachable features, including a pre-term foetal doll which can be housed in a separate uterus. Like Chovet's model, du Coudray's obstetrical machine was mechanized with flowing liquids mimicking blood flow, and various pulleys and levers that could be engaged to further show the mechanics of labour. Besides its animation, the most notable feature of du Coudray's machine is its puffiness – it looks very much like an inflatable woman – an effect achieved by covering bony surfaces and stuffing cavities with flesh-coloured cloth or leather.

No extant model of a British obstetrical machine exists, and information about them must be pieced together from newspaper advertisements, midwifery treatises, teaching syllabi, and students' accounts of their use. Moreover, while du Coudray provides a visual example of what an eighteenth-century obstetrical machine looked like, her puffy machine was not representative of all British devices of this sort. This is evident from the glass obstetrical machine used by Richard Manningham, an early London midwife and likely the first midwife in Britain to use a machine. Manningham was familiar with unusual claims about human birth, as he was one of a cadre of medical men who examined the rabbit breeder Mary Toft in 1726. He also opened Britain's first known lying-in facility in 1739, a short-lived enterprise with the dual goal of delivering women and training local midwives. His *Abstract of Midwifry For the Use of the Lying-in Infirmary* (1741), an outline of his teaching at the facility, repeatedly mentions the importance of a glass machine.

Calling it 'our *Glass Machine*', and 'our *great* Machine', Manningham never describes his apparatus, but he does emphasize that students must engage in regular practice on it, first by observation and then by hands-on practice, before they can examine and deliver real women.[23] Calling midwifery 'the Work of the Hands', Manningham felt that instrument use in childbirth was largely unnecessary and that careful practice on his device developed manual dexterity and skill, so that when properly trained, a midwife's hands could largely substitute for instruments.[24] He claims his machine not only provides 'the greatest Opportunity of *forming* [...] Hands for Practice, and informing [...] *Judgment* at the same Time', it also allows the 'Manner of Touching or Handling Women' to be perfected.[25]

The fact that Manningham's machine taught students how to perform pelvic examinations (*touching*) as well as how to apply their hands during all cases of natural and difficult labours suggests that his glass woman was technically sophisticated. Peering inside the transparent glass to see the different positions of the child – whose composition is unknown – students could visualize different malpresentations of the child such as a breech or transverse birth, or a shoulder presenting first. They could also observe and then respond to obstetrical emergencies such as sudden haemorrhaging (*flooding*), a cord wrapped around the baby's neck, or a prolapsed uterus. Though Manningham advised female midwives to call for the assistance of male midwives when they encountered difficulties, he did teach midwifery to both sexes on his machine and was so convinced of its efficacy that he offered a 'Single Lecture in Midwifery on the Glass Machine' to 'Women with Child, their Parents, or other discreet Persons', so that they could learn how to choose a competent midwife.[26]

Manningham's desire to educate the general public on his device was an anomaly, as the vast majority of obstetrical machines were used to train, not evaluate, midwives. In 1750 Thomas Young, the father of the School of Obstetrics at the University of Edinburgh, published an outline of the 22 midwifery lectures that he offered to male and female students.[27] On the title page of the work, Young claims that '*natural, difficult* and *preternatural* Labours, [will be] demonstrated upon Machines made in Imitation of Women and Children'. This statement that 'Machines are made in Imitation of Women and Children' is one almost invariably repeated in any print mention of men midwives' machines. While this aim of machines to duplicate the experience of pregnancy and childbirth is undeniable, without descriptions of what machines looked like and how they functioned, one cannot say for certain that all machines had moving parts. This is particularly true when one considers that in the eighteenth century one meaning of the word 'machine' was simply *the human body*. That said, the latter half of the eighteenth century witnessed 'a flurry of attempts to simulate with machinery the physiological processes and cognitive behaviors of living creatures', such as 'machines with soft skin, flexible lips, and delicate, jointed fingers. These machines not only wrote, drew, and played musical instruments but also breathed, ate, and defecated'.[28] Used solely as popular entertainment, the most famous of these devices was Jacques Vaucanson's mechanical Duck, which was first displayed in Paris in 1738.[29] This artificial bird not only moved its body and preened its feathers but also ate, drank, digested food, and defecated.[30] While obstetrical machines had a serious pedagogical function, and all models may not have been mechanized, they should still be viewed as an Enlightenment attempt to approximate nature, in this case the changes that occur within the maternal body during pregnancy, labour, and birth.

Young left no descriptions of his machines, but in the 1750 outline of his teaching he emphasizes that 'all the Variety of natural, difficult and preter-natural Labours [will be] demonstrated upon Machines' and 10 of his 22 lectures are devoted to hands-on demonstrations, including techniques to extract the placenta, administer clysters (enemas), and deliver with various kinds of instruments.[31] Without a larger, more complexly rendered model of a pregnant woman that could mimic labour and various deliveries, such demonstrations would be impossible. He also explains that reproductive anatomy will be 'shown on natural detached Pieces, and artificial Wax ones' and that 'artificial Orifices' will be used to demonstrate 'the different Shape and Changes of the internal Orifice' or cervix.[32] Whether these orifices could be positioned within his replicas of pregnant women is not known, but the fact that his 'artificial Orifices' represented different stages of cervical dilation and effacement and that natural and difficult labours were shown on machines strongly suggests that Young's devices were not static, three-dimensional models of the female body; rather, they were artificial bodies that contained moving parts.

In the 1750s, a number of men midwives began to advertise machines in their midwifery courses, and all of them use the phrase, or some variation of it, that 'machines are made in imitation of real women and children'. In just over a two-year period (August 1753 to October 1755) four separate practitioners – Christopher Kelly, Felix MacDonough, John Martin, and Hugh Crawford – announced the use of obstetrical machines in their forthcoming midwifery courses.[33] Two of the four practitioners were respectable medical men. The first, the Irish man-midwife Christopher Kelly, was a member of the Royal College of Physicians. In his advertisements Kelly identifies himself as a 'Surgeon', but some time towards the end of 1756 he became one of the men-midwives at the British Lying-in Hospital.[34] George Macaulay was one of his peers, and soon after Kelly's appointment the two jointly developed a procedure to induce premature labour in women with distorted pelvises. Kelly even communicated the results of this work to a young Thomas Denman, who several decades later became the leading man-midwife of late eighteenth-century London.[35] In 1757 Kelly published outlines of his eighteen midwifery lectures. At the conclusion of lecture thirteen, on 'præternatural Labours where the Child is in a wrong Position', Kelly notes that he will display 'a curious Subject with a gravid *Uterus* well preserved, at the full Time of Pregnancy, in which the Child (a very large one) presents with the Breech, the Placenta is also preserved in the curious Situation it was found in'.[36] This preserved specimen of a breech birth should not be confused with Kelly's machines, since many men-midwives used both obstetrical machines and various artificial and preserved specimens in their teaching. In a notice in the *London Evening Post* (1 January 1760) Kelly highlights this point by claiming that his forthcoming lectures will be 'illustrated by a compleat Sett of artificial Women and Children, a Collection of necessary Preparations, and also by real Labours'.

The second man-midwife to advertise in London papers that he used machines in his midwifery courses is Felix MacDonough. A member of the company of Surgeons, MacDonough founded the General Lying-in Hospital in 1752 and in 1768 published a study of midwifery patients at the facility, presenting the number of women delivered each year, 'their parishes of origin, their social circumstances and marital status, and the numbers of easy and difficult deliveries'.[37] In his midwifery advertisement, MacDonough states that pupils of both sexes are granted free admission to his first lecture. He also claims that he is an expert in difficult births, particularly those involving the likelihood that a child's large head will become lodged in the pelvis. He goes on to say that demonstrations of these cases will occur first on his machines, and later, as opportunities arise, on live women. Little is known of the remaining two practitioners, John Martin and Hugh Crawford. Both claim they are surgeons; Crawford also identifies himself as a man-midwife – and following a pattern typical of the time, Crawford offers a new course of midwifery lectures each fortnight.

The use of obstetrical machines was not some fad utilized by opportunistic men-midwives with little or no training, nor was it a mid-century phenomenon. Henry Khron, a member of the Royal College of Physicians and physician and man-midwife to The Queen's Hospital for Lying-in Married Women, also used them.[38] In 1769 Khron was elected joint physician and man-midwife to the Middlesex Hospital, along with Thomas Denman, who, in his joint teaching with William Osborn, is also likely to have used machines.[39] Two advertisements for Khron's midwifery teaching have been located, the first from 1766 and the second from 1788.[40] In the former, Khron advertises a new course of midwifery lectures to be held at his house in Dean Street, Soho, where pupils will receive explanation of childbirth 'on artificial machines, resembling nature, and also confirmed by real subjects that are delivered at the Doctor's Hospital'. Twenty-two years later, Khron gave notice that his teaching would occur at two locations and that 'Pupils will have an Opportunity of being instructed in the operative Part, on a new and improved Phantom, performing by mechanical Construction all the Functions of Nature'.

Khron's 1788 advertisement suggests that at least in London the market had become so saturated with these teaching aids that some practitioners felt compelled to publicize that their machines were of a new and improved design, and thus better than those of their competitors. John Leake, a physician man-midwife to the Westminster New Lying-in Hospital and a member of the Royal College of Physicians, took this idea of novelty to such an extreme that he advertised a newly constructed machine in London newspapers for eight years (1762–1770).[41] In the earliest-known advertisement, he claims that 'an artificial Representation of each difficult Labour' will be 'clearly demonstrated' by anatomical preparations and 'Machines of a new Construction, made for that Purpose, in exact imitation of real Women and Children'. For a brief time, he also publicized that prospective students could obtain a course syllabus and view 'the APPARATUS' at his residence in Craven Street in the Strand.[42] At the end of 1770, Leake, for some reason, stopped mentioning obstetrical machines in newspaper advertisements for his teaching. This does not mean, though, that he stopped using them.

Leake's *Introduction to the Theory and Practice of Midwifery* (1787) includes a section entitled 'Use of OBSTETRIC APPARATUS'. In it, Leake claims that

difficult Labours will be artificially represented on Machines of a new Construction, substituted for the real bodies of Women and Children. In the first, [part of the course] all the parts concerned in PARTURITION are fabricated upon the Female Skeleton, in exact imitation of Nature; and in the last, the effect of Pressure on the Infant's head, will be exemplified by an artificial Fœtus.[43]

As indicated, Leake not only used real skeletons in his devices but he also had an artificial foetus with a partially collapsible head. He also states that students can practise on 'an artificial Uterus, which contracts on the hand of the Operator (by imperceptible means)'.[44] What 'improvements' Leake made to his machines during his 25 years of using them may not be known, but as is indicated by these statements, his machines were not static renditions of the female body. The foetus and uterus actually moved.

Movement also occurred in Leake's earlier machines. In a 1767 outline of his teaching, Leake claims that he will show 'A natural Labour artificially represented on Machinery (in a Manner not hitherto attempted) distinctly and minutely shewing the *gradual Dilation* of the *Os Uteri* [cervix] and *Protrusion* of the *Membranes* [amniotic sac]; with their alternate *Distension* and *Relaxation*, as the *Pains* [contractions] come on and go off'.[45] In addition to these features, his machinery included foetuses with pliable cranial bones and an amniotic sac that could show evacuation of fluid 'by a Discharge of Air'.[46] Moreover, as with many machines, Leake's 'Artificial Woman and Child' allowed students to first visualize and then practise difficult labours and forceps application, and at the conclusion of the twelfth lecture – there were eighteen total – he promises to discuss 'the Insufficiency of the *Glass Uterus*, in demonstrating the Manner how the *Child* is to be turn'd in *Twin Cases*, or otherwise' – a statement which indicates that in constructing his machines, Leake used material other than glass.[47]

Thomas White, a member of the Royal College of Physicians who practised midwifery and medicine in Manchester, provides further evidence of the mechanization of some obstetrical machines and demonstrates that machines were not specific to London or Edinburgh. A 1787 syllabus of his midwifery lectures contains a two-page section entitled 'Of the Intent, and Real Advantage of an Apparatus, in demonstrating the Practical Part of Midwifery'.[48] Using rhetoric that echoes Leake's 1787 remarks, White first explains his fee schedule and the efficacy of using machines before mentioning that his apparatus includes 'an artificial Uterus, of a New Construction, which contracts uniformly on the body of the infant, from the fundus [that portion opposite the cervix] to the cervix uteri'.[49] While uterine contractions were a staple of mechanized machines, White took this idea a step further to demonstrate a uterus after birth that 'contracts itself in the middle like an hour-glass [...] so as to obstruct the extraction of the placenta'.[50] Like Leake, White also invited students interested in taking his course to view the apparatus at his lecture room, where, presumably, he demonstrated how his contracting uterus would be used in his teaching.

Whether obstetrical machines moved or not, they clearly had a complex relationship with women's bodies. As is suggested by the commonly used phrase 'Machines made in imitation of real women and children', they were viewed as practical substitutes for live women. Richard Manningham, Thomas Young, John Leake, and Thomas White all emphasize that, through repeat visualization and hands-on practice on these devices, students gain requisite dexterity and skill that they could transfer to the bodies of pregnant women. Constructing machines in such a way that they replicated the living maternal body, then, was key. These artificial, yet real, bodies had to mimic the look, feel, and touch of live bodies, and all bones and organs – the pelvic basin, uterus, amniotic sac, cervix, placenta, and vagina – had to have the same shape, dimensions, and placement that occurred in living women. Relying on advancements in preservation techniques and waxwork injections, some midwives used natural body parts. Madame du Coudray first used real pelvic bones but then began to use wicker and other artificial material, which she then fashioned into the artificial female bodies she created.[51]

Other midwives, like Dr Horsley, used both natural and artificial matter. In a 1783 advertisement for his teaching, he purports to have 'a curious Artificial Apparatus, as also a Natural one' to show 'all the parts concerned in Gestation' as well as 'natural methods of assisting Nature in all sorts of labors'.[52] This notice appeared soon after the death of William Hunter, and at the end of it, Horsley even advertises that he has 'some exceeding valuable and very useful Gravid Uterus's' for sale that he had made for the late doctor. In an early critique of William Smellie's teaching and practice, William Douglas not only emphasizes the need for machines to approximate living bodies but he also felt that they should incorporate real bodies within them. In his estimation, 'every good Master should use a natural *Fœtus* in his Machine', and Smellie's machines are inferior because he chose to use 'little stuffed Babies, which have rather amused, than instructed' the pupils he sought to teach.[53]

Exact simulation of the female body, however, had its challenges. If natural bodies or body parts were used, one had to know how to preserve and prepare the various parts. One also had to know how to put the various parts together so that the machine looked and felt natural and was durable enough to allow for repeated hands-on practice. At the same time, the machine had to impart whatever information about pregnancy and birth the individual midwife wanted to communicate to students. Thomas White and John Leake felt that midwives and anatomists should consult on the design and construction of machines because devices made by mere mechanics without any medical knowledge 'do much harm, by misinforming the judgment of the student, and giving him a false idea of nature, both in the *touch*, *figure*, and *disposition* of the several parts'.[54] In an early advertisement of his midwifery teaching, Christopher Kelly also suggested that machines should be carefully crafted:

THE ART of MIDWIFRY completely taught; by an Imitation of the most approved Method; whereby the Theory and Practice of that Art are communicated in the most plain and intelligible Manner; the former by Machinery, on which the various Cases that occur in Practice are very naturally represented, and the most successful Methods of relieving the same first distinctly shewn, and then repeated by each Pupil, whereby the truest Ideas thereof are imprinted on the Memory; and the latter on Nature.[55]

Machines that are only gross estimations of nature cannot convey essential truths ('truest Ideas') about gestation and childbirth that should be 'imprinted on the Memory' of students and then used in the care of living women. Hidden within this notice, then, is the belief that not only should machines have the look and feel of reproductive organs but they should also replicate the physiological processes of pregnancy, labour, and delivery. Speaking of 'the most approved Method' of imitation and 'the truest Ideas' to impart, Kelly suggests fascination and reverence for the female body mingled with the belief that human life could be simulated.

The eighteenth century does not seem to have objected to student midwives examining artificial women and children, but it did have objections to male midwives viewing and handling the bodies of actual women. Throughout the century debate raged about the possibility and, for some, the certainty, that men-midwives were lecherous and raised impure thoughts (and reactions) in their female patients.[56] This alleged impropriety of men-midwives towards pregnant women explains, in part, why some men-midwives felt that teaching students on artificial bodies was preferable to teaching on real women. John Leake claimed 'that living Bodies are very improper Subjects for initiating Pupils in the operative Part of this Art [midwifery]'; a statement repeated verbatim by Thomas White.[57] Leake goes on to claim that training 'on real Subjects, [leads] to the manifest Danger of the Patient and the Ruin of their own Reputation'.[58] Richard Manningham makes a similar claim when he reminds students that 'Women in Labour ought always to be treated with all imaginable Tenderness and Humanity' and that by proper and diligent training on machines 'we secure our Women from all Injuries, which would happen from Pupils, attempting Deliveries, before they are duly inform'd'.[59] Undoubtedly men-midwives' reasons for using machines in their teaching were multiple and varied; still, it seems clear that machines allowed men-midwives to be closer to, and distanced from, the actual women they sought to serve. By using artificial women, they could limit students' contact with real women, protect the latter from unnecessary physical injury, and, for a time, keep their own and their patients' reputations intact.

The man-midwife whose practice best illustrates the importance of obstetrical machines in eighteenth-century British midwifery practice is William Smellie. Smellie began constructing and using obstetrical machines in 1740 after first seeing them used by Grégoire in Paris.[60] Deciding that Grégoire's machines were inferior, Smellie went about building his own devices and used them in his teaching until his retirement to Scotland in 1758.[61] John Harvie, who trained under Smellie and married a niece of Smellie's wife, inherited the machines and Smellie's medical collection, and wasted no time in advertising to prospective students that 'Dr. Smellie being retired into the Country, takes this Method to inform such Gentlemen [...] that he has left all his Machines and Preparations with Dr. Harvie; who will Fulfill all his Engagements'.[62] When Harvie died in 1770, Smellie's collection of machines, medical books and prints, instruments, and anatomical specimens went up for auction.[63]

One of the machines passed into the hands of William Hunter, who then sold it to the Irish man-midwife Edward Foster. Foster lived and worked in Dublin, and once he received the machine, the following announcement appeared in the Dublin papers:

> On Tuesday the 22nd of November next, will commence *a Course of Lectures and Demonstrations upon the Theory and Practice of Midwifery*; in which the Principles of that Art will be distinctly explained, its most extensive Branches (including the Diseases peculiar to Women and Child) will be methodically taught, and its several Operations clearly demonstrated, upon Machines of the best Construction, by Edward Foster, M.D. at his House, No. 13, in Anglesea-street, and at the hour immediately following, the Anatomical Lectures in the College. Having at considerable Expence, and with much Trouble, procured from Doctor Hunter, Professor of Anatomy in London, and Physician to the Queen, that celebrated Apparatus, upon which the late ingenious and learned Dr. Smellie formed above nine Hundred Accoucheurs, exclusive of female Students, in a Series of two hundred and eighty Courses of Lectures (as he declares in the Preface of his *Treatise on Midwifery*), and this being the first and only Apparatus that has yet made its Way into this Kingdom, Dr. *Foster* is determined to adhere to his Resolution of delivering two Courses of Lectures every Winter, during the private Anatomical Course of the College, and one or two Courses during the Summer.[64]

Recent scholarship fails to recognize the importance of this advertisement, choosing instead to argue that it illustrates how Smellie's machine 'surpasses the goal of being merely a simulator of the childbirth drama' to 'become a veritable factory for churning out man-midwives'.[65] An alternative and, it seems to me, more correct way to interpret this advertisement is to recognize it as evidence of the inordinate respect and value given to Smellie's machines by his peers. Deemed so important, this one obstetrical machine, built by Smellie some time before 1758, passed through the hands of John Harvie and William Hunter before it was purchased by Foster in 1770 and shipped from London to Dublin to be used by Foster in his midwifery teaching. Foster could have built his own machine in his native Dublin at much less expense; instead, he chose to spend his time and money in procuring this one apparatus, and then announcing in the local newspaper that he had it in his possession.

Its longevity and fame is comparable to another machine advertised for sale in 1783. This device, which may have been made by the same Grégoire with whom Smellie first trained, is described as 'that Ingenious Machine well known in the Universities of Paris and Edinburgh'. It 'was made by the most eminent Accoucheur and Professor of Midwifery in Paris' and like all sophisticated devices, it was used to teach normal and difficult labours.[66] Rather than condemn the legacy of machines as examples of male midwifery run amuck, scholars could see these machines for what they were: sophisticated replications of the maternal body that reflected and shaped the empirical practice of midwifery.

The 1770 sale catalogue of Smellie's medical effects records more than fifty medical books, a number of prints, drawings, and instruments, and a variety of wet and dry preparations centred on female reproduction. It also lists four machines, four artificial uteri, five artificial foetuses or foetal heads, and five rings of different sizes to explain cervical dilation. This material clearly shows that in their quest to depict natural and unnatural labours and certain conditions of pregnancy and childbirth men-midwives often had more than one machine in their possession. Smellie's first machine was 'contrived for explaining all natural and easy Labours, and likewise difficult Labours'.[67] His second machine depicted a narrowed and distorted pelvic cavity, while his third machine had a uterus that contracted and dilated, upon which 'every kind of Labour may be explained'.[68] The fourth machine is said to have been the most recent and 'the most perfect', as it had a detachable uterus and 'Appendages'.[69] Among the uteri were two made of glass, one made of leather, and one whose composition is not specified. Some of the foetal heads were detachable; one 'artificial Child' was 'pretty much used' and at least two others were made to explain what happens to the foetal head when it was necessary to dismantle it in utero by a crotchet.[70]

The fact that some machines and foetuses were old and others newly made indicates that Smellie did not use just one set of machinery throughout his career, or one type of material; rather, he continually worked to improve upon the design and construction of his various devices. His teaching with machines was so influential that it even spawned a second generation of admirers. Margaret Stephen, one of the few women to author a midwifery treatise, praised the instruction she received from her teacher, a former pupil of Smellie who used machines.[71] She went on to replicate this practice by having various preparations and 'a machine which I believe few teachers can equal', which she used to teach women how to use forceps and turn the child in the womb.[72]

To conclude this essay, I would like to provide descriptions of Smellie's machines. Petrus Camper, a former student of Smellie and a renowned anatomist in his own right, claimed that in his midwifery classes Smellie 'explains the osteology of the pelvis in both a healthy and in a morbid misshapen state [...] by using the dead bodies of women' but he 'much more clearly [...] used other exhibits specially prepared for the purpose'.[73] These 'other exhibits' may be Smellie's machines or they may be normal, or abnormally shaped female skeletons or pelvic bones. Other students who discuss Smellie's machines invariably remark upon his use of skeletons and how his 'frame of human bone' adds to the naturalness and technical sophistication of his machines. One reports that the machines 'are composed of real Bones, mounted and covered with artificial Ligaments, Muscles, and Cuticle, to give them the true Motion, Shape, and Beauty of Natural Bodies'.[74] Peter Camper, who also mentions that the skeletal frame adds in the machine's movement, claims that the machine's cavity encloses 'working models', which show 'the contraction of both the internal and external os, [opening of the cervix into the uterus and the vagina] the generation of water in parturition and the dilatation [*sic.*] of the os uteri [opening of the cervix into the vagina]'.[75] How Smellie was able to mimic the contraction of the entire cervical canal and then, as labour advanced, the dilation of the cervical opening into the vagina is astounding. Another feat of anatomical engineering is secure placement of these models within the pelvic cavity. Smellie did recognize that in non-pregnant women the round and broad ligaments were fairly slack and that only when the uterus rose in pregnancy was this slack taken up – like a slingshot being drawn back for fire. Perhaps he used specially preserved human ligaments to keep his models secure, since it is reported that 'the contents of the Abdomen, are imitated with great Exactness'.[76]

While Smellie chose not to use infant cadavers in his machine, his foetuses are not the small waxen dolls or little stuffed babies that his detractors claimed they were. As Camper attests, they 'are all artificially made of wood according to the natural dimensions, shapes and methods of jointing. The bones of the head work just as in the actual living foetuses, the nose is inset and the jaw is movable'.[77] A second account of Smellie's foetuses claims 'the children ... are likewise, excellently contriv'd, they having all the Motions of the Joints. Their Craniums are so formed, as to give way to any Force exerted, and are so elastick, that the pressure is no sooner taken off, [then] they return to their natural Equalities'.[78] With their movable jaws and necks, and pliable cranial bones, these foetuses allowed students to practise various manoeuvres to reposition the child in the womb so it could be delivered in the natural posture with its head facing the mother's back and its chin tucked in. At least one of Smellie's foetuses also allowed students to practise embryotomy, or piecemeal extraction of the child while in the birth canal. In the days before anaesthesia, when Caesarean operations were rarely practised, knowledge of such a procedure, though rarely performed, was vital in cases where the mother's small or distorted pelvis prevented a successful vaginal birth.

Much more could be said about the obstetrical machines of Smellie and other men-midwives, including their relationship to anatomical models such as those mentioned at the beginning of this essay, their comparative use in other European countries, and the detailed studies of parturition and birth, from living and dead subjects, that aided midwives in the design and construction of their machines. Male midwifery practice was regularly, and loudly, critiqued by certain individuals during the period, but there seems to have been no comparable outcry over obstetrical machines or the treatment of poor pregnant women, which a number of men-midwives used as a supplement to machines by delivering them, usually without charge, in their homes or in lying-in hospitals. Further inquiry into these issues, with a focus on class and gender, seems in order. Some male midwives taught female pupils on their machines, typically in separate classes; others did not, and of those who did, one wonders what midwifery curriculum, including instrument use, was taught. Margaret Stephen learned forceps application on machines, then taught it the same way in her 30-year career teaching female pupils.[79] Was her experience a lone case, or did obstetrical machines provide women with an avenue into the increasingly male-dominated venue of male midwifery? Though many questions remain unanswered, what this essay has aimed to accomplish is simply this: to document the widespread use of obstetrical machines in eighteenth-century Britain so that they can be placed firmly within the history of science, gynaecology, and midwifery.

NOTES

1. F. J. Cole, 'History of the Anatomical Museum', *A Miscellany Presented to John Macdonald Mackay, LL.D. July 1914*, ed. Oliver Elton (Liverpool, UK: Liverpool University Press, 1914), pp. 302–317 (p. 305).
2. Anita Guerrini, 'Anatomists and Entrepreneurs in Early Eighteenth-Century London', *Journal of the History of Medicine and Allied Sciences*, 59.2 (2004): 219–39 (224).
3. Nehemiah Grew, *Musaeum Regalis Societatis; or, A Catalogue and Description of the Natural and Artificial Rarities belonging to the Royal Society* (1681; London: Hugh Newman, 1694), pp. 3, 6, 8.
4. Captain Laskey, *A General Account of the Hunterian Museum, Glasgow* (Glasgow, UK: John Smith and Son, 1813), p. 51. For discussion of how Hunter's plaster *casts* correspond to illustrations in his atlas, see N. A. McCulloch, D. Russell, and S. W. McDonald, 'William Hunter's Casts of the Gravid Uterus at the University of Glasgow', *Clinical Anatomy*, 14.3 (2001): 210–17.
5. Thomas Schnalke, *Diseases in Wax: The History of the Medical Moulage*, trans. Kathy Spatschek (Carol Stream, Ill: Quintessence Books, 1995), p. 29. Pamela Pilbeam claims that Desnoues brought his models to London in 1727 and 1730. See her

Madame Tussaud and the History of Waxworks (London: Hambledon and London, 2003), p. 5.

6. Marta Poggesi, 'The Wax Figure Collection in "La Specola" in Florence', *Encyclopaedia Anatomica: Museo La Specola Florence*, ed. Monika von Düring, Georges Didi-Huberman, and Marta Poggesi (Köln, Germany: Taschen, 1999), pp. 6–25 (p. 21).

7. Mr. Christopher Cock, *A Catalogue of Several Curious Figures of Human Anatomy in Wax, taken from the life. With several other valuable preparations (the works of the late ingenious Mons. Denoue, of Paris, who was forty years in making these excellent emblems of nature) … Which will be sold by auction … on Tuesday the 11th of May, 1736* (London, 1736), pp. 4–7, 9–13.

8. Cock, *A Catalogue*, pp. 10–11.

9. 'Proposals for making Anatomies of human Bodies in colour'd wax after the manner of those belonging to the Sieur Desnoues', by Abraham Chovet, surgeon (1732); and 'A proposal to make anatomies of human bodies in coloured wax by A. Chovet' (1732): Royal Society Library (RefNo RBO/17/33 and JBC/14). For Chovet's reading of these proposals, see John H. Appleby, 'Human Curiosities and the Royal Society, 1699–1751', *Notes and Records of the Royal Society of London*, 50.1 (1996): 13–27 (14).

10. A. W. Bates, '"Indecent and Demoralising Representations": Public Anatomy Museums in mid-Victorian England', *Medical History*, 52.1 (2008): 1–22 (3–4).

11. The *London Daily Advertiser*, 28 December 1754, 25 August 1755; Anon., *An explanation of the figure of anatomy, wherein the circulation of the blood is made visible, through glass veins and arteries with the actions of the hearts and lungs; As also, The Course of the Blood from the Mother to the Child, and from the Child to the Mother … Adorned with a copper-plate, Wherein The Structure of the Heart is design'd, and the Glass Vessels exactly represented in their Order, as they are in the Figure to which they are to be referred* (London, 1737); Anon., *An explanation of the figure of anatomy, wherein the circulation of the blood is made visible thro' glass veins and arteries. With the actions of the heart and lungs… Adorned with a copper-plate: … to be seen at B. Rackstrow's in Fleet-Street, at one shilling each person* (London, 1747).

12. Rackstrow's Museum, *A Descriptive Catalogue (giving a full explanation) of Rackstrow's Museum: consisting of a large and very valuable collection of most curious anatomical figures, and real preparations; also figures resembling life* (London, 1784), pp. 6–7.

13. An early version of this essay appeared as 'William Smellie's Use of Obstetrical Machines and the Poor', *Studies in Eighteenth-Century Culture*, 29 (2001): 65–86. Many of the texts mentioned in the following discussion can be found in Pam Lieske (ed.), *Eighteenth-Century British Midwifery*, 12 vols. (London: Pickering and Chatto, 2007–2009).

14. Beginning in the early eighteenth century, obstetrical machines for midwifery teaching also appeared in France, Germany, Italy, and Sweden. See Urs Boschung, 'Geburtschilfliche Lehrmodelle: Notizen zur Geschichte des Phantoms und der Hysteroplasmata', *Gesnerus*, 38 (1981): 59–68; and Gerhard Ritter, 'Das Geburtschilfliche Phantom im 18. Jarhundert', *Medizinhistorisches Journal*, 1 (1996): 127–43.

15. The *Public Advertiser*, 8 May 1755.

16. A likely example of a less sophisticated machine comes from Bartholomew di Dominiceti, a physician who practised in Bristol. On 25 March 1760, Dominiceti

ran a notice in The *London Evening Post* promoting the spa-like amenities he offered patients who lodged with him, including hot and cold baths, a 'Lead machine', various devices to promote sweating, circulation, and salivating, medicinal remedies, and a full laboratory. Near the end of the notice, he claims he has '400 Anatomical Pieces; such as Skeletons, dissected Men in different postures, united and separated' and male and female anatomical specimens. He also has 'a Number of curious Pieces in Midwifery, representing the different Situations of Children in the Matrix [uterus], & c. with all the Operations and Apparatuses in Surgery and Midwifery'. Given Dominiceti's widespread interests, his machines were probably more for display than for serious hands-on education.

17. Adrian Wilson, *The Making of Man-Midwifery: Childbirth in England, 1660–1770* (Cambridge, MS: Harvard University Press, 1995), pp. 115, 125. See also Herbert Spencer, *The History of British Midwifery from 1650 to 1800* (1927; New York: AMS Press, 1978), pp. 16, 46.
18. Primary texts on Smellie and his critics, and on male/female midwifery debates, can be found in Pam Lieske, *Eighteenth-Century British Midwifery*, vols. 5 and 7.
19. William Smellie, *A Treatise on the Theory and Practice of Midwifery*, vol. 1 (London: D. Wilson 1752), p. v.
20. William Smellie, *A sett of anatomical tables, with explanations, and an abridgement, of the practice of midwifery, with a view to illustrate a treatise on that subject, and collection of cases* (London, 1754).
21. Bonnie Blackwell, 'Tristram Shandy and the Theater of the Mechanical Mother', *ELH: English Literary History*, 68.1 (2001): 81–133 (91); and Meghan Burke, 'Making Mother Obsolete: Eliza Fenwick's Secresy and the Masculine Appropriation of Maternity', *Eighteenth-Century Fiction*, 21.3 (2009): 357–84 (371).
22. Nina Rattner Gelbart, *The King's Midwife: A History and Mystery of Madame du Coudray* (Berkeley, CA: University of California Press, 1999), p. 62.
23. Richard Manningham, *An Abstract of Midwifry For the Use of the Lying-in Infirmary* (London, 1744), pp. i, v, vi, 10, n. pag., 15, 21, 22. (pagination incomplete). See *London Evening Post*, 12 April 1740, for a recently discovered newspaper advertisement of Manningham's midwifery teaching with a Glass Matrix.
24. Manningham, *An Abstract of Midwifry*, p. vi.
25. Manningham, *An Abstract of Midwifry*, p. vi.
26. Manningham, *An Abstract of Midwifry*, pp. 21–26.
27. Thomas Young, *A Course of Lectures Upon Midwifery* (Edinburgh, 1750).
28. Jessica Riskin, 'Eighteenth-Century Wetware', *Representations*, 83.1 (2003): 97–125 (97–98; 104).
29. Jessica Riskin, 'The Defacating Duck, or, the Ambiguous Origins of Aritificial Life', *Critical Inquiry*, 29.4 (Summer 2003): 599–633 (599).
30. Riskin, 'The Defacating Duck', pp. 599, 608.
31. Young, *A Course of Lectures*, p. 1.
32. Young, *A Course of Lectures*, pp. 4–5.
33. Kelly: *Daily Advertiser*, 25 August 1753, 5 October 1754, 19 October 1754, 28 December 1754, 4 January 1755; *London Evening Post*, 7 May 1754, 30 July 1754. MacDonogh: *London Evening Post*, 13 October 1753. Martin: *Daily Advertiser* 25 August 1755; *Public Advertiser* 30 October 1755. Crawford: *Daily Advertiser*, 16 October 1754, 19 October 1754, 28 December 1754, 4 January 1755; *Public Advertiser* 27 March 1755, 24 April 1755, 8 May 1755.

34. Susan Lawrence, *Charitable Knowledge: Hospital Pupils and Practitioners in Eighteenth-Century London* (Cambridge, UK: Cambridge University Press, 1996), p. 186.

35. Lisa Forman Cody, *Birthing the Nation: Sex, Science, and the Conception of Eighteenth-Century Britons* (Oxford: Oxford University Press, 2005), p. 248; Spencer, *The History of British Midwifery*, pp. 138–39.

36. Christopher Kelly, *A Course of Lectures on Midwifery* (London, 1757), p. 12

37. Wilson, *The Making of Man-midwifery*, pp. 147, 151; Lisa Forman Cody, 'Living and Dying in Georgian London's Lying-in Hospitals', *Bulletin of the History of Medicine*, 78.2 (2004): 309–48 (321).

38. *The Court and City Kalendar: or, a gentleman's register, for the year 1764*, 4th ed. (London, 1764), p. 175.

39. Khron and Denman's joint appointment to the Middlesex Hospital was announced in the *Lloyd's Evening Post*, 1 November 1769. Denman was exposed to obstetrical machines through his study under William Smellie. In addition, in 1770, he and Osborn bought a teaching apparatus from Dr Cooper for £120, *ODNB* (http://www.oxforddnb.com/view/article/7494, accessed 25 July 2007).

40. *Gazetteer and New Daily Advertiser*, 30 September 1766; *St. James Chronicle or the British Evening Post*, 11 September 1788.

41. *Public Advertiser*, 5 January 1762, 16 February 1765, 19 March 1765, 8 January 1766, 18 December 1766, 6 June 1767, 20 January 1768, 21 September 1768; *St. James Chronicle or the British Evening Post*, 16 September 1769, *Gazetteer and New Daily Advertiser*, 5 October 1770.

42. *Public Advertiser*, 16 February 1765.

43. John Leake, *Introduction to the Theory and Practice of Midwifery* (London, printed for R. Baldwin and A. Murray, 1787), pp. 79–80.

44. Leake, *Introduction to the Theory and Practice of Midwifery*, p. 80.

45. John Leake, *A Course of Lectures on the Theory and Practice of Midwifery* (London, 1767), p. 1.

46. Leake, *A Course of Lectures*, pp. 10–11.

47. Leake, *A Course of Lectures*, pp. 12–13.

48. Thomas White, *A Syllabus of Lectures, on the Theory and Practice of Midwifery* (Manchester, UK: Harrop, 1787).

49. White, *A Syllabus of Lectures*, p. 8.

50. White, *A Syllabus of Lectures*, p. 8.

51. Gelbart, *The King's Midwife*, pp. 61–2.

52. *Morning Herald* and *Daily Advertiser*, 30 September 1783.

53. William Douglas, *A Letter to Dr. Smelle [sic.] Shewing the Impropriety of his New-Invented Wooden Forceps; as also the absurdity of his method of Teaching and Practising Midwifery* (London, J. Roberts, 1748), p. 19.

54. White, *A Syllabus of Lectures*, p. 8; Leake, *A Course of Lectures*, n. pag.

55. *Daily Advertiser*, 25 August 1753.

56. A number of primary texts condemning male midwifery practice can be found in Lieske, *Eighteenth-Century British Midwifery*, vols. 2, 5, and 7.

57. Leake, *A Course of Lectures*, n. pag.; White, *A Syllabus of Lectures*, p. 2.

58. Leake, *A Course of Lectures*, n. pag.

59. Manningham, *An Abstract of Midwifry*, pp. vi–vii.

60. John Glaister, *Dr. William Smellie and his Contemporaries: A Contribution to the*

History of Midwifery in the Eighteenth Century (Glasgow, UK: James Maclehose & Sons, 1894), p. 26.

61. The year of Smellie's retirement is typically given as 1759, but as the following advertisement from Harvie makes clear, Smellie retired in 1758.

62. Walter Radcliffe, *Milestones in Midwifery and the Secret Instrument: The Birth of the Midwifery Forceps* (Bristol, John Wright and Sons, 1967), p. 61; Robert William Johnstone, *William Smellie: The Master of British Midwifery* (Edinburgh: E. and S. Livingstone, 1952), p. 28. Harvie received his midwifery certificate from Smellie on 1 December 1757 (Royal College of Obstetricians and Gynaecologists GB 1538 S52/1). Newspaper notices announcing that Harvie has inherited Smellie's machines appeared in the *London Evening Post*, 23 May 1758, 25 May, 1758; and the *Public Advertiser* 24 May 1758, 29 May 1758. The quotation cited is identical in all four notices.

63. Samuel Paterson, *A Catalogue of the Entire and Inestimable Apparatus for Lectures in Midwifery … by the Late Ingenious Dr. William Smellie, Deceased* (London, 1770).

64. *Freeman's Journal*, 27 September 1774; quoted in Thomas Percy Claude Kirkpatrick and Henry Jellet, *Book of the Rotunda Hospital: An Illustrated History of the Dublin Lying-in Hospital from its Foundation in 1745 until the Present Time* (London: Adlard and Son, Bartholomew Press, 1913), p. 81.

65. Blackwell, *'Tristram Shandy'*, pp. 95–96. Blackwell's quotation of the notice varies slightly from the one presented here.

66. *Morning Herald and Daily Advertiser*, 30 December 1783.

67. Paterson, *A Catalogue*, p. 6.

68. Paterson, *A Catalogue*, p. 6.

69. Paterson, *A Catalogue*, p. 6.

70. Paterson, *A Catalogue*, p. 6.

71. Margaret Stephen, *Domestic Midwife: or, The Best Means of Preventing Danger in Child-Birth Considered* (London: S.W. Fores, 1795), p. 18.

72. Stephen, *Domestic Midwife*, p. 4. Stephen's teacher may have been Harvie or perhaps Colin MacKenzie, who was a senior assistant of Smellie's until the two parted ways in 1754. Mackenzie subsequently had a successful career teaching midwifery in London and maintained a private lying-in establishment. He is known to have used machines and preparations in his courses. See W. I. C. Morris, 'Colin MacKenzie M.D. (St. Andrews): An Estranged Pupil of William Smellie', *British Journal of Obstetrics and Gynaecology*, 82.10 (1975): 769–74 (773) and *ODNB* (http://www.oxforddnb.com/view/article/94832, accessed 4 January 2008).

73. Quoted in Johnstone, *William Smellie*, p. 26.

74. 'An Answer to a late Pamphlet, Intituled, "A Letter to Dr. Smellie; Shewing the Impropriety of his new invented Wooden Forceps"' (London: C. Corbet, [1748?]), p. 17.

75. Peter Camper, quoted in Johnstone, *William Smellie*, pp. 26–27.

76. 'An Answer', p. 17.

77. Peter Camper, quoted in Johnstone, *William Smellie*, pp. 26–7.

78. *A Short Comparative View of the Practice of Surgery in the French Hospitals: With Some Remarks on the Study of Anatomy and Midwifery. The whole endeavouring to prove, that the advantages to students, … are greater at London, than at Paris* (London, Jacob Robinson, 1750), pp. 49–50.

79. Stephen, *Domestic Midwife*, p. 17.

6

Transcending the Sexed Body: Reason, Sympathy, and 'Thinking Machines' in the Debates over Male Midwifery

SHEENA SOMMERS

By the end of the eighteenth century male physicians had replaced female midwives as the preferred birthing attendants among the aristocracy and wealthy middle class. How the private world of the lying-in, which derived its authority from women's experiential knowledge of birth and reproduction, had become the domain of the male physician is a complicated and yet often over-simplified story.[1] The eighteenth- and early nineteenth-century debates over the man-midwife illuminate complex and competing discourses surrounding the nature of men, women, and the reproductive body. Through an analysis of selected works published during this period, this essay will highlight the ways in which advocates both for and against the use of male midwives drew upon the wider Enlightenment discourses surrounding natural law, sexual difference and reason to bolster their claims. The repositioning of reproductive matters in the public forum entailed new ways of thinking about how the 'truths' of the body were to be ascertained. Birth and maternity increasingly came to be defined as matters that could only be fully managed and understood through detailed, objective, and professional learning, rather than through experiential knowledge. As the traditional foundations for female midwifery came under attack it was the man-midwife who was best able to harness the growing faith in reason and science and to position himself as working in the interests of the emergent public sphere.

Scholars such as Lisa Cody have done much to question simplistic explanations for the triumph of the man-midwife in England, highlighting not only their claims to superior anatomical knowledge and skill but also their successful appropriation of qualities more traditionally associated with femininity.[2] Drawing upon the insights of Cody, this essay will further explore the contested ideological terrain of the midwifery debates. Throughout this period male midwives worked hard to position themselves as embodiments of an idealized masculinity; yet their success in this venture depended not only upon their capacity to negotiate and transcend the boundaries of the public and private as Cody maintains but also upon their ability to respond to the virulent attacks of their opponents. Only by analysing the terms of the debate, including the ways in which each side sought to construe itself and its opponent, can the success of man-midwifery be explained.

The problem of sexual impropriety was perhaps the most damning of the issues for male practice and as such, this matter became of central importance to the man-midwives' subsequent self-constructions. It was precisely in response to ongoing concerns about sexual immodesty that the man-midwife mapped out his unique professionalism. In appropriating empathetic qualities for himself and in rendering female sympathy dubious, the male practitioner claimed a rational compassion that was uniquely removed from any association with a specifically sexed body. The man-midwife's capacity to transcend the limitations of his own sex was set in stark contrast to the practice of women. The relationship between female practitioners and their patients was problematized by the advocates of male midwifery as one that was too close to allow female practitioners the necessary distance required to achieve objective understanding. In appropriating empathetic qualities for himself and in rendering female sympathy dubious, the male practitioner claimed a rational compassion that was uniquely removed from any association with a specifically sexed body – a claim I will discuss later.

Two explanations have traditionally been put forward by historians to elucidate the replacement of female midwives by male practitioners in the birthing chamber: fashion and forceps.[3] The design of the forceps was made public between 1733 and 1735 after being a closely guarded secret of the Chamberlen family.[4] The revolutionary nature of this new device meant that the male practitioner, previously called in generally only during the final moments of a difficult birth in order to save the mother and deliver a dead child, was now equipped with the means to save the woman *and* deliver a live infant. Indeed, according to Adrian Wilson, it was only with the introduction of this instrument that the 'imaginative horizon of male obstetric practice shift[ed] beyond the delivery of a dead child'.[5] Previously, the instrument of the surgeon or male midwife used in cases of obstructed births was the crotchet, a sharp hook designed to pull out the head of a lifeless infant. The image of the male practitioner suffered due to his association with such instruments. Nevertheless, once it became known that a male practitioner could deliver a *living* child, the fear associated with the sight of a surgeon during lying-in was replaced with hope in cases of difficult births. Female practitioners were put at a distinct disadvantage, as the use of instruments was forbidden to them. According to Wilson, the rise of the professional male midwife was a result of this momentum; the less women feared the male practitioner, the earlier they would call him in, and the earlier he arrived, the greater chance there was of a successful delivery.[6]

The second reason generally given for the shift towards the use of male practitioners is fashion. According to Roy Porter, the fashionable appeal of the male practitioner during the age of Enlightenment stemmed from the desire among wealthy mothers-to-be to obtain practitioners who were 'smooth, polite and confident', in contrast to the 'traditional lower-class and uncouth women'.[7] For Wilson, acquiring the services of a man-midwife worked as a means for elite women to distinguish themselves from women further down the social scale.[8] Among the aristocracy and wealthy middle class, the man-midwife came to represent yet another element of conspicuous consumption. Thus Wilson concludes that male practitioners were 'turned into midwives not by their own desire but through the choices of women'.[9]

Such arguments illuminate the important role played by mothers-to-be in the shift towards the use of male practitioners. Yet, the question remains as to how male midwives narrated their own intervention and growing involvement in the field. While the fashionable appeal of the man-midwife may have played a part in women's decisions to employ a male practitioner, women and their families were unlikely to make such an important decision solely on this basis. The man-midwives and their advocates were, therefore, keen to highlight their professionalism and skill, most often leaving references to their fashionable appeal as fodder for their opponents. Convincing women and their families to forgo female midwives required a sustained effort by male practitioners, one which could hardly have been achieved without underscoring their perceived superior abilities in the field.

From the vantage of our own time, it is not too difficult to see who emerged victorious in the battle for control of birth and reproduction. Eighteenth- and nineteenth-century denunciations of the man-midwife nevertheless suggest that the male practitioner, despite his claims to superior skill, faced a multitude of opponents both within and outside the medical community. A thriving practice was never solely a matter of technical know-how and the man-midwife had to work hard to counter attacks concerning impropriety by cultivating an appropriate gentlemanly demeanour, particularly if he wished to have access to the most lucrative clientele. The development of male midwifery was, from the outset, fraught with a host of difficulties. Aside from the fact that it was a fairly recent invention, its connotations not only as a female practice but also as a manual art made its practitioners subject to criticism and continued exclusion from the sphere of the university-trained physician. With a few exceptions, midwifery went unrecognized by the three main bodies governing the field of medicine in England throughout the eighteenth century.[10] Thus, in England, regulation and training in midwifery existed in a somewhat haphazard state, while on the Continent municipal regulation was becoming increasingly common.[11]

The belief that women's bodies were inaccessible to male practitioners had promoted the authority of female midwives and validated their traditional position as arbiters of female bodily truth. Throughout the eighteenth century, however, knowledge about the reproductive body became viewed increasingly, both inside and outside the medical community, as an acquisition 'attainable through "rational-critical" means rather than personal bodily experience'.[12] This period witnessed an explosion of printed works which dealt with matters of sex and reproduction, from midwifery and medical manuals to sex advice literature and erotica.[13] As Cody's work demonstrates, concerns over population, disease, and sexual reproduction progressively found their way into the coffee houses, newspapers, and public forums, as did debates on the use of male midwives.[14]

Male practitioners advertised their services, held public lectures on midwifery and established philanthropic enterprises.[15] In so doing, the male practitioner of midwifery was not only involved in a process of redefining pregnancy and childbirth as matters for public discussion and debate but was also engaged in a project of self-fashioning. With his supposedly superior learning and skill, the emergent obstetrician repositioned himself as an objective interlocutor of the female body. His claims to objectivity were, however, as Cody's work has shown, situated alongside the possession of very personal qualities such as compassion and sympathy.[16] While these characteristics had been regarded as forming the very basis for female midwifery – as women's sympathy was deemed to stem from shared experience and intuitive understanding – the man-midwife appropriated these qualities for himself and, simultaneously, rendered such characteristics in women suspect. It was, to a certain degree, precisely the distance of the male practitioner from the sufferings of childbirth that allowed him the objectivity apparently needed to arrive at reproductive truths. Male practitioners quite successfully presented themselves as the necessary intermediaries between women's bodies and reproductive knowledge.

THE EVIDENCE OF NATURE

So long as knowledge about the female reproductive body was seen to stem from feeling and experience, the male practitioner would have little place in the birthing chamber. The inherent unnaturalness of a man in the birthing chamber formed a standardized part of attacks directed against male practice. As many eighteenth-century contemporaries were quick to remark, even the term 'man-midwife' was an oxymoron. Nature had become one of the watchwords of eighteenth-century polemics and was frequently used in the midwife debates. It was used as an umbrella term which could be stretched to provide ammunition for either side of the debate, encompassing all that was good and decent about female midwifery, or outlining women's natural inadequacies as practitioners. References to nature worked on a variety of levels. Since traditionally women had attended births, female midwives and their advocates argued that this was the most natural route, one which had already stood the test of time.[17] Some works suggested that it was dangerous for men to expose the secrets of women's nature, that male practice was fundamentally inconsistent with the tender nature of women, and that the presence of men in the birthing chamber actually worked to halt and disturb the natural process of labour.[18] According to the opponents of male practice, it was nature herself that rendered women inevitably more fit for midwifery. Women did not need extensive medical knowledge of anatomy to perform the work of midwifery as 'nature [was] the book, [and] experience the guide'.[19] Women's intuition, along with their experiential knowledge, was thus positioned in opposition to male artifice and professional learning.

The physical differences between men and women made it obvious to many that men were simply not cut out for this particular branch of medicine. Women's hands, for instance, were designed for such undertakings, owing to a certain 'softness, flexibility, and dexterity of hand, palpably denied to the men'.[20] In contrast, men's hands were said to be much too large. As a result, they needed to resort to the use of instruments which, it was argued, did far more harm than good.[21] Hamilton Fitzwilliams, author of medical handbooks – particularly those on women's health, thus asked the reader to compare the damage a woman could cause with her hands to that done by a man with his 'levers, his crotchets, his forceps, his perforators, and the rest of his murderous instruments'.[22] Elizabeth Nihell, a practising midwife and author of a birthing manual, worked to portray the female hand as the 'essential obstetric instrument'.[23] The tenderness of a woman's hands served merely as the physical manifestation of her tenderness of feeling; her delicate hands were simply a reminder of her innate ability to sympathize with the sufferings of other women. Only women, wrote the anonymous author of *The Danger and Immodesty of the Present too General Custom* (1772), could have a 'tenderness for their own sex in labour, which it is impossible men can ever equal'.[24]

Women's sympathy, unlike men's, was deemed natural by the proponents of female midwifery since only they could have actually 'felt the pains and the anxieties attending child-birth'.[25] Thus women, according to Nihell, had an 'irresistible instinct' that made them the most obvious choice of birthing attendants.[26] In opposition to female 'instinct', she suggested that men who engaged in the study and practice of midwifery actually spoiled their minds with such 'undigested studies'.[27] Nihell was dextrous in her use of rhetorical reversals and the physical metaphor of digestion worked to highlight the innate unnaturalness of a man attempting to pursue this practice. While traditionally it was held that too much study would ruin the body and mind of women, in this case Nihell turned the tables, arguing that studies in midwifery were, to a man, so foreign that his body and mind were quite simply incapable of ingesting them.

With all of these arguments in favour of female midwives what, then, according to the opponents of male practitioners, had caused the women of Europe to flock to male midwives? Fashion, particularly of the French flavour, provided one of the most compelling explanations and again was set in direct contrast to nature. According to Nihell, 'too many women' had been 'miserably mislead by fashion as to prefer the betraying [of] the cause of their own sex, and the subjecting [of] themselves to those who deceive them with false hopes'.[28] Nihell went even further in portraying the male midwife as antithetical to nature by drawing upon the most sacred of all eighteenth-century images: the maternal breast. In a final stab at the practice, Nihell maintained that at this rate she would not be surprised if 'dry-nursing became fashionable', with the man-midwife arguing that 'water-gruel or scotch-porridge was a much more healthy aliment for new-born infants than the milk of the female breast'.[29] The symbol of nursing held important significance during this period and Nihell's use of this iconic image worked to spell out women's natural abilities over male artifice.[30]

Some works went even further, arguing that male practice was in fact a symptom of a diseased civilization. Thus, Dr John Stevens attributed this 'noxious weed' which had cast its 'shadow far and wide' to the unchecked luxury of European civilization as a whole.[31] Indeed, the contrast between civilization and the natural world found full force in the various racialized comparisons between European civilization and 'other' populations. Good European women were apparently surrendering themselves to practices that even the most immodest and uncivilized women would never dream of. To make matters worse, these women of Christendom were, according to some, doing so with great 'pleasure and satisfaction'.[32] Fitzwilliams maintained that even the 'wild Indian, the uncivilized negro, the untutored savage, and even the Hottentot woman would revolt with disgust at the idea of the presence of a male practitioner in the sanctuary of childbirth'.[33] She would 'feel polluted by his filthy and unhallowed touch – would shrink with horror from the disgusting exposure of her person to which the *delicate*, and *refined*, and *Christian* women of Europe [...] submit without reluctance and shame'.[34] As Stevens argued, quoting another physician, even an 'oriental mother [...] would sooner die than seek the assistance of a man in her hour of travail'.[35]

Nature did not, of course, long remain the sole property of anti-male midwifery arguments. Male midwives countered these attacks with references to their own understandings of natural law. The increasing interest in, and understanding of, the biological differences between men and women served as ammunition for the attacks against the use of female midwives. The belief that women had far more sensitive nervous systems, for instance, suggested to some that they were excessively susceptible to the impressions of the senses and had difficulty, therefore, in distinguishing between what was real and what was not, a tendency that would have disastrous consequences in the birthing chamber. According to the man-midwife John Leake, women's delicate bodily frame – rather than making them particularly fit for such endeavours – as we saw above with reference to the female hand – led inevitably to a delicacy of mind liable to 'many excesses and inordinate motions'.[36] According to their opponents, female midwives frequently made errors of judgement because their 'passions led them astray'.[37] Women's natural sympathy for other women, rather than aiding their practice was actually seen to hinder it. As Cody maintains, while many men-midwives and their advocates certainly emphasized the fact that women were by nature creatures of feeling, they were, however, unfortunately always 'feeling incorrectly'.[38]

Male practitioners could not afford to give over the whole realm of feeling and sympathy to the female sex. In their writings, men-midwives stressed their own superior rationality and their ability for 'masculine sympathy'. According to Leake, for those practitioners 'blessed with sympathy and a benevolence of heart', the profession will 'afford a most exalted pleasure', especially, he goes on, 'where such assistance is given to women, who are to be considered as the weaker sex and unable to help each other'.[39] The man-midwife combined feeling with rationality, sympathy with objective understanding. The surgeon Louis Lapeyre likewise maintained that the male midwife must not only be educated but also 'endowed with a sensitivity of soul'.[40] He should be able to 'sympathize with the evils and afflictions which human nature is liable to; he must be extremely compassionate, especially with regards to the pain to which the sex to whose service he has devoted his talents and labours, is so subject'.[41] In his deportment, he must remain simple and modest in order to 'shew forth the probity and rectitude of his heart' alongside that 'cool composure, sedateness and presence of mind'.[42] In sympathizing with the 'evils and afflictions to which human nature is liable to' from the vantage point of rational observer, the male professional claimed to be both in the service of this humanity while simultaneously transcending the excessive feeling said to characterize female practice.

Not all male practitioners and writers adhered to the notion that female feeling exceeded that of men's. Lapeyre himself was quite willing to forgo his tenderness of soul and extreme compassion when making reference to the 'lowest class of human beings' – the female midwives.[43] Lapeyre reversed the arguments surrounding innate female sympathy by suggesting that female midwives were in fact the ones guilty of having an 'unfeeling heart'.[44] His portrayal of the female midwife drew upon traditional motifs of the doting old woman, callous, ignorant and full of 'superannuated gossip'.[45] According to Lapeyre, the traditional midwife was little more than an 'animal with nothing of the woman left'.[46] In depicting female midwives as predominantly older, presumably post-menopausal women, Lapeyre's writings alluded to a long and popular history whereby older women were portrayed as malevolent creatures, incapable of empathetic feeling and forever jealous of younger, childbearing women.[47] Lapeyre's portrayal sought to displace the basis for female midwifery, namely the argument that there was a natural sisterly affection between women based upon equality and shared experience that qualified women to practise the art. By depicting the female midwife as an older woman, this similitude was shattered, the relationship between female practitioner and her patient instead becoming one fraught with envy and ineptitude.[48]

SEXUAL KNOWLEDGE AND INTIMATE ENCOUNTERS

While nature and feeling worked on numerous levels in the arguments over the man-midwife, the problem of sex was even more forcefully played out in ways which could both disturb and titillate the reader. Male midwifery was construed by its opponents as a perversity that had the potential to destroy marriages, families and, subsequently, the whole basis upon which the state rested. Male practitioners had to walk a very fine line in this regard and defend themselves against the suggestion that they operated in secret and with private designs.[49] The private designs of the male practitioner were particularly threatening when one reflected upon his superior anatomical and sexual knowledge. Thus, while some opponents portrayed man-midwifery as an effeminate and unmanly profession, most of the attacks were directed against their tendency towards the darker side of male passions.

The sexual danger posed by the man-midwife did not escape his opponents. As Fitzwilliams maintained, all men 'love lovely women' and that passion is 'so strongly implanted in our nature, that even the wisest and best of men have […] violated and outraged […] the doctrines and legislation of the marriage bond'.[50] The 'passions of the man', wrote the anonymous author of *Junonesia* (1838), are 'by sight and touch liable to be excited'.[51] This work went on to describe in extensive detail how each of the senses (excluding taste) became aroused in the close contact with women that male practitioners enjoyed. The sight of a beautiful bosom, the tangible feel of a woman's soft skin, and her frailness of voice all worked inevitably to lead a man to 'seek the fruition of his desires'.[52] Nor did the author wish to pass over the olfactory sense which apparently 'all naturalists know … is extremely powerful in many animals'.[53] The litany of all of these powerful sense impressions which drove the practitioner to falter suggested, according to this author, that the man-midwife could hardly be considered 'a free agent'.[54]

Other opponents were less forgiving in their description of men's motives in midwifery and suggested contrarily that male practitioners were entirely conscious and wilful with regard to achieving a certain perverse satisfaction. In Steven's attack, he 'quotes' a practising man-midwife who apparently told him that

> We [the man-midwives] have the opportunity of receiving the favours of the fair with greatest facility, and on extensive scale. We buy our gratifi-cations at a cheap rate; we obtain profit and pleasure at the same time – a pretty girl, the thanks and gratitude both of herself and her cara sposa, and, what is more, are paid too in the bargain.[55]

The notion that the male practitioner operated with selfish motives was taken up by Nihell as well. She maintained that male practitioners operated with private designs, while female midwives were dutiful servants of the public good.[56] According to Nihell, the male midwives sought to 'drive out of the practice those who stand in the way of their private interest'.[57]

While the superior knowledge possessed by male practitioners was precisely one of the arguments used in favour of men-midwives, such knowledge could be used equally by their opponents to discredit them. The male practitioner, according to the author of *Junonesia*, 'knows every touch, and all variety of fingering'.[58] He was 'expert in amorous arts', his profession had taught him 'where to place his finger upon the *clitoris*', which, according to the author, was the 'master-key to the accomplishments of his desires'.[59] Some writers attempted a little more subtlety, pretending themselves too modest to describe what the male practitioners were in fact doing in their practice that was so horrifying and contrary to sexual propriety. In Fitzwilliams' work, for instance, the author claimed that it was difficult for him to discuss what male midwives actually do. Thus, to 'avoid sullying my pages', he writes, he shall not describe the details of the 'pawing and *fingering*, the *peeping* and *prying*, the *trying* and *taking of pains*, and the rest of the abominations of the *touching* and *tailing* gentry'.[60] Authors such as Fitzwilliams sexualized their texts while simultaneously lamenting the need to do so, in effect blaming the men-midwives for their own titillating and sullied pages.[61]

It was precisely this sexual knowledge that allegedly made it so difficult for female patients to resist the doctor's advances. What woman, asked Nihell, could 'refuse a man, to whom nothing of that has been refused?'[62] His expert touch made it 'next to impossible for a woman of warm temperament to preserve her virtue'.[63] Indeed, according to Dr W. Beach, an American physician cited by Dr Stevens, women were 'more susceptible to temptation during pregnancy than at any other time'.[64] Even if, asks the author of *Junonesia*, the sensations that affect both the male practitioner and his female patient could be put aside for some time, how could the doctor not remember in retrospect the 'delicate confirmation of her limbs, their luxuriant fullness and proportions, or the texture and complexion of her skin[?]'[65] The female patient likewise would not soon forget that 'as well by touch as by sight, he [the man-midwife] knows her in person already too intimately'.[66] The possibility of separating the man from the medical professional was, according to his opponents, a ludicrous proposition. The man being a professional cannot 'obliterate the idea in her [the female patient's] breast that he is nevertheless a man'.[67] The author of *The Danger and Immodesty* thus offered what s/he felt would work as a permanent solution to this problem. For, s/he writes, if men '*must* be *introduced* to the *privacies* of women, I would earnestly recommend it as the MOST ESSENTIAL *qualification* requisite TO PREPARE them for the study, that they submit to having their VOICES *made delicate*'.[68] This last comment illustrates again the fact that the man-midwife's claim to transcending manly passions was not enough to convince his opponents. While perhaps only a jest, by advocating castration this writer reaffirms the sexual danger posed by men-midwives. The only way for a man to pursue this practice was to undergo a very physical process, one that could, unlike transcendental reason, take the man out of the male practitioner.

TRANSCENDING THE SEXED BODY

While many opponents stressed the preposterousness of a man being able to attend to women in the birthing chamber without having his passions inflamed, male practitioners countered these arguments by portraying themselves as professionals transcending the passions of their sex. In order to remove the threat posed by male sexuality, the male practitioners needed to downplay any reference to their own sexed bodies. Using the gendered discourse of male rationality, male practitioners simultaneously attempted to unsex themselves, in effect, taking the sting, or at least the man, out of the man-midwife.

This transcendence of a specifically located, sexed body through the use of reason was part of the broader cultural dialogues that came out of the emerging field of seventeenth-century scientific inquiry. The increasing interest in interrogating the secrets of nature accentuated what had already become a fairly central metaphor of scientific endeavour: that of a male subject penetrating the secrets of female nature.[69] Men's dominion over the natural world was set in contrast to a seeming 'incompatibility between female nature and women's capacity to control nature'.[70] Within naturalist science women were positioned as the particular, the offshoot of the male sex, and, in another sense, the embodiment of a generalized, unchanging nature.[71] Depicted as creatures of nature, women could hardly position themselves as objective interlocutors of the natural world.

As the laws of nature came increasingly to be seen as above and beyond human politics, the male practitioner sought to position himself as objective investigator of the natural world. The gendered discourses of transcendent reason were thus deployed in favour of men's advancement in the field of midwifery. Male practitioners were nevertheless forced to walk the fine line of embodying masculine qualities while simultaneously circumventing any association with their own sexed bodies. While the tracts against the use of male midwives emphasize the irrefutability of sexual difference as one of the reasons why men should be excluded from this field of practice, male practitioners and their advocates sought to counter these accusations by denying the relevance of their own bodies and those of their patients. The man-midwife straddled two competing and yet overlapping ideas. Being born a man, he was inherently more suited for rational thought than was his female counterpart, and yet, it was precisely this possession of reason that allowed him to transcend the natural desires of the body. In redefining childbirth as a medical condition in need of professional supervision, male practitioners not only helped to create new understandings of the maternal body but were also involved in the process of constructing a new kind of male medical professional, one able to show compassion without passion.[72]

It was claimed, therefore, that the man-midwife adopted his profession not out of some perverse fascination or private motivation, but rather out of a sense of 'gratitude to his mother' and a natural 'kinship with women'.[73] Lapeyre, for instance, attempted to deny accusations of impropriety by stating that those employed in this profession were actually immune to what other men might call the 'beauty, charms, attractives [*sic*], [and] incentives' of the female sex.[74] Where other males saw, perhaps, a beautiful young woman, the man-midwife saw nothing but an 'assemblage of nerves, cartilages, muscles, [and] fibers'.[75] Having been exposed to so many women in his practice, the 'presence of such objects makes not the least impression on him'.[76] This was due to the fact that man, according to Lapeyre, desired only that thing whose 'value is augmented in proportion to the difficulty which attends [its] attainment'.[77] As an example of this, Lapeyre also utilized a racialized analogy informing the reader that in the practice of his art, the man-midwife is akin to Europeans in America who, generally unaccustomed to seeing public nudity, might at first experience something of a 'tumult', but soon, through habit and daily exposure, feel nothing. The 'frame of mind peculiar to those in his profession' armed the practitioner with a genuine indifference to female enticements.[78]

Beyond the passions of the body, the man-midwife, according to Lapeyre, was himself truly 'a being who, in a moral sense, may be said to belong to neither sex'.[79] Faced merely with a 'bundle of nerves', the male practitioner became himself no more than 'a thinking machine'.[80] As the female patient was reduced to a body without sex, Lapeyre construed the man-midwife as a mind/machine capable of transcending his own sexed body. This mechanistic analogy was part of a shift in Enlightenment thought concerning the nature of the universe and the individual's place therein. According to Jean Donnison, 'the impact of this "masculine", mechanistic philosophy' with regard to the shifting nature of medical practice, 'cannot be underestimated'.[81] Lapeyre's portrayal of the medical practitioner's relationship to his female patients aptly mirrors this transition. Lapeyre and his ilk represented the new mechanical universe engaged in the pursuit of reproductive truths, while the female patients he attended to were contrarily portrayed in more organic metaphors as bodies or body parts.

This kind of portrayal in Lapeyre's work was related to the more general decline in the importance of the patient's subjective self-reporting in medical encounters that began in the eighteenth century. Porter argues that the relationship of the physician to his patients for most of the early modern period involved a significant amount of participation from the patient, as physical examinations were an infrequent part of the duties of a physician. The subjective narrative of the patient, her description of her ailments, symptoms, lifestyle, medical history and so on, was, therefore, paramount in the doctor's diagnosis.[82] In the burgeoning field of man-midwifery, however, new techniques that focused upon manual operations carried out by the practitioner, such as podalic version, pelvic manipulation, and the use of forceps, were related to a decreasing significance of the woman's own account of her condition.[83] Eve Keller's analysis of eighteenth-century medical casebooks illustrates this quite well. The declining importance of the female patient as subject in these texts was coupled with her subsequent relegation to the status of silent object, composed of dismembered parts.[84] The female patient in these works became either 'irrelevant or obviated altogether', while the other birth attendants became merely the 'backdrop to the author's self-construction'.[85] According to Ernelle Fife's analysis of the differing discourses used in the writings of male and female midwives, the former opted for a linear, analytical technical style of writing which tended to position women more as physical bodies lacking subjectivity.[86] As a collection of organs and body parts, the female patient possessed neither sex nor subjectivity.

While this desexing of both the patient and the medical practitioner worked to counter attacks regarding the impropriety of the man-midwife, some authors went beyond a merely defensive stance and reversed the arguments surrounding sexual passions altogether. Tobias Smollet, novelist and practitioner of midwifery, turned the tables of perversity and sexual appetite onto the female practitioner. In his virulent attack against Elizabeth Nihell, he not only called her a 'lunatic' with the fluency of a 'fish woman', but went so far as to call into question the purity of her motivations for practising midwifery. Smollet claimed that Nihell had made reference in her writings to a technique that midwives sometimes used, whereby she would place her hand upon the lower abdomen of a woman in labour in order to ease her pain. Smollet seized upon this admission in order to portray the female midwife as sexually suspect. Thus he writes that 'just how far Mrs. Nihell's shrewd, supple, sensitive fingers, may be qualified for the act of titillation' he did not wish to ponder too deeply.[87] Smollet's attack on Nihell reversed the naturalness of a woman as birth attendant motivated by sisterly love and replaced it with the suggestion of unnatural female sexuality. Thus, while the 'thrust of many attacks against man-midwives had been (and continued to be well into the nineteenth century) that they operated secretly with private designs', these same arguments could also be used to make women's interest in the field of midwifery seem itself unnatural and representative of deviant sexuality.[88] Whereas Lapeyre's portrayal above sought to displace the similarity between women, Smollet instead rendered it dubious. By drawing attention to this moment of touch between two women, the author sought to highlight the unnatural closeness between the female midwife and her patient.

CONCLUSION

The debates over the man-midwife became a battleground for rival interests as they drew upon a variety of intellectual shifts that were taking place throughout the eighteenth and nineteenth centuries. The tracts discussed above, while often complicated and contradictory, nevertheless represent competing modes of knowing. As experiential understanding began to be replaced with reason as the basis upon which knowledge about the body could be obtained, the man-midwife gained an increasing foothold in the field of midwifery. Portraying themselves as rational and sympathetic professionals, the man-midwives transformed themselves from hack surgeons to cultivated specialists.

Nature, as we have seen, was used as an argument both for and against the use of male practitioners. While women's innate feeling for other women was generally deemed greater than that of men's on both sides of the divide, women's sympathy increasingly became construed in extreme cases as a perversity, but more generally as that which rendered them incapable of arriving at scientific truths. The rational sympathy of the male practitioner, on the other hand, enabled him to engage in this practice with a reasoned objectivity as a 'thinking machine', transcending the passions of the body. The authors in favour of male advancement in this field aimed, therefore, to neutralize any reference to the sexed bodies of both themselves and their patients. In order to defuse references to manly passions, these authors drew upon the emergent gendered discourse of transcendental reason. The unsexing of the male practitioner was related to the emergence of a new individual, one coded as 'universal' and therefore beyond the common confines of sex. Thus, while proponents of female midwifery continued to argue that female practice served the public well and that women were capable of reason and professionalism, female practitioners were increasingly defined in terms of their biological make-up. Hence, the female practitioner could not (like her male adversaries) forgo her own sex in order to arrive at transcendent truths. While the female patient might be seen by the man-midwife as no more than a sexless 'bundle of nerves', the female midwife, contrarily, could not escape her own sexed body and all the consequences and limitations this entailed.

The man-midwife quite successfully portrayed himself as working in the interests of the emerging public sphere. While women and their advocates continued to make reference to the public good, they were frequently regarded as the objects, rather than the executors, of enquiry. Investigations into the peculiarities of the female body were, moreover, inevitably investigations into what it meant to be a man. In remapping the maternal body, the man-midwife gave birth to himself. The knowledge which obstetrical studies entailed had therefore as much to do with the medical professional's self-presentations as it did with any specific truths about female anatomy.

NOTES

1. As Lisa Forman Cody argues, historical narratives concerning the wresting of control over the female body by the masculine medical profession have generally taken two paths, one highlighting the progressive accomplishments of medical technologies, and the other viewing this 'progress' as more accurately a reflection of the increasing domination of women and their bodies by a misogynist profession. See Lisa Forman Cody, 'The Politics of Reproduction: From Midwives' Alternative Public Sphere to the Public Spectacle of Man Midwifery', *Eighteenth-Century*

Studies, 32.4 (1999): 477. Doreen Evenden and David Harley have separately noted the traditionally negative views of medical historians in their depictions of early modern female midwives, see Doreen Evenden, *The Midwives of Seventeenth-Century London* (Cambridge, UK: Cambridge University Press, 2000); and David Harley, 'English Archives, Local History, and the Study of Early Modern Midwifery', *Archives*, 21 (1994): 152. Mary Daly, on the other hand, suggests that the shift away from female midwives amounts to a 'gynaecological crusade to shorten women's lives' (*Gyn/ecology: The Metaethics of Radical Feminism* (London: The Women's Press, 1979), p. 260). See also Barbara Ehrenreich and Deirdre English, *Witches, Midwives and Nurses* (Old Westbury, NY: Feminist Press, 1973).

2. Lisa Cody, *Birthing the Nation: Sex, Science, and the Conception of Eighteenth-Century Britons* (Oxford: Oxford University Press, 2005).
3. Adrian Wilson, *The Making of Man-Midwifery: Childbirth in England 1660–1770* (Cambridge, MA: Harvard University Press, 1995), p. 3.
4. Wilson, *The Making of Man-Midwifery*, p. 3.
5. Wilson, *The Making of Man-Midwifery*, p. 57.
6. Wilson, *The Making of Man-Midwifery*, p. 97
7. Roy Porter and Dorothy Porter, *Patient's Progress: Doctors and Doctoring in Eighteenth-Century England* (Cambridge, UK: Polity Press, 1989), p. 181.
8. Wilson, *The Making of Man-Midwifery*, p. 187.
9. Wilson, *The Making of Man-Midwifery*, p. 192.
10. The Royal College of Physicians (founded in 1518), The Company of Barber-Surgeons (founded in 1540) and The Society of Apothecaries (founded in 1617) all refused to provide any certificate of qualification or licence for the practice of midwifery for most of the century. See Jean Donnison, *Midwives and Medical Men: A History of the Struggle for the Control of Childbirth* (London: Historical Publications, 1988), pp. 50–71.
11. Donnison, *Midwives and Medical Men*, p. 25. Many of the most prominent eighteenth-century midwives were thus Scottish men who had trained in Edinburgh and had come to London to make their careers. For a detailed analysis of the importance of the Scottish influence on man-midwifery in England see Cody, *Birthing the Nation*, pp. 152–97
12. Cody, 'Politics of Reproduction', p. 483.
13. Roy Porter and Lesley Hall, *The Facts of Life: The Creation of Sexual Knowledge in Britain, 1650–1950* (New Haven, CT: Yale University Press, 1995) p. 33.
14. Cody, 'Politics of Reproduction', p. 483.
15. Cody, 'Politics of Reproduction', p. 486.
16. Cody, *Birthing the Nation. Sex, Science, and the Conception of Eighteenth-Century Britons* (Oxford: Oxford University Press, 2005).
17. John Stevens, *Man-Midwifery Exposed* (London: W. Horsell, 1849), p. 2.
18. Stevens, *Man-Midwifery Exposed*, pp. 4–5.
19. Anon., *Junonesia; or Women Rescued* (London: W. Kidd, 1838), pp. 34–35.
20. Elizabeth Nihell, *A Treatise on the Art of Midwifery* (London: A. Morley, 1760), p. 89.
21. William Douglas, M.D., *A Letter to Dr. Smellie* (London: J. Roberts, 1748), pp. 18, 25.
22. Hamilton Fitzwilliams, *Death Blow to He or Man Midwifery* (London: Claridge & Co., 1850), pp. 9–10.

23. Wilson, *The Making of Man-Midwifery*, p. 198.
24. Anon., *Danger and Immodesty of the Present too General Custom* (London: J. Wilkie, 1772), p. 29. It has recently been suggested by Lisa Cody that Elizabeth Nihell may have been the author of this work. See Cody, *Birthing the Nation*, p. 185.
25. *Danger and Immodesty*, p. 29.
26. Nihell, *A Treatise*, p. 90.
27. Nihell, *A Treatise*, pp. 61–62.
28. Nihell, *A Treatise*, p. 5.
29. Nihell, *A Treatise*, p. 190.
30. According to Amanda Gilroy, in a 'backlash against wet-nursing, maternal breast-feeding became the symbol of maternal virtue, domestic economy and national responsibility' (see Amanda Gilroy, 'Candid Advice to the Fair Sex', in *Body Matters: Feminism, Textuality and Corporeality*, ed. Avril Horner and Angela Keane (Manchester, UK: Manchester University Press, 2000), p. 18). While wet-nursing was actually at its height around mid-century, a large body of work began pouring out, reprimanding women for not feeding their own children and highlighting the numerous health benefits of breastfeeding. See also Simon Richter, 'Wet-nursing, Onanism, and the Breast in Eighteenth-Century Germany', *Journal of the History of Sexuality*, 7 (1996), pp. 1–22.
31. Stevens, *Man-Midwifery Exposed*, p. 3.
32. Fitzwilliams, *Death Blow*, p. 6.
33. Fitzwilliams, *Death Blow*, p. 5.
34. Fitzwilliams, *Death Blow*, pp. 5–6.
35. Stevens, *Man-Midwifery Exposed*, p. 5.
36. John Leake, *A Lecture Introductory to the Theory and Practice of Midwifery*, 3rd ed. (London: 1773), p. 26.
37. Cody, 'Politics of Reproduction', p. 486.
38. Cody, 'Politics of Reproduction', p. 486.
39. Leake, *A Lecture*, p. 54.
40. Louis Lapeyre, *An Enquiry into the Merits of These Two Important Questions* (London: S. Bladon, 1772), pp. 44–45.
41. Lapeyre, *An Enquiry*, pp. 44–45.
42. Lapeyre, *An Enquiry*, pp. 44–45.
43. Lapeyre, *An Enquiry*, p. 29.
44. Lapeyre, *An Enquiry*, pp. 36–37.
45. Lapeyre, *An Enquiry*, pp. 36–37.
46. Louis Lapeyre, *An Enquiry…Whether Women with Child Ought to Prefer the Assistance of Their own Sex* (London: S. Bladon, 1772), p. 35.
47. See Cindy McCreery, 'Lustful Widows and Old Maids in Late Eighteenth-Century Caricatures', in K. Kittredge (ed.), *Lewd and Notorious: Female Transgression in the Eighteenth Century* (Ann Arbor, MI: University of Michigan Press, 2003); Lyndal Roper, *Oedipus and the Devil: Witchcraft, Sexuality and Religion in Early Modern Europe* (London: Routledge, 1994).
48. Here Lapeyre, rather than criticize female similitude as that which rendered the female practitioner incapable of objective understandings, displaces this bond by way of distancing the female midwife from her patient through a generational divide.
49. Cody, 'The Politics of Reproduction', p. 484.

50. Fitzwilliams, *Death Blow*, p. 36.

51. *Junonesia*, p. 141.

52. *Junonesia*, pp. 70–71.

53. *Junonesia*, p. 72.

54. *Junonesia*, p. 141.

55. Stevens, *Man-Midwifery Exposed*, p. 6.

56. Nihell, *A Treatise*, p. vii.

57. Nihell, *A Treatise*, p. vi.

58. *Junonesia*, p. 143.

59. *Junonesia*, p. 141.

60. Fitzwilliams, *Death Blow*, p. 26.

61. Wilson's work shows that this kind of tactic was not uncommon in anti-male midwife tracts (Wilson, *The Making of Man-Midwifery*, p. 198).

62. Nihell, *A Treatise*, p. 234.

63. *Junonesia*, p. 143.

64. Wooster Beach, *An Improved System of Midwifery*, 17, as cited in Stevens, *Man-Midwifery Exposed*, p. 5.

65. *Junonesia*, p. 138.

66. *Junonesia*, p. 138.

67. *Junonesia*, p. 138.

68. *Danger and Immodesty*, p. 43.

69. Eve Keller, *Reflections on Gender and Science* (New Haven, CT: Yale University Press, 1985), p. 3.

70. Lieselotte Steinbrügge, *The Moral Sex: Women's Nature in the French Enlightenment*, trans. Pamela E. Selwyn (New York: Oxford University Press, 1995), p. 28.

71. Steinbrügger, *The Moral Sex*, p. 28.

72. According to Eve Keller, medical practitioners' self-constructions have been 'relatively unexplored' by historians. See Keller, 'The Subject of Touch: Medical Authority in Early Modern Midwifery', in *Sensible Flesh: On Touch in Early Modern Culture*, ed. Elizabeth D. Harvey (Philadelphia, PA: University of Pennsylvania Press, 2003), p. 68.

73. Cody, 'Politics of Reproduction', p. 488.

74. Lapeyre, *An Enquiry*, p. 61.

75. Lapeyre, *An Enquiry*, p. 61.

76. Lapeyre, *An Enquiry*, p. 55.

77. Lapeyre, *An Enquiry*, p. 57.

78. Lapeyre, *An Enquiry*, p. 61.

79. Lapeyre, *An Enquiry*, p. 61.

80. Lapeyre, *An Enquiry*, p. 61.

81. Donnison, *Midwives and Medical Men*, p. 33.

82. Porter, 'The Rise of the Physical Examination', in *Medicine and the Five Senses*, ed. W. F. Bynum and Roy Porter (Cambridge, UK: Cambridge University Press, 1993), p. 182.

83. While touch had generally been associated with the feminine, according to Eve Keller it was reconceptualized in the late seventeenth and eighteenth centuries, becoming, in the work of the man-midwives, 'aligned with the masculine attributes of reason and decorous action' (Keller, 'The Subject of Touch: Medical Authority in Early Modern Midwifery', in *Sensible Flesh*, p. 70). For earlier evidence of this

repositioning by anatomists see Bettina Mathes, 'As Long as a Swan's Neck?: The Significance of the "Enlarged" Clitoris for Early Modern Anatomy', in *Sensible Flesh*, pp. 103–24.

84. Keller, 'The Subject of Touch', in *Sensible Flesh*, p. 70.
85. Keller, 'The Subject of Touch', in *Sensible Flesh*, p. 70.
86. Ernelle Fife, 'Gender and Professionalism in Eighteenth-Century Midwifery', *Women's Writing* 11.2 (2004): 185–200.
87. Tobias Smollett, *The Critical Review*, 9 (1760): 187–97, cited by Cody, in 'Politics of Reproduction', p. 487.
88. Cody, 'The Politics of Reproduction' p. 484. See also Porter, 'A Touch of Danger: The Man-Midwife as Sexual Predator', in *Sexual Underworlds of the Enlightenment*, ed. G. S. Rousseau and Roy Porter, (Manchester, UK: Manchester University Press, 1987): pp. 206–31.

7

Emma Martin and the Manhandled Womb in Early Victorian England

DOMINIC JANES

In early Victorian England pregnancy and childbirth were matters of both medical and spiritual concern. In this paper I will be exploring the way in which these two realms of knowledge and discourse were brought together when a radical feminist, Emma Martin, rebelled against her religious upbringing and came to dedicate the final years of her life, not simply to women, but to their wombs. She did this by lecturing on gynaecology and practising as a freelance midwife. By doing so she was not simply rejecting religious practice for that of science, but was connecting with the female embodiment of fertility, which was for her the original and essential core of human existence. In so doing she was fighting against the Christian-sponsored domination of worship by men and also combating contemporary attempts to promote the role of men as midwives. In between her years as a Baptist housewife and those as a midwife she spent some time (after she had separated from her husband) lecturing from a radical socialist viewpoint. It was towards the end of this period that she published one of her most remarkable discourses: *Baptism: A Pagan Rite* (1844). In this text she argued for the symbolic centrality of the uterus in human cultural life. For example, she contended that the origins of religion lay in fertility cults in which devotees of male and female elements competed:

> Those who supposed the influence of the male was greatest, instituted the worship of the Linga, of which the round towers of Ireland, the Phallus of India, Egypt and Greece, the Cross and the Lord's Supper are varieties; while those who held the contrary opinion, viz. that the female had the greatest share in the production of the new being, established the worship of the Yoni, – from which the cavern worship of India, the Pyramids of Egypt, and the rite of Baptism by water proceeded.[1]

As the title of her tract suggests, she was interested in focusing on the primal antiquity of worship of the Yoni (female reproductive organs). In writing this piece she was inspired by a tradition of comparative religion that had been developed and popularized since the Reformation by anti-clerical comparisons of Roman Catholicism with pagan worship. However, where many male writers on such topics focused on the supposed primacy of phallic devotion, for Martin it was the body of the female which had been the true and central focus of worship.

In this essay, I will explore the way in which Martin came to criticize her original Baptist beliefs and practices through a process of thinking not about the female body as a problematic object in need of male religious and medical discipline, but *with* the female person as a creative subject. This interdisciplinary project requires engagement with topics (notably the histories of science and religion) that are often seen as distinct. Yet in early Victorian England, religious, moral, and medical discourses not only competed but also influenced each other. Research into ideas of embodiment in this period can benefit from an approach similar to that taken by Esther Pasztory in *Thinking with Things: Toward a New Vision of Art* (University of Texas Press, 2005). In this book Pasztory provides suggestive insight into the ways in which diverse textual discourses can be found to interact with objects in order to produce sophisticated understandings of the world. In her analysis, the cultural meaning of, for instance, the body, is established not only through changing textual discourses concerning the body but also via evolving practices and performances of the body itself. The need for such approaches can be seen in the work of Kathleen Canning, who has concluded that there has been 'a veritable flood' of works on the body in history, but these mostly 'invoke the body [...] without referring to anything specifically identifiable as body, bodily or embodied'.[2] Pasztory, in contrast, has not been content to relegate the embodied world to a secondary status in comparison to structures of 'meaning' produced in textual discourses led and shaped by men. In a similar way, Martin reacted against what she regarded as the downgrading of what appeared to her to be the central importance of female embodiment in religious, antiquarian, and medical discourse. In so doing she rejected elements of male discourses on both spirituality and medicine and displaced them by focusing on women's lived experience. By concentrating on the body and on embodied truths, Emma Martin effectively argued that women had superior, inside knowledge of their own bodies and should shake themselves free of male descriptions and interference.

BAPTISTS AND OWENITES

Emma Martin was a person of passionate beliefs, but the nature of those beliefs changed drastically over her lifetime. At the age of seventeen she joined a small sect called the Particular Baptists.[3] The first such Calvinistic Baptist group had formed in 1633 in East London. They held that Christ had died only for the elect (for those of their number who had been baptized) rather than, as the General Baptists believed, for all people. Although there were no priests in a sacerdotal sense (priesthood for Baptists was something awful pertaining to Hindus and Catholics), the leadership of the communities remained very much in the hands of men.[4] Women nonconformists (a term in general use by the mid-nineteenth century) were restricted in their roles.[5] While it was respectable for women to disseminate the creative efforts of men through participating in tract distribution, female creative expression through preaching (often dismissed as 'ranting') was not.[6] Such limited opportunities for an active role for women in their congregations may have appeared even more meagre in the face of the fact that only one-third of the members of Baptist churches were men at this time.[7] The 'woman with a cause' was a recognized, but also a mocked and stereotyped figure in early Victorian England. Part of the reason for this was that such a public role was hard to reconcile with middle-class notions of domestic propriety.[8] Emma Martin, however, was willing to pay the social price of assuming a role of strident social advocacy for the rights of women.

It took several years of mounting resentment to convince her to leave the Particular Baptists. After all, she had invested much energy in the roles allowed her. From the age of eighteen she had run a school and been active in distributing tracts. Furthermore, in 1831 she had married another Baptist, Isaac Luther Martin, and they had had three daughters. She was very unhappy in the marriage and a combination of dissatisfaction with her home and her church life appears to have led her to begin attending radical lectures. Initially she attacked the anti-religious ideas she heard there but was speedily won over. At the end of 1839 Isaac moved the family to London. Barbara Taylor has written perhaps the most detailed account of this period.[9] According to her the key event took place in February of that year when Martin was 'transfixed' by hearing Alexander Campbell, one of the Utopian socialist Robert Owen's leading followers.[10] Shortly afterwards, Martin separated from her husband, took her children, and became a lecturer for the Owenites in her own right.

Robert Owen's movement was intended to bring about a revolution in society, since he argued in favour of communitarian modes of production. He fought against traditional marriage 'bonds' as being based not on love but on property ownership and he argued for less formal and more equal companionate relationships.[11] The very fact that lecturing for a small salary was open to Owenite women was a testament to the movement's radicalism. Martin used the new freedom of expression open to her to turn on her previous beliefs and practices. In so doing she developed a systematic explanation for Baptist failings which drew on widespread cultural suspicions of the practice of baptism by immersion. The sprinkling of water on the brow of infants was the standard practice of the Church of England, and for many who supported this practice there was something quite improper about the Baptist use of 'plunging'. The fact that concern was mostly focused upon the immersion of young ladies by male Baptist ministers indicates the widespread apprehension that the nature of this impropriety was in some sense sexual. This led to the publication of horrified accounts such that of an anonymous writer who reported hearing

> the shrill scream of a woman as she felt herself going under the water. Another [scream] arose with the struggling of the young person, who succeeded in wrenching herself from the minister's grasp, and fell with a loud splash into the baptistery. More than once I recall that people fainted in the water: I distinctly retain the image of the ghastly and death-like countenance of a woman, as her head hung back, wet and motionless, over the arm of the person who dragged her into the vestry.[12]

Such alarming events could prove fatal, for the same writer reported that another woman experienced fever, delirium, and death after baptism in cold water.[13] The implications here are clearly related to medical danger. Yet there was more to it than that. On another occasion, this writer saw young women 'decked out in decorated caps, and white vestments, far more tastefully arranged than simple convenience required', and marked the manner by which they were 'severally plunged by the minister, and then, as my eye followed each of them, drenched and dripping (a spectacle anything but impressive)' they were led away.[14] This author tells us that he walked off into the countryside and read the Bible amid flowers and fresh air, having escaped from such an infamous display of soaked chemises. For male writers, the problem was not so much the manhandling of the women, however, as the circumstances in which this took place. It was contended that cold water was injurious to the allegedly fragile nature of the female frame and that women's moral respectability was also endangered, since immersion took place in front of mixed crowds including men, who might find the spectacle erotic. For instance, another text of the time argued that such a 'profuse exhibition of the person' was but an opportunity for cloth to fall enticingly away from the neck and bust.[15] Would men, it was asked, not blush to have their wives and daughters baptized in such circumstances by other males?[16] Immersion was, in short, 'a distressing rite to womanly weakness and modesty, and opposed to manly self-respect'. Are not those to be dipped 'in a state of terror, of both body and mind? Have they not, while being plunged, sometimes convulsively sobbed, and even screamed aloud?'[17] It was alleged that ministers wore waders under their gowns and postponed baptism of the sick: 'surely then, danger is sometimes anticipated, even by persons who loudly dilate on the safety and pleasure of being popped under water in a baptistery!'[18]

Such claims were, of course, vigorously contested. Baptists replied that such injuries were figments of the imagination and that immersions were witnessed by people with 'the most solemn and tender impressions generally and commonly manifested'.[19] It was not immodest, since there were female attendants who went with the devotees to change their clothes and to ensure that they were dressed 'most abundantly and carefully'.[20] However, the feeling was occasionally expressed that the event should be in some sense a stressful trial. One writer viewed immersion in positive terms as a lesser type of the shame that Christ suffered on the cross.[21] Being baptized was seen by those with such views as possessing a spiritual richness which derived from abjection of the body. As one Baptist hymn asked,

> Hast thou for me the cross endured,
> And all the shame despised?
> And shall I be ashamed, O Lord,
> With thee to be baptised?[22]

On leaving the Baptists Emma Martin was free to counter suggestions of the morally improving nature of female suffering and denounce male manhandlings of women in the baptismal pool. However, the way she explained this situation was strikingly original in that she represented these religious performances as explicitly phallic disruptions of female selfhood and sanctity. Rather than simply accusing Baptist ministers of prurient recklessness she challenged the entire right of men to participate in such a rite of symbolic rebirth.

ANTIQUARIANS AND MIDWIVES

By the end of the nineteenth century holy wells associated with medieval saints start to appear in popular English folklore in the form of interesting, if ultimately pagan, folk customs.[23] When Emma Martin was writing, however, assertion of links between pagan springs and Christian modes of healing and regeneration was a radical act and one which was, for many people, scandalous. But Martin, in *Baptism: A Pagan Rite*, went much further, in that she understood sexualized readings of the modern ceremony of baptism as reflecting its original ritual purpose. In this work she identified that the first places of worship were caves. She wrote that 'the cave was no inapt symbol of the womb', which was worshipped because divine creation was the primal mystery.[24] In the second stage of religious evolution there took place a struggle between the phallus/lingam as a focus for devotion (as seen in the last supper and the cross), and the uterus-vagina/yoni (as in the pyramids of Egypt, baptism, and the caves in India).[25] Christ's worship was taken over by phallocentric devotees of the cross during the Middle Ages, but the original reality was different. Jesus was born in a cave, then baptized in a river and then buried in a cave, before he rose again.[26] Since Martin regarded rivers as ritual substitutes for caves, she was indicating that the cult of Christ was, in origin, symbolically female. Water, she asserted, which 'washes away the defilements of the body, may aptly represent the purification of the mind', but that purification was the result of female regenerative agency.[27]

Ironically, however, the textual origins of this 'genitalization' of the landscape lay in the male world of eighteenth-century erotica, in which sexualized readings were applied to a range of political, religious, commercial and domestic contexts. In these forms of text, 'representations homed in on points where gender and geography merged, situating eroticized female bodies in sexualized locations that were appropriately dark and deep – caves, grottoes, groves, and shut rooms, all metaphors for female bodies and parts'.[28] The audience for such learned erotica was substantially the same as that for works of antiquarian erudition. A key figure in this world of connoisseurs and libertines was William Hamilton, diplomat and collector, who heard of a surviving 'phallic cult' north of Naples in which wax images were offered at a local church by women in the hope of ensuring their fertility. He was interested in the cult because it 'offer[ed] a fresh proof of the similitude of the Popish and Pagan religion'.[29] In May 1785 he travelled to the location and examples of the phallic images were sent to the British Museum.[30] Hamilton described the cult to Richard Payne Knight, who published on the subject in his *Discourse on the Worship of Priapus* in 1786.[31] This was to be the most influential book on the subject of fertility cults, but its explicit phallocentricity appears to have been resisted by Emma Martin, who relied, by contrast, on the researches of Godfrey Higgins, an antiquarian from Doncaster who was interested in both uterine and phallic imagery. Higgins' method was based on 'discovering' nomenclatural similarities (Christ and Chrishna, for example) and identifying objects that were shaped like genitalia. For instance he noted 'clefts' in rocks in India, adding that among the Celts 'the early Christians called these things *Cunni Diaboli*, and from the former of these words came the vulgar appellation for the membrum foemineum in England'.[32] The section of Higgins' work quoted by Martin is one in which he emphasizes the companionate marriage

of the male and female principles. According to him, active masculine fire
was the first element, but passive feminine water was his 'assistant', 'the agent
by which everything was born again, or regenerated', since without water the
sun could not produce life.[33]

Higgins was, therefore, notable among writers on comparative religion
in that he evoked notions of gendered partnership, but Emma Martin
went further. For her, the female principle was of primary rather than
secondary importance. What she did was to reignite the radical potential of
such comparative religion by fixing on the notion that men had perverted
the original religious practices. Martin did not, at this point, believe in
the resurrection of ancient religion. She stated that 'there is no creative
intelligence that requires of any man prayer' and that one might as well
perform Christian baptism as use 'one of those [rituals] by which the Hindoo
worshipper honours the Goddess Kale [sic.], as mentioned in the Missionary
Quarterly Papers'.[34] However, she did want to spell out what she regarded
as the core cultural truth of the importance of the female body, a truth that
had become obscured by male textual and physical interference.

Martin thus transcended traditions of male erotica. She condemned
Baptist ministers for treating the baptismal pool not as a symbol of the
sacred womb, but as a passive space in which to act out male penetrative
manhandling of the female body. The minister standing in the pool was
pretending that his aggressive act of immersion was a creative act of spiritual
rebirth when it was, in fact, an act of symbolic violence towards the female
body and its fertility. Not only that, but Martin also challenged male writers
on fertility religion who had a strong tendency to focus on the phallus as
the active agent of creation and who sought to relegate the uterus to the
role of a vital but passive counterpart. She also differed from male devotees
of comparative religion because she did not see such studies as an amusing
pastime for gentlemen of leisure and the revelation of such topics as the
subject for ribald entertainment. It is instructive, for instance, to compare
her serious denunciation of Baptist preachers with that of Robert Taylor,
who wrote that:

> The Baptae or Baptists were an effeminate and debauched order of Pagan
> priests [...]. They take their name from their stated dippings and washings,
> by way of purification, though it seems they were dipped in warm water,
> and were to be made clean and pure, that they might wallow and defile
> themselves the more, as their nocturnal rites consisted chiefly of lascivious
> dances and other abominations. The Baptists, or Anabaptists, as they
> are called, continue as an order of religionists among Christians, under
> precisely the same name.[35]

Taylor was a sometime Anglican priest who put on in London remarkable and blasphemous shows which were burlesque parodies of religion.[36] His writings on the Baptists effectively summon up images of erotic spectacle. His revelations of Baptist impropriety, therefore, had nothing much to do with the liberation of women and their bodies, and everything to do with the fact that he earned his living by selling tickets to his voyeuristic shows after he was thrown out of the Church of England.

In 1845 Emma Martin ceased to preach the Owenite gospel and devoted her professional life to women and their bodies by becoming a midwife.[37] It is clear that she had become disillusioned with the Owenites. It is possible that she had come to realize that the movement, though radical, was still led by a man who was not about to renounce his patriarchal role as intellectual leader. Martin trained as a midwife at the Royal Adelaide Lying-in Hospital, but the rule of the Royal Maternity Charity that required prayer at the bedside meant that she had to practise freelance.[38] She also lectured on gynaecology. In so doing she entered the final phase of her struggle against illegitimate male authority. It had long been assumed that midwifery was naturally the preserve of women. However, Roy Porter has noted, of the later eighteenth century, that 'unblemished morals and religious orthodoxy rather than medical skill were the criteria of fitness to attend births, because midwives so easily fell under suspicion of colluding in illegitimacy, abortion and infanticide'.[39] Such suspicion of female collusion meant that the fathers who paid the medical bills in upper and middle class families increasingly preferred to employ men to assist in childbirth. This meant that 'by the turn of the nineteenth century, men-midwives and other men of science had established a cultural authority over sex and birth'.[40] Yet the medical training of men-midwives was insufficient to ward off thoughts of their erotic involvement with their patients and this led to the development of a new phase of moral panic with claims that 'sexual innuendoes and accusations thus turned medicine into a scandalous travesty at the crossroads between fear and farce'.[41] This meant that 'despite repeated proposals for the rehabilitation and regulation of midwives, none of these had come to fruition' and that by the early nineteenth century 'the stigma attaching to the occupation was such that educated entrants to it were rare indeed'.[42] Medical reform after the arrival of the man-midwife was, therefore, slow in coming. The first English Hospital for Women did open in Red Lion Square, Holborn, in 1842, close to Emma Martin's practice. However, it had to face accusations that its services were mainly used by fallen women and that it acted inappropriately to palliate the results of vice.[43] As a former Owenite and a woman who had separated from her husband, Martin would have fallen under similar moral suspicion and it is possible that her last years were impoverished ones, since her clients were unlikely to have been women from wealthy and respectable households.

CONCLUSION

In her study, *Eve and the New Jerusalem: Socialism and Feminism in the Nineteenth Century* (1983), Barbara Taylor acknowledges the role of Emma Martin in the struggle for women's rights, but she also comments that, in the tract on baptism, Martin's argument has a 'strangely Freudian twist'.[44] Freud was, of course, not writing on sexual symbolism until half a century later, but the term 'Freudian' is sometimes used in casual speech as a code word for an apparently peculiar obsession of a writer or a speaker with sexual symbolism. I want to emphasize that this was not Emma Martin's concern. What she did attempt to do was to wrench debates on religion away from the arcane preoccupations of denominational differences centred on phallocentric social politics, and to insist on the importance of women's bodies. Furthermore, in her professional life she asserted the final importance of engagement with the practices of female health over participation in male-dominated realms of discourse. In the tract that I have been discussing she employed the textual tradition of comparative religion, which was itself rooted in assumptions of phallic supremacy, to assert that a primitive celebration of female fertility had, in the baptismal pool, been turned into a tragic expression of male dominance over women and their bodies. The outrage with which female speech on the subject of sex was often greeted inevitably limited the scope for other women to develop her ideas. In the United States a notable exception was the socialist and suffragist Eliza Burt Gamble, who argued that Protestantism represented the highest form of the attempt to eradicate the female divine, since it was 'the most intensely masculine of all religious schemes'.[45]

After Emma Martin died in 1851, her intellectual work in this area lacked immediate successors. Nevertheless, her example can be seen as indicative of the way in which an early Victorian feminist sought to engage with enmeshed and hostile religious and medical discourses. If, as Ornella Moscucci has argued, gynaecology was seen at this time to be the study of the 'whole woman', and as being a discipline which 'fused the physical, psychological and the moral aspects of femininity', then Martin's work can be seen to have been centrally situated in a battle for the control of human reproduction and its related values and meanings.[46] Gamble and Martin were isolated figures (Gamble less so than Martin because she lived fifty years later), yet the assertion of combined female physicality and spirituality was, of course, to play a major role in the development of feminism in the twentieth century. Those who have embraced the worship of the Earth Mother over recent decades had, if not a fellow believer, at least a kindred spirit in a woman who had spent much of her life toiling in the apparently uncompromising moral and social landscape of early Victorian England.[47] In her professional practice Martin wished to bring embodiment to the fore.[48] Martin was arguing that textual obsessions with male desire and disgust were obscuring an essential bodily truth: that the essence of regeneration lay not in an act of priapic exuberance (the end result of a fetishistic manipulation of body parts by men) but in the wondrous female gestation of a newborn child.

NOTES

1. Emma Martin, *Baptism: A Pagan Rite* (London: Watson, 1844), p. 8.

2. Kathleen Canning, 'The Body as Method? Reflections on the Place of the Body in Gender History', *Gender and History*, 11 (1999): 499–513 (499).

3. Kenneth Dix, *Strict and Particular: English Strict and Particular Baptists in the Nineteenth Century* (Didcot, UK: Baptist Historical Society, 2001); and Geoffrey Ralph Breed, *Particular Baptists in Victorian England and Their Strict Communion Organizations* (Didcot, UK: Baptist Historical Society, 2003).

4. Anon., 'Native Royal Patronage of the Buddhist Religion', *The Investigator*, 1 (1841): 49–52 (52).

5. Linda Wilson, 'Nonconformist Obituaries: How Stereotyped was their View of Women?', *Women of Faith in Victorian Culture: Reassessing the 'Angel in the House'*, ed. Anne Hogan and Andrew Bradstock (Basingstoke, UK: Macmillan, 1998), pp. 145–58 (p. 156).

6. Olive Anderson, 'Women Preachers in Mid-Victorian Britain: Some Reflections on Feminism, Popular Religion and Social Change', *Historical Journal*, 12 (1969): 467–84 (468).

7. Clive D. Field, 'Adam and Eve: Gender in the English Free Church Constituency', *Journal of Ecclesiastical History*, 44 (1993): 63–79 (66, Table 2).

8. Suzanne Rickard, 'Victorian Women with Causes: Writing, Religion and Action', in *Women, Religion and Feminism in Britain, 1750–1900*, ed. Sue Morgan (Basingstoke, UK: Palgrave Macmillan, 2002), pp. 139–57.

9. Barbara Taylor, *Eve and the New Jerusalem: Socialism and Feminism in the Nineteenth Century* (London: Virago, 1983), pp. 130–55.

10. Taylor, *Eve and the New Jerusalem*, p. 133; W. Hamish Fraser, *Alexander Campbell and the Search for Socialism* (Manchester, UK: Holyoake Books, 1996).

11. John Fletcher Clews Harrison, *Robert Owen and the Owenites in Britain and America: The Quest for the New Moral World* (London: Routledge and Kegan Paul, 1969), pp. 56–59.

12. Anon., *Confessions of a Convert, From Baptism in Water to Baptism by Water* (London: John Snow, 1845).

13. Anon., *Confessions of a Convert*, p. 18.

14. Anon., *Confessions of a Convert*, p. 45.

15. Anon., *Can Women Regenerate Society?* (London: John W. Parker, 1844), pp. 59–60.

16. Anon., *Immersion not Christian Baptism* (London: Simpkin, Marshall and Co., c.1851), p. 4.

17. Thomas Mills, *The True Mode of Baptism Investigated; Being a Plain and Compendious Summary of Evidences in Favour of Sprinkling, and Against Immersion* (London: John Snow, 1849), pp. 145–46.

18. W. Thorn, *Dipping not Baptizing* (London: Jackson and Walford, 1832), p. 24.

19. Benjamin Coxhead, *Remarks Related to Christian Baptism* (London: G. Wightman, 1832), p. 108.

20. Coxhead, *Remarks Related to Christian Baptism*, p. 112.

21. Coxhead, *Remarks Related to Christian Baptism*, p. 110.

22. Anon., '*Pouring and Sprinkling Versus Baptism*', Tracts on Christian Baptism, 5 (Leicester, UK: Baptist Depository for Tracts and Sabbath School Publications, n.d.), p. 8.

23. See, for instance, Robert Charles Hope, *The Legendary Lore of the Holy Wells of England, including Rivers, Lakes, Fountains and Springs* (London: Elliot Stock, 1893) and M. Quiller-Couch and L. Quiller-Couch, *Ancient and Holy Wells of Cornwall* (London: C. J. Clark, 1894).

24. Martin, *Baptism*, p. 9.

25. Martin, *Baptism*, pp. 8, 12.

26. Martin, *Baptism*, p. 13.

27. Martin, *Baptism*, p. 15.

28. Paul Griffiths, Review of Karen Harvey, 'Reading Sex in the Eighteenth Century: Bodies and Gender in English Erotic Culture' (Cambridge, UK: Cambridge University Press, 2004), *Journal of British Studies*, 45 (2006): 661–63 (662).

29. Lee Alexander Stone, *The Story of Phallicism With Other Essays on Related Subjects by Eminent Authorities*, 2 vols. (Chicago, Ill: Pascal Covici, 1927), Vol. 1, p. 95.

30. Giancarlo Carabelli, M560–4: 'Gli ex Voto di Isernia al British Museum', Annali dell'Università di Ferrara, Nuova Serie, Sezione III, Filosophia, Discussion Paper 35 (Ferrara: Università degli Studi di Ferrara, 1994); and *In the Image of Priapus* (London: Duckworth, 1996).

31. See Richard Payne Knight, *A Discourse on the Worship of Priapus, and its Connection with the Mystic Theology of the Ancients ... A New Edition. To which is Added an Essay* [by Thomas Wright and others] *on the Worship of the Generative Powers during the Middle Ages of Western Europe* (1786; London: Chiswick Press, 1865).

32. Godfrey Higgins, *Anacalypsis: An Attempt to Draw Aside the Veil of the Saitic Isis; or an Inquiry into the Origin of Languages, Nations and Religions*, 2 vols. (London: Longman, 1836), Vol. 1, p. 346.

33. Higgins, *Anacalypsis*, Vol. 1, p. 529.

34. Emma Martin, quoted in *Women without Superstition: 'No Gods – no Masters', Collected Writings of Women Freethinkers of the Nineteenth and Twentieth Centuries*, ed. Annie Laurie Gaylor (Madison, WN: Freedom from Religion Foundation, 1997), pp. 99–100.

35. Robert Taylor, *The Diegesis; Being a Discovery of the Origin, Evidences, and Early History of Christianity, Never Yet Before or Elsewhere so Fully and Faithfully Set Forth* (London: Richard Carlisle, 1829) pp. 208–209. Compare Robert Taylor, *Syntagma of the Evidences of the Christian Religion. Being a Vindication of the Manifesto of the Christian Evidence Society, Against the Assaults of the Christian Instruction Society Through Their Deputy, J. P. S., Commonly Reported to be Dr. John Pye Smith, of Homerton* (London: Richard Carlisle, 1828).

36. Iain McCalman, 'Popular Irreligion in Early Victorian England: Infidel Preachers and Radical Theatricality in 1830s London', in *Religion and Irreligion in Victorian Society: Essays in Honor of R. K. Webb*, ed. R. W. Davis and R. J. Helmstadter (London: Routledge, 1992), pp. 51–67.

37. Gaylor, *Women without Superstition*, pp. 93–101.

38. Taylor, *Eve and the New Jerusalem*, p. 155.

39. Roy Porter, *Bodies Politic: Disease, Death and Doctors in Britain, 1650–1900* (London: Reaktion Books, 2001), p. 225.

40. Lisa Forman Cody, *Birthing the Nation: Sex, Science, and the Conception of Eighteenth-Century Britons* (Oxford: Oxford University Press, 2005), p. 269. See also D. Harley, 'Ignorant Midwives: A Persistent Stereotype', *Society for the Social History of Medicine, Bulletin* 28 (1981): 6–9.

41. Porter, *Bodies Politic*, p. 227; Ludmilla Jordanova, *Nature Displayed: Gender, Science and Medicine, 1760–1820* (Harlow, UK: Longman, 1999), pp. 23–24.

42. Jean Donnison, *Midwives and Medical Men: A History of the Struggle for the Control of Childbirth* (Historical Publications, 1988), p. 70.

43. Omella Moscucci, *The Science of Woman* (Cambridge, UK: Cambridge University Press, 1990), pp. 75–76, 86.

44. Taylor, *Eve and the New Jerusalem*, p. 145.

45. Eliza Burt Gamble, 'Sex, the Foundation of the God Idea' (1897), in L. E. Stone, *The Story of Phallicism with other Essays on Related Subjects by Eminent Authorities*, 2 vols. (Chicago, Ill: Pascal Covici, 1927), Vol. 1, pp. 143–256 (pp. 144, 150, 180, 244). Gamble's connection between religion, sex and feminism is also clear from her other book, *The Evolution of Woman. An Inquiry into the Dogma of her Inferiority to Man* (New York: G. P. Putnam, 1894).

46. Moscucci, *Science of Woman*, p. 103.

47. Melissa Leach, 'Earth Mother Myths and other Ecofeminist Fables: How a Strategic Notion Rose and Fell', *Development and Change*, 38.1 (2007): 67–85.

48. Canning, 'The Body as Method?', p. 499.

8

Narrating the Victorian Vagina: Charlotte Brontë and the Masturbating Woman

EMMA L. E. REES

In 1989 Eve Kosofsky Sedgwick claimed that the discipline of gynaecology emerged in the nineteenth century as a response to cultural and medical anxieties over female masturbation. Sedgwick, in her controversial article 'Jane Austen and the Masturbating Girl', argued for a rereading of *Sense and Sensibility* (1811) that allowed for the possibility of a homoerotic, or even autoerotic, identity for the novel's Dashwood sisters.[1] While Sedgwick's approach might be described as anachronistic or even exclusionary (it implies that readers who cannot see in Austen's text what Sedgwick sees have been blinded by their own heterosexist assumptions), it does present a useful model for the juxtaposition of historical and literary texts. That is, in forging audacious links between texts in an attempt to reveal what has previously been unsaid, unheard, or unexamined, Sedgwick illustrates the impossibility of locating an objective 'meaning' in canonical literary works. In this essay I echo Sedgwick as I explore the rich, albeit tangential, allusiveness produced by the juxtaposition of literary and non-literary texts. In exploring Victorian gynaecological treatises and a novel, Charlotte Brontë's *Villette* (1853), I identify a provocative cultural narrative of staged propriety and silent restraint.

This essay, then, tells the story of how certain Victorian lives intersect and coalesce. What comes into view from the merging of the canonical and the non-canonical, the fictional and the real, is an account of how the individual sexual subject struggles to make sense of its identity in relation to the secret and unspoken complexities of the female body. This account begins in the operating theatre and ends in a dramatic theatre. In both theatres the female body is specularized: pathologized in the one, and idolized in the other in the person of the actress Rachel, reimagined by Brontë in the sexually mesmeric persona of Vashti. To write about Victorian

women's sexual identities is to examine the revelation of the previously
concealed, and to encounter the apparent cultural eradication of women
themselves: of American and European women who had strikingly little
knowledge, or ownership, of their own bodies. The transfer from midwives
to doctors of medical control over women's bodies and sexual identities in the
mid-nineteenth century led to the emergence of gynaecology as a discrete
therapeutic discipline. In America, Ephraim McDowell, W. H. Byford, and
J. Marion Sims were gynaecological pioneers. Sims, for example, who spent
much of his working life in France, perfected his technique for the repair of
vesicovaginal fistulas on slave women in the US – without anaesthesia – and
the design of speculum that bears his name is still in use today. In the UK
Robert Lawson Tait and William Tyler Smith were among the first British
gynaecologists. This male domination of the field was not challenged until
the late 1890s when, in Providence, Rhode Island, one of the first women
gynaecologists, Helen Putnam, began practising.

The very nature of gynaecology and its cultural association with the
figure of the midwife complicated its emergence: 'the mere fact that a
woman's practice gave "birth" to modern obstetrics was [...] damaging to the
reputation of obstetrics'.[2] Further, the gender-specific focus of the discipline
rendered it unique in medical circles. As Ornella Moscucci argues, 'the
physiology and pathology of the male sexual system simply *were not seen* to
define men's nature. Although gynaecology does have a male counterpart
in genito-urinary medicine, it is perhaps no coincidence that attempts to
redefine urology as the "science of masculinity" have been unsuccessful in
the past'.[3] In Victorian gynaecological praxis it is not objective fact that
materializes, but a *theory* of conduct and morality. The foundation of much
Victorian gynaecological praxis was not objective *fact* but rather a *theory*
of social and moral control, and 'there were big disparities in the medical
sophistication' of Victorian doctors to the extent that medical science was
'a weapon used by men to rationalize the perpetuation of traditional sex
roles'.[4] To quote Moscucci again, 'nineteenth-century gynaecologists were
not merely technicians or males bringing cultural constructs of femininity
into the gynaecological encounter; they were also individuals pursuing an
occupation for financial gain, and as such they should be studied as part of
a network of social and economic relations'.[5]

In many of the gynaecological and obstetric discourses of the period
the 'unresisting body' of the woman became melded with other bodies, so
that 'individual women dissolve into one enormous, universal uterus – a
disembodied, faintly threatening womb'.[6] The debilitating, identity-erasing
essentialism of such discourses was widespread, and, as other chapters in this
book demonstrate, traditionally female occupations such as midwifery were
being overtaken by male practitioners. The 'accoucheur' or male midwife was

widely viewed with suspicion; not only was he blamed for a marked increase in recorded cases of puerperal fever but he was also frequently accused of rape. He occupied a peculiar ideological and social position. On the one hand his maleness ostensibly allowed him the authority to participate in the discourse of male primacy in gynaecology and obstetrics; on the other, it was inevitable that his masculinity would be regarded as a threat, since his movement between public and private places was replicated in his practice: 'the "invasion" of the accoucheur into this private architectural space [the lying-in bedroom] stood for the imagined, but sometimes literal penetration of the bodily space of the woman herself'.[7] The science of women's bodies in the mid to late nineteenth century, then, necessitated the careful social negotiation of professional roles. It was a site of manoeuvring for authority and respectability: General Practitioners and obstetrician-accoucheurs like Tyler Smith, for example, did much to dissociate themselves from female midwives. As Mary Poovey demonstrates, Tyler Smith rewrote 'obstetric history in terms of an exclusively male genealogy', citing William Harvey, Peter Chamberlen, and William Hunter as the 'fathers' of obstetrics in an article for *The Lancet* in 1847.[8] Women were inevitably the victims of this jostling for professional status and the rush for 'progress' meant that new practices, such as the use of anaesthesia in childbirth, often had fatal consequences for mother and baby.

One doctor who entered this complex burgeoning gynaecological network was Alfred Poulet, the eminent adjutant surgeon-major of the hospital in Val-de-Grâce, Paris. In 1880 Poulet published the second volume of his *Treatise on Foreign Bodies in Surgical Practice*, listing the objects he had removed from the bodies of young women in his care, and citing cases recounted by his peers in Great Britain and America. Poulet's list of the most commonly occurring foreign bodies removed from vaginas is striking in its mundane nature and suggests that female masturbation, attempts at medical self-help, abortion, and sexual abuse constituted the unspoken reality of women's lives in the period. Spools of thread, needle cases, boxes of pomade, hairpins and hairbrushes and, in Poulet's language, more 'innocuous' objects such as pessaries and sponges, were removed.[9]

Embedded in Poulet's apparently dispassionate medical discourse is a shadow-narrative of pain, secrecy, and fear. In one case study Poulet recounts the story of a woman whose identity is forever lost to – or protected from – the inquisitive eyes of history. She was not a particularly wealthy woman – we know, for example, that her hairbrush was made of wood, not silver. At 28 years of age, Poulet tells his readers, the woman was 'surprised by some one entering her room as she was introducing a cedarwood brush into her vagina'; quickly she 'seated herself in order to conceal the act in which she was engaged, and the stick of wood was suddenly pushed through the posterior wall of the vagina into the peritoneal cavity'.[10] An actor in her own performance of decorum, since, 'as a general rule, a *modest* woman seldom desires any sexual gratification for herself', this woman lived in the most unimaginable pain and terror for eight months: the brush had ruptured her vagina, its handle becoming lodged in her intestines.[11] She presented to her doctor finally, the pain presumably having grown too much to bear. The brush was removed and she died of peritonitis four days later. Secrecy and concealment characterize this woman's story from first to last: her solitary masturbatory activity could not be admitted. Nor could the consequent injury, for that would be to reveal that the original act had been carried out. A warped, but entirely culturally consistent, notion of modesty killed her.

Such attitudes to female masturbation and modesty permeated the culture of the late nineteenth century. William Acton, writing in 1857, had claimed in his *Functions and Disorders of the Reproductive Organs* that 'masturbation may be best described as an habitual incontinence eminently productive of disease' but that 'the majority of women (happily for them) are not very much troubled with sexual feeling of any kind'.[12] Further, for Acton, 'the vagina was the source of most venereal poisons. [...] Implicit in Acton's work is the notion that women are diseased by virtue of being female'.[13] A decade later, in 1866, Isaac Baker Brown would write on masturbation leading to clitoral hypertrophy: 'The deplorable effects of this baneful habit', he wrote, 'both on the physical and mental health, have been less considered in the case of females than of males'.[14] Baker Brown was an advocate of amputation of the clitoris by scissors, a 'radical cure [which] is [...] fortunately in our hands'.[15] For Baker Brown female masturbation posed a threat to the status quo not least because, he believed, it caused sterility, which, in turn, would lead to an unnatural role for women as sexual but not reproductive beings, akin to prostitutes; he argued that excision could scarcely be considered a mutilation since 'the clitoris is not an essential part of the generative system'.[16] In short, Baker Brown's notorious clitoridectomies epitomized the era's conflation of the physiological, psychological, and moral aspects of women's health.[17]

Instead of attempting to eradicate the lethal modesty of the silent masturbating woman, Poulet paradoxically reinforces cultural condemnation of what he terms 'masturbation and lewdness'.[18] He writes of how 'more than nine-tenths of the cases [of foreign bodies found in the female urethra and bladder] belong, in fact, to this category [of masturbation], and are observed in females varying from fourteen to thirty years of age, and addicted to the solitary vice'.[19] Such censorious language is hardly calculated to encourage Poulet's peers to make women feel able to seek gynaecological assistance. This, of course, meant that not only was female autoeroticism concealed for as long as possible – sometimes even to the point of death – but so, too, were cases of sexual assault (a notable omission from the 1861 Offences Against the

Person Act is a statutory definition of the crime of rape).[20] Arguably, then, the emergent discipline of gynaecology did not so much liberate women from ignorance as redefine how that ignorance could be culturally managed. In his accounts of how foreign bodies come to be lodged in his patients' bodies in the first place, Poulet creates a morally informed taxonomy, which means that not all women are equally represented or, one imagines, treated. In discussing the extraction of foreign bodies from the urethra, for example, he delineates between a variety of different reasons for insertion:

> Malice [...] probably accounts for the presence of foreign bodies, like needles, in very young children of the ages of two, three, or four years. Insanity also plays some part, and we must perhaps call upon this cause in order to account for the abnormal relapses of the introduction of foreign bodies which have nothing in common with those employed by masturbators in procuring the artificial sensations of pleasure [...]. The lunatic under Sonnie-Moret's observation, to whom reference has been made so frequently, has also, in a suicidal attempt, pushed a small package of cut iron wires into the urethra.[21]

In narrating the Victorian vagina, or, in the cases just cited, the Victorian urethra, Poulet merges discourses at once explicit, reproving, and coy. His language is characterized not by objective praxis but is informed instead by his own prejudices of class, race, and gender. Similarly, Poulet's patients' bodies bear the scars of their own narratives of fear – fear of pregnancy and of pleasure: in short, a fear of every facet of their sexual selves.

Poulet's language of confession and admonition serves to keep the vagina secret and to keep himself in business. In his narrative women are paraded before the reader like specimens at Kahn's anatomical museum: 'a peasant woman' follows a 'robust servant'; an eighteen year-old girl bearing 'the stamp of idiocy produced by the habit of masturbation' dies alone of vaginal perforations, and their suffering is almost always presented as being self-inflicted.[22] What lay behind the insertion of foreign objects, pessaries in particular, was not only masturbation but also the attempted self-cure of uterine prolapse, and what Poulet terms the 'criminal purpose' of abortion.[23] Victorian contraceptive methods focused primarily on the woman's body. With a plethora of douches, pessaries, and sponges being advocated and inserted into vaginas, it is little wonder that such practices often led to infection and illness.[24] In her *Nymphomania: a History* (2001) Carol Groneman argues that 'the physical evidence [...] might have led to multiple explanations, including sexual abuse or attempted abortion. Instead, many physicians saw these women as temptresses, not victims'.[25] The language of guilt is pervasive: women were, according to Poulet, inserting objects into themselves to engage in 'secret practices' and doctors needed to be 'aided by the *confessions* of the patients' regarding their 'wilfulness [...] vicious habits' and 'lewd practices'.[26] Because little distinction was drawn between abuse, abortion, and masturbation, Poulet's patients were vilified, which led to their 'depraved habits' being vilified too.[27]

The attitudes of early European gynaecologists such as Poulet had much in common with those of their antecedents and counterparts across the Atlantic. The career of Charles D. Meigs, for example, seems to have been motivated by an eccentric combination of morality, paternalism, and philanthropy. Despite his highly unconventional upbringing (he was educated briefly by Cherokee Indians), Meigs' practice and beliefs were very much in accordance with the European gynaecologist-moralists. His wife, too, performed her conventional role with considerable vigour – Meigs' obituarist tells us that Mary Meigs, mother to ten children 'cared not for the glitter of fashion and found ample space for the exercise of her true privileges without bustling in the crowd and joining in angry discussions on woman's rights'.[28]

Meigs published *Woman: her Diseases and Remedies* in 1848, while based in Philadelphia. His style is flamboyant and literary as he frames his thoughts on all aspects of women's sexual health in an epistolary form addressed 'To the Students of My Class, in the Session of 1846–47'.[29] In Letter XIII Meigs attempts to justify his ostentatious writing style, which could, he is well aware, draw censure from his peers, being 'below the dignity of medical composition, and a complete innovation on the time-honoured solemnity of the powdered wig, square-toed shoes and buckles, and gold-headed cane of the medical faculty'.[30] It is in this letter that his readers meet the imaginary 22-year old 'Helen Blanque' (her surname presumably being a play on words designed to suggest anonymity). As we shall see, Meigs had a passion for the theatre, and the description of his meeting with Blanque employs images of staging and display; rarely has a record of a consultation sounded so sumptuous:

> When I called at 11 o'clock in the morning, I found her reposing in a luxurious *fauteuil* and her slippered feet rested on a low ottoman. The apartment was richly furnished with mirrors, and chandeliers, and candelabras, and carved sofas, with chairs of every form and hue. A fragrant bouquet stood upon the little table near her, by half a dozen volumes, some of which were opened and lying on their faces, as if taken up and laid down in disgust; her hair was in curls, but carelessly; and the *tout ensemble* of the young lady was expressive of languor and indifference, if not of pain or distress.[31]

Helen is presented as suffering from anaemia, the symptoms of which include hypochondria or lethargy – the theatrical tableau, with its opulent furnishings, vanity-inspiring mirrors and discarded novels, prepares the readers for this diagnosis, and it is up to Meigs to promise to restore Helen to health: 'wait a little till I cure you, and you shall, with the blessing, have two cheeks like the sunny side of an apple; and those pale lips shall pout like twin cherries'.[32] Helen's ennui would also, for many of Meigs' readers, have identified her as a participant in 'the solitary vice', as one of Poulet's reprehensible masturbators (one not unlike Sedgwick's Marianne), but one who – presumably because of her 'luxurious' social station – deserves cure over admonishment. By contrast, a later case of a girl who was 'very anemic and nervous' and whose 'vice became more and more deep rooted' resulted in her doctor, Démétrius Alexandre Zambaco, believing it 'necessary to change tactics and treat her severely, even with the most cruel brutality. Corporal punishment was resorted to, in particular the whip'.[33] Meigs' more humane observations are in keeping with those of social purity campaigners like Elizabeth Blackwell, a colleague of Florence Nightingale, who became the first woman to be awarded a medical degree in America. In her *Counsel to Parents on the Moral Education of their Children in Relation to Sex* (1878), Blackwell warned against, to use Meigs' expression, the 'languor and indifference' that young women like Helen might display. 'At an early age', Blackwell proposed, 'self-control can be taught. It is a principle which grows by exercise. The more the brain asserts its power of Will over the automatic actions of the body, the stronger may become the control of reason over sensations and instincts'.[34]

In encouraging Helen to undertake physical exercise Meigs quotes Seneca (there happens to be a fifteenth-century Venetian copy of Seneca's letters to Lucilius on Helen's pier table) and bemoans the lack of exercise that 'railroads [...] and steamboats' encourage in the modern world when, in antiquity, 'Galatea could run, or even fly' as she disappeared into the willow copse.[35] Because Helen is no Galatea (neither the nymph nor Pygmalion's living statue) but is 'etiolated like a celery', Meigs prescribes brisk daily walks and iron pills and reports that 'in twenty days, I met her as beautiful as a Houri; with a gait like Hygiea, and a cheek that might put Euphrosyne or Hebe to "a palpable and open shame"'.[36] Meigs' account of this case is striking on many levels. The discourse is more of social class and flirtation than of medicine (one of Meigs' detractors elsewhere called him an 'obstetrical dandy' to which Meigs replied: 'at my age and with twenty grandchildren!').[37] Crucially, Helen's condition is presented as one where *taxis*, or touch, is avoided:

> Such cases do not at all require that the lady should be subjected to the grief and vexation inseparable from a medical exploration by taxis [...]. Do not compel the young girl then to submit to the debasement of a vaginal examination [...]. When it *is* necessary it is not a debasement. She is a

fool to refuse it; and if you be a physician, in deed and in truth, with the missionary heart and soul of a physician, God's messenger, I say she is twice a fool to decline your proffered aid.[38]

The issue of touch in gynaecological practice was a live one and was subject to much debate. The skill – and the threat – of the accoucheur was regarded as residing in his fingers, and Tyler Smith, in an anatomically troubling image, argued that 'the obstetrician who has by long practice acquired the *tactus eruditus* in perfection may almost be said to have the end of his finger armed with an eye'.[39] By comparing Helen to exemplary women and by making a point of the absence of touch in his diagnosis, Meigs was effectively mythologizing the female form: Helen's *physical* purity is represented as being emblematic of her *moral* wholesomeness.

Meigs' evocation, in the case of 'Helen', of the fictional Galatea as the perfect woman may, unconsciously at least, have been a nod at Elisa Félix, a Swiss-born Jewish actor who became famous under her stage name of 'Rachel' and who toured extensively in Europe in the 1840s and early 1850s, travelling through the US in the autumn and early winter of 1855. These dates mean that by the time Meigs was writing the fourth edition of his book he could have seen her perform – certainly his writings suggest he did. The roles Rachel took were tragic and serious, and ultimately served to reinforce notions of submissive femininity. When Meigs possibly saw her she was playing Virginius's daughter, Virginia, in the play of the same name by James Sheridan Knowles (1820). Knowles' play, based loosely on Shakespeare's *Titus Andronicus* (1592), has as its key theme a father 'protecting' his daughter's sexual reputation by killing her.[40] Rachel had played Galatea throughout Europe and was perhaps best known for her role in Racine's *Phèdre* (1677), in which, as the eponymous heroine, she drank poison to assuage her guilt at her incestuous desires for her stepson Hippolyte. Virginia, Phèdre, Galatea: each woman ultimately subsumes her sexual autonomy in the cause of a controlling man. In each role potentially unruly sexual desire is halted, be it by poison, murder, or by the sculptor's practised hand.

Meigs was a creative writer manqué – his equally hyperbolic obituarist tells us that he 'could not help embellishing the substance of his prelections by word-ornament which was not always taken from the vernacular. His love for the beautiful was ingrained in his philosophy, and gave a colouring both to his written and spoken compositions'.[41] He found in Rachel the means to make gynaecology artistic, and female sexuality both erotic and extinguishable. In Letter IV, 'Sexual Peculiarities', Meigs shares with his students what he perceives to be the characteristics of 'woman'. Physically, 'she differs from man in her stature, which is lower; in her weight, which is less; in her form, which is more gracile and beautiful'.[42] Artistically she has inspired men throughout history: 'Versailles and Marli, and the Trianons, had never been built for *men*'; spiritually 'the household altar is her place of worship and service. The Forum is too angry for her. The Curia is too grave and high'.[43] Intellectually, woman's ideal is the Venus de Medici, and Praxiteles' work is praised. 'Compare her', writes Meigs of Venus, 'with the Apollo of the Belvidere – she has a head almost too small for intellect, but just big enough for love'.[44] This Pygmalion-like invocation of statuary as the ideal is particularly poignant given Rachel's renown for playing the role of Galatea. The Pygmalion myth centres on the fantasy of a silent woman's body which is controlled by an authoritative male gaze. It could almost be a metaphor for the gynaecology of the mid nineteenth century, and is fundamental to explaining Meigs' extravagant enthusiasm for Rachel. He writes:

> Among the wonderful exceptions of power in women, there is perhaps none on record so extraordinary as that of the actress Rachel. The power of that woman's eloquence seems superhuman, and I must doubt whether the most splendid orators of antiquity, or the most powerful senators of modern times, could vie with the potent and spell-weaving accents and gestures of that extraordinary creature. A word, a look, a sign, a *pleno rotundoque ore* effusion of thoughts that breathed and words that burned, overbore me that I could no longer look at her face and figure, but compelled me to avert my eyes from the intolerable blaze of genius that flashed like a glory all about the pretended daughter of Virginius.[45]

The somatic impact that Rachel has on the doctor is immediately undermined in a way that removes any sense of agency from her: 'Although I believe that Rachel was the most eloquent human being that has lived, she was mainly so in the use of others' thoughts and others' words. As to her own power of imagination, reasoning or judgment, I presume they were those of a play actress'.[46]

Critics have argued recently that Rachel actually brought to the passive role of Galatea a power and agency: 'Rachel is [...] not simply an art-object, but is confirmed in her own person as an artist, self-consciously and deliberately fashioning herself, usurping the right of the sculptor, and as such defying the constraints of Galatea's situation, and the terms both of her reification and incarnation'.[47] By contrast, in drawing a distinction between 'the pretended daughter of Virginius' and 'a play actress', Meigs reinforces his argument that 'woman' is muse, not artist; object, not subject. Rachel-as-Virginia, in her autonomy and verbal power, momentarily threatens Meigs' world view, but she is reined in at last.

This act of reining in would have been informed in part by Meigs' Victorian belief in the links between acting and prostitution. The prostitute was recurrently portrayed as having a physically and morally contaminated

– and contaminating – body to the point where even her identity *as a woman* was compromised. Acton, writing in 1857, claimed:

> What is a prostitute! She is a woman who gives for money that which she ought to give only for love; who ministers to passion and lust alone, to the exclusion and extinction of all the higher qualities [...] She is a woman with half the woman gone, and that half containing all that elevates her nature, leaving her a mere instrument of impurity.[48]

In her exemplary work *Actresses As Working Women* (1991), Tracy C. Davis argued that 'the popular association between actresses and prostitutes [...] persisted throughout the nineteenth century because Victorians recognized that acting and whoring were the occupations of self-sufficient women who plied their trade in public places [... and who were] objects of desire whose company was purchased through commercial exchange'.[49] The logical and perceived effects of such self-sufficiency (and, after all, what is masturbation but a repudiation of the necessity of reliance on another?) are precisely what intimidated Meigs, Acton, and their contemporaries.

Rachel's fame was such that many of her contemporaries used her as inspiration for their own artistic inventions. Disraeli's Josephine in *Tancred* (1847) represents her, and, despite his anti-Semitic opinions on Rachel, G. H. Lewes could not help falling for her enchantments too, writing about her repeatedly from the 1850s through to his *Actors and the Art of Acting* of 1875.[50] The energy of Rachel is present, too, in George Eliot's *Daniel Deronda* (1876), as Gwendolen aspires to surpass 'that thin Jewess' Rachel (interestingly, Hermione is the character ultimately opted for, *The Winter's Tale* (1611) being a reworking of the Pygmalion/Galatea myth).[51]

Having seen Rachel on stage in London in 1851, while working on *Villette* (1853), Charlotte Brontë created the character of Vashti. In the theatre with Dr John, Lucy Snowe (her name, coincidentally at least, recalls for us Meigs' own 'Helen Blanque') gazes in yearning wonder at Vashti/Rachel:

> For awhile – a long while – I thought it was only a woman, though an unique woman, who moved in might and grace before this multitude. By-and-by I recognised my mistake. Behold! I found upon her something neither of woman nor of man: in each of her eyes sat a devil. These evil forces bore her through the tragedy, kept up her feeble strength – for she was but a frail creature; and as the action rose and the stir deepened, how wildly they shook her with their passions of the pit! They wrote HELL on her straight, haughty brow. They tuned her voice to the note of torment. They writhed her regal face to a demoniac mask. Hate and Murder and Madness incarnate, she stood.
>
> It was a marvellous sight: a mighty revelation.
>
> It was a spectacle low, horrible, immoral.

[...] Suffering had struck that stage empress; and she stood before her audience neither yielding to, nor enduring, nor in finite measure, resenting it: she stood locked in struggle, rigid in resistance. She stood, not dressed, but draped in pale antique folds, long and regular like sculpture. A background and entourage and flooring of deepest crimson threw her out, white like alabaster – like silver: rather be it said, like Death.[52]

In Vashti's presence Lucy grows utterly self-absorbed: 'The strong magnetism of genius drew my heart out of its wonted orbit', reading in the actor's movements an alternative mode of ardent being.[53] She experiences what one critic has termed Rachel's 'fusion of passionate life with marbled restraint'.[54] By contrast, as if to remind Lucy of the real world, Dr John, in a manoeuvre not unlike Dr Meigs', 'judged [... Vashti] as a woman, not an artist', looking on the charismatic actress with an 'almost callous' smile.[55] As Vashti's midnight death scene is about to reach its climax, the entire audience is held in suspense so that even Dr John 'bit in his under lip and knit his brow', and in the hushed, crowded theatre only Vashti's 'throes' can be heard as the tragic figure who has experienced 'the rape of every faculty' is beheld.[56] Before the scene's climax can be reached, however, the audience's pleasure is abruptly cut short, and anxious voices, 'pregnant with omen' interrupt the drama as people begin to panic, 'rushing, crushing – a blind, selfish, cruel chaos'.[57] As the theatre catches fire Lucy looks at her companion: 'And Dr. John? Reader, I see him yet, with his look of comely courage and cordial calm'.[58] Faced with passion and (literal) heat, Dr John remains impassively controlled, and presented with 'Vashti, or even Lucy's warm feelings for him, he is cold and unmoved'.[59]

Vashti, however, is not the only depiction of female sexuality encountered by Lucy, and nor is Dr John the novel's only male figure of clinical restraint. The episode in the theatre, where Lucy's responses to the audience's panic are restricted and controlled by Dr John, recalls an earlier encounter, and a similar control, this time exerted by M. Paul. Such control is, of course, logical in a cultural climate where medical and gynaecological discourses informed even the world of artistic representation until, as Sally Shuttleworth argues, 'the creation of the feminine in male-executed art is directly allied to the medical construction of women'.[60] In the gallery Lucy gazes over a 'cordon of protection stretched before' a painting of Cleopatra, the 'dusk and portly Venus of the Nile'.[61] M. Paul also functions as a 'cordon of protection'. He is horrified not only by the fact that Lucy has come to the gallery alone with Dr John but also because of her focus on the body of Cleopatra. He attempts to distract Lucy by turning her away from Cleopatra to face instead a series of four paintings called 'La vie d'une femme'. Tellingly, Lucy finds these tableaux 'flat, dead, pale and formal'.[62] Her gaze is repeatedly pulled away from their lifeless representation of the four ages of woman – maid,

bride, mother, widow – to the vivid potency of 'the indolent gipsy-giantess'
Cleopatra.[63] As medical men like Acton, Tyler Smith, Poulet, and Meigs
attempted to redirect the focus of 'respectable' women away from their
sexuality and towards more 'modest' pursuits, so is M. Paul's entreaty for
Lucy to look away somewhat in vain. It is also deeply hypocritical – a fact
not missed by Brontë's coolly ironic narrator: 'I noticed, by the way, that he
looked at the picture himself quite at his ease, and for a very long while: he
did not, however, neglect to glance from time to time my way, in order, I
suppose, to make sure that I was obeying orders and not breaking bounds'.[64]

Lucy is aware that the 'bounds' are there and that they have the potential
to be broken, but whenever such transgression is about to be realized in the
novel it is frustrated by a literal or moral conflagration. Lucy's encounters
with both Cleopatra and Vashti blaze in direct opposition to the 'snowy'
sensuality she is forced to affect. On first seeing the well-fed, voluptuous
sensuality of Cleopatra, Lucy's language is mocking: 'She lay half-reclined on
a couch: why, it would be difficult to say; broad daylight blazed round her'.[65]
Reminiscent of the pose of Helen Blanque, Cleopatra's air of immorality
and languid excess can neither make sense nor find a fulfilling, candid
articulation in the stifling world of propriety which Lucy inhabits.

As her spectators detach her natural body from her ideational one,
Eliza Félix, the woman behind the stage construct 'Rachel', is done away
with, emblematizing the eradication of autonomous female sexual identity
by nineteenth-century gynaecologists. Such was Rachel's skill that, in
subsuming herself entirely into roles of passive or repentant women, her
private self was, paradoxically, *kept* private within the public arena of
performance. The secrecy and shame surrounding women's bodies was not
so much *de*mythologized by doctors like Poulet and Meigs, but was rather
re-emphasized and reinvigorated by their endeavours to project their morally
unpolluted vision of what it meant to be a woman; women's *actual* bodies and
desires risked being hindrances to the *image* of passive femininity propagated
by the gynaecologists. Poulet's language of scolding and ignominy and
Meigs' Praxitelean aspirations for his patients, while ostensibly packaged as
medically supportive, simultaneously urged women to distance their private
desires from their public personae.

The rhetoric each doctor used functioned as a distraction from the very
real agonies of gynaecological ailments. The cedarwood brush lodged in a
28-year old's body was slowly killing her, while the doctors best qualified
to help her spoke only of embarrassment – the shame that prevented her
seeking help because of the shame of the autoerotic impulse which led to the
accident in the first place. Any possibility of a sexual identity is hidden, like
Lucy Snowe's precious, symbolically freighted letters from Dr John which
she furtively buries under the pear tree: 'I cleared away the ivy, and found

the hole; it was large enough to receive the jar, and I thrust it deep in'.[66] 'I was not', writes Lucy, 'only going to hide a treasure – I meant also to bury a grief'.[67] Indeed, emblems of quite literally encapsulated female sexuality abound in the novel; Lucy compulsively conceals objects in boxes, drawers, and desks, and is, of course, 'haunted' by the figure of the nun whose own sexual transgressions had been punished by a living entombment. Under Madame Beck's roof her host's constant surveillance leads to secrecy and jealous privacy; like Poulet's patient she must conceal her desires.[68] When she comes close to engaging in a meaningful relationship with M. Paul she signifies herself as shut away, secret, and confined:

> And taking from the open desk the little box, I put it into his hand.
> 'It lay ready in my lap this morning', I continued; 'and if Monsieur had been rather more patient, and Mademoiselle St Pierre less interfering – perhaps I should say, too, if *I* had been calmer and wiser – I should have given it then'.
> He looked at the box: I saw its clear warm tint and bright azure circlet, pleased his eye. I told him to open it.[69]

The potential for eruption which haunted authentic autonomous female sexual identity was smoothed over by Dr Meigs, was demonized by Dr Poulet, was repressed by M. Paul, and was extinguished by Dr John. As Lucy Snowe herself expressed it, 'doctors are so self-opinionated, so immovable in their dry, materialist views'.[70] The promise of the mid-century emergence of gynaecology as a discipline, and its concomitant struggle to demonize female sexual passion might finally, perhaps, be likened to the fate of Vashti. In Brontë's novel she ignites in Lucy Snowe a passion which, unable to burn in Lucy's body, finds its displaced expression in the body of the theatre itself. 'On our way back we repassed the theatre', Lucy reports, 'all was silence and darkness: the roaring, rushing crowd all vanished and gone – the lamps, as well as the incipient fire, extinct and forgotten. Next morning's papers explained that it was but some loose drapery on which a spark had fallen, and which had blazed up and been quenched in a moment'.[71] The non-canonical texts examined in this essay suggest that that 'quenching' of 'incipient fire' may just as well have been in the bodies of the text's women as in the building Lucy beholds.[72]

NOTES

1. Eve Kosofsky Sedgwick, 'Jane Austen and the Masturbating Girl', *Critical Inquiry*, 17 (1991): 818–37.
2. Mary Poovey, *Uneven Developments: The Ideological Work of Gender in Mid-Victorian England* (London: Virago, 1988), p. 40.

3. Ornella Moscucci, *The Science of Woman: Gynaecology and Gender in England 1800–1929* (Cambridge, UK: Cambridge University Press, 1990), p. 32. Italics in original.

4. Michael Mason, *The Making of Victorian Sexuality* (Oxford: Oxford University Press, 1994), p. 179; Cynthia Eagle Russett, *Sexual Science: The Victorian Construction of Womanhood* (Cambridge, MA: Harvard University Press, 1989), p. 191.

5. Moscucci, *The Science of Woman*, p. 42.

6. Poovey, *Uneven Developments*, pp. 29, 35.

7. Alison Bashford, *Purity and Pollution: Gender, Embodiment and Victorian Medicine* (Basingstoke, UK: Macmillan, 1998), p. 70.

8. Poovey, *Uneven Developments*, pp. 40, 216 n. 60.

9. Alfred Poulet, *A Treatise on Foreign Bodies in Surgical Practice*, 2 vols. (New York: William Wood and Co., 1880), Vol. 2, p. 190.

10. Poulet, *A Treatise on Foreign Bodies*, p. 196. Gould and Pyle describe this same case, but as involving a pencil rather than a brush. See George M. Gould and Walter L. Pyle, 'Surgical Anomalies of the Genito-Urinary System', *Anomalies and Curiosities of Medicine* (W. B. Saunders, 1896), Project Gutenberg, available at http://www.gutenberg.org/etext/747 (accessed 7 December 2010).

11. William Acton, *The Functions and Disorders of the Reproductive Organs* (1857), quoted in *The Sexuality Debates*, ed. Sheila Jeffreys (London: Routledge & Kegan Paul, 1987), pp. 57–73 (p. 62). Italics added.

12. Acton, *The Functions and Disorders*, pp. 57, 61.

13. Mary Spongberg, *Feminizing Venereal Disease: The Body of the Prostitute in Nineteenth-Century Medical Discourse* (Basingstoke, UK: Macmillan, 1997), pp. 47, 49.

14. Isaac Baker Brown, *On Some Diseases of Woman Admitting Surgical Treatment* (1866), quoted in *The Sexuality Debates*, ed. Jeffreys, pp. 27–41 (p. 27).

15. Brown, *On Some Diseases of Woman*, p. 27.

16. Brown, *On Some Diseases of Woman*, p. 29.

17. On Baker Brown see Elizabeth Sheehan, 'Victorian Clitoridectomy: Isaac Baker Brown and His Harmless Operative Procedure', *Medical Anthropology Newsletter*, 12.4 (1981): 9–15. See also Isaac Baker Brown, *Curability of Certain Forms of Insanity, Epilepsy, Catalepsy and Hysteria in Females* (1866), quoted in *The Sexuality Debates*, ed. Jeffreys, pp. 11–26. Baker Brown's callously cavalier attitude is summed up in one of his case studies where he was eager to see the effects of having 'divided the clitoris subcutaneously' since 'this being [his ...] first operation [he ...] did not know the consequences of performing the operation in this manner' (p. 12).

18. Poulet, *A Treatise on Foreign Bodies*, p. 208.

19. Poulet, *A Treatise on Foreign Bodies*, p. 208.

20. For more on the Act and on how 'the Victorians' desire to preserve innocence and reinforce female morality produced a complex and contradictory discourse full of linguistic reticence and innuendo', see Kim Stevenson, '"Crimes of Moral Outrage": Victorian Encryptions of Sexual Violence', in *Criminal Conversations: Victorian Crimes, Social Panic, and Moral Outrage*, ed. Judith Rowbotham and Kim Stevenson (Columbus, OH: Ohio State University Press, 2005), pp. 232–46 (p. 244).

21. Poulet, *A Treatise on Foreign Bodies*, p. 208.

22. Poulet, *A Treatise on Foreign Bodies*, pp. 194, 189, 195. On women-only sessions at Kahn's anatomical museum in the West End of London see Mason, *The Making of Victorian Sexuality*, pp. 190–91.

23. Poulet, *A Treatise on Foreign Bodies*, p. 202.

24. Charles Knowlton had been, in his *Fruits of Philosophy: Or the Private Companion of Young Married People* (1832), one advocate of the use of the vaginal douche as contraceptive aid, for the promotion of which he was briefly imprisoned in Massachusetts. See Mason, *The Making of Victorian Sexuality*, p. 58.

25. Carol Groneman, *Nymphomania: A History* (London: Fusion, 2001), p. 35.

26. Poulet, *A Treatise on Foreign Bodies*, pp. 202, 205, 207, 238, 191. Italics added.

27. Poulet, *A Treatise on Foreign Bodies*, p. 222.

28. Information on Meigs' life is drawn mainly from John Bell, 'Obituary Notice of Charles D. Meigs M.D.', *Proceedings of the American Philosophical Society*, 13.90 (1873): 170–79 (170). By the time he died, Meigs had more than forty grandchildren of whom at least thirteen had predeceased him.

29. Charles D. Meigs, *Woman: Her Diseases and Remedies* (1851; Philadelphia, PA: Blanchard and Lea, 1859), frontispiece. The book proved a commercial success and ran to several editions, the fourth (the one I have used for this essay) appearing in 1859.

30. Meigs, *Woman*, p. 187.

31. Meigs, *Woman*, p. 188.

32. Meigs, *Woman*, p. 191.

33. Démétrius Alexandre Zambaco, 'Onanisme avec Troubles Nerveux chez deux Petites Filles' (1882), trans. Jeffrey Moussaieff Masson and Marianne Loring as 'Masturbation and Psychological Problems in Two Little Girls', in Jeffrey Masson, *A Dark Science: Women, Sexuality, and Psychiatry in the Nineteenth Century* (New York: Noonday, 1988), pp. 63, 65. Zambaco's treatise is the one discussed by Sedgwick in her 'Jane Austen and the Masturbating Girl'.

34. Elizabeth Blackwell, *Counsel to Parents on the Moral Education of their Children in Relation to Sex* (1878; London: Hatchards, 1884), p. 64.

35. Meigs, *Woman*, p. 201.

36. Meigs, *Woman*, pp. 203, 207. Another nineteenth-century gynaecologist who had recourse to Classical references in order to illustrate his work was Tyler Smith. See Helen King, *Midwifery, Obstetrics and the Rise of Gynaecology: The Uses of a Sixteenth-Century Compendium* (London: Ashgate, 2007), p. 168.

37. King, *Midwifery, Obstetrics and the Rise of Gynaecology*, p. 209.

38. King, *Midwifery, Obstetrics and the Rise of Gynaecology*, p. 187. Elsewhere, Meigs, still discussing 'Helen Blanque', refers to pelvic examination as 'the shocking *ultima ratio*' (p. 208).

39. William Tyler Smith, *The Modern Practice of Midwifery: A Course of Lectures on Obstetrics Delivered at St. Mary's Hospital, London* (De Witt, 1858), p. 361.

40. On American performances of Knowles' play see Robin O. Warren, 'They Were Always Doing Shakespeare: Antebellum Southern Actresses and Shakespearean Appropriation', *Borrowers and Lenders: The Journal of Shakespeare and Appropriation*, 1:1 (2005), available at http://www.borrowers.uga.edu/cocoon/borrowers/pdf?id=781416 (accessed 7 December 2010).

41. Bell, 'Obituary Notice', p. 174.

42. Meigs, *Woman*, p. 55.

43. Meigs, *Woman*, pp. 56, 58.

44. Meigs, *Woman*, p. 60.

45. Meigs, *Woman*, p. 59.

46. Meigs, *Woman*, p. 59.

47. Gail Marshall, *Actresses on the Victorian Stage: Feminine Performance and the Galatea Myth* (Cambridge, UK: Cambridge University Press, 1998), p. 49.

48. William Acton, *Prostitution Considered in its Social and Sanitary Aspects* (1857), quoted in *The Sexuality Debates*, ed. Jeffreys, pp. 42–56 (p. 42).

49. Tracy C. Davis, *Actresses as Working Women: Their Social identity in Victorian Culture* (London: Routledge, 1991), p. 100.

50. An excellent essay on Rachel's influence on Victorian writers is John Stokes, 'Rachel's "terrible beauty": An Actress among the Novelists', *English Literary History*, 51.4 (1984): 771–93.

51. George Eliot, *Daniel Deronda* (1876; Oxford: Oxford University Press, 1998), p. 44.

52. Charlotte Brontë, *Villette* (1853; London: Penguin, 1979), p. 339.

53. Brontë, *Villette*, p. 340.

54. Marshall, *Actresses on the Victorian Stage*, p. 48.

55. Brontë, *Villette*, p. 342. On 'the denigration and ambivalence that Brontë has displayed here towards female passion and suffering', see Diane Long Hoeveler, 'Smoke and Mirrors: Internalizing the Magic Lantern Show in *Villette*', *Gothic Technologies: Visuality in the Romantic Era*, available at http://www.rc.umd.edu/praxis/gothic/hoeveler/hoeveler.html (accessed 12 April 2009).

56. Brontë, *Villette*, p. 342.

57. Brontë, *Villette*, p. 342.

58. Brontë, *Villette*, p. 342.

59. John Maynard, *Charlotte Brontë and Sexuality* (Cambridge, UK: Cambridge University Press, 1984), p. 191.

60. Sally Shuttleworth, *Charlotte Brontë and Victorian Psychology* (Cambridge, UK: Cambridge University Press, 1996), p. 238.

61. Shuttleworth, *Charlotte Brontë*, pp. 275, 281. For more on the symbolism of this cordon, see Heather Glen, *Charlotte Brontë: The Imagination in History* (Oxford: Oxford University Press, 2002), p. 205.

62. Brontë, *Villette*, p. 277.

63. Brontë, *Villette*, p. 278.

64. Brontë, *Villette*, p. 278.

65. Brontë, *Villette*, p. 275.

66. Brontë, *Villette*, p. 380.

67. Brontë, *Villette*, p. 380.

68. Heather Glen also comments on the number of *things* which are hidden, secreted, and put away in the novel. See Glen, *Charlotte Brontë*, p. 215.

69. Brontë, *Villette*, p. 433.

70. Brontë, *Villette*, p. 338.

71. Brontë, *Villette*, p. 347.

72. For more on Lucy Snowe's 'inner conflict between assertive sensuality and ascetic submission' see Sandra M. Gilbert and Susan Gubar, *The Madwoman in the Attic: the Woman Writer and the Nineteenth-Century Literary Imagination* (1979; New Haven, CT: Yale University Press, 2000), pp. 412–13.

9

'Those Parts Peculiar to Her Organization': Some Observations on the History of Pelvimetry, a Nearly Forgotten Obstetric Sub-speciality

JOANNA GRANT

In an unsigned piece published in the *Journal of Psychological Medicine and Mental Pathology* in 1851, the anonymous author takes a moment to indulge in a fulsome description of the marvels of the female pelvis and its fleshy accessories:

> It is in that portion of the body in immediate connexion with those parts peculiar to her organization that the greatest beauty of form is found in woman, as though they were the *fons et origo* of corporeal as well as mental loveliness [...] the contours of the back are of the most admirable purity; the region of the kidneys is elongated, the scapulae scarcely visible; the loins grandly curved forwards, the haunches prominent and rounded; in short, the posterior surface of the torso in woman is unquestionably the *chef d'oeuvre* of nature.[1]

Anonymous's anatomical Venus delights with her beauty founded on her fertility; her magnificent soft curves seem meant to indicate her physical and spiritual readiness for woman's most supposedly sacred task: childbearing.

Unfortunately, there is a problem here. For all we and Anonymous know, the beautiful loins of this ostensibly healthy female specimen might conceal a multitude of anatomical sins. Her pelvic conformation might be twisted and contracted in eccentric ways due to a host of possible factors: heredity, accident, or diseases. In an age devoid of many of our modern techniques for foetal imaging and surgical intervention, each birthing case represented a possible threat to the life of both mother and child.

This essay discusses the origins and some of the major features of an almost forgotten sub-speciality of obstetrics: pelvimetry, whose practitioners sought to learn all they could about the anatomy and possible malformations of the female pelvis with the aim of facilitating safer, shorter labours and the delivery of living children with less risk to mother and child. In her study of the rise of the modern science of obstetrics and gynaecology in England and America, *The Science of Woman*, Ornella Moscucci mentions pelvimetry in passing, remarking that it 'remains to date totally unexplored'.[2] A discussion of some of the most important practitioners, terms, instruments, and issues associated with this forerunner of modern imaging and surgical techniques helps the student of medical history to examine, from a fresh yet complementary perspective, some of the 'uneven developments' of nineteenth and early twentieth-century gender science, a collection of practices and assumptions as 'bound up with the representation of reality' as with material social relations and practices.[3] Thus an exploration of pelvimetry's history in the period under review (c. 1850–c. 1950) can profitably take its place beside histories of other obsolete obstetric and gynaecological practices such as the use of chloroform and ovariotomy as we seek to counter tendencies towards teleology in our understanding of the history of medical and cultural practices.

A review of a sample of pelvimetry texts drawn from the medical literature of the period, cross-referenced with standard texts in the field, enables us to make observations about some of the common themes that emerge from this chorus of invested experts and practitioners. Firstly, we can situate the tone and stated objectives of these instrument- and technique-touting texts within the context of two broader historical developments charted by Adrian Wilson and Ornella Moscucci. In his *The Making of Man-midwifery: Childbirth in England, 1660–1770*, Wilson seeks to complicate the more simplistic model of paradigm shift previously accepted by social historians committed to a Foucauldian view of the utter medicalization of women's bodies in this period. While Wilson concurs with Moscucci that the years from 1750 to 1950 saw the triumph of the professional medical man over the midwife, Wilson argues that changing patterns of class affiliation and aspiration drove educated, wealthy women to turn away from a 'woman's culture', increasingly stigmatized as old-fashioned, and to embrace a rising medical profession that seemed to offer 'fashion', 'progress', and 'status' to its female consumers. Pelvimetry's valorization of an 'empirical aesthetic' of efficient engineering 'offered [...] woman [...] not the chance of independence, but rather the opportunity for a new form of dependence upon men'.[4] The growth of literacy, compulsory education, and imperial anxieties combine in strange and compelling ways in this literature, as patients, practitioners, and cultures seek strange bedfellows in the quest for agency and status.

The discipline of pelvimetry grew out of craniometry and other subspecialities of Victorian racial science. Indeed, pelvimetry was employed as an important means of establishing differences between the races, a fact confirmed by J. G. Garson, MD in an article entitled 'Pelvimetry' that appeared in *The Journal of Anatomy and Physiology, Normal and Pathological* in 1882: 'Perhaps next in importance to the form of the skull as indicating race-characters may be placed that of the pelvis'.[5] Pelvimetry, then, embraced the teleological aim of offering empirical evidence to underwrite the premise of white Western racial superiority. Garson's listing of the fourteen measurements required for typing the pelvis, including such parameters as 'Width between the posterior margin of the acetabulum and the symphisis pubis', spoke of objective, verifiable certainty.[6] We might say the same of some of the names and descriptions of Garson's tools of the trade:

> 1. An osteometer, an instrument similar to that used by shoemakers for measuring the width of the foot, but with metal uprights, the extremities of which terminate each in a fine point; 2. An instrument like that used by hatters to measure the internal diameters of hats; and 3. A goniometer for measuring angles.[7]

Garson's sharing of his preferred techniques and instruments indicates a change in the nature of the obstetric profession. Wilson tells us about the secrecy and guildlike structure of the profession of the obstetric surgeon/early man-midwife in the years leading up to a cultural sea change during the later eighteenth century.[8] Dynasties like the Chamberlens would keep their forceps and other tools a closely guarded family secret. Now we see the emergence of a self-governing, peer-reviewed medical establishment benefiting from doctrines of intellectual property and the desire for advertising and what we might call the 'branding' of instruments and techniques. Additionally, Garson's proliferation of measurements serves as an introduction to one of the major strands of this narrative: the tendency of scientists in this period to strip away the messy physicality of the body and to replace it with pure, sterile information. And the success with which this narrative of rationalization was greeted by women on both sides of the Atlantic testifies to the pull this fusion of fact and [fantasy] exercised over the imaginations of women, the eventual consumers of the therapeutic practices developed and debated in the medical literature.

An important theme in the discourse of pelvimetry is the attempt to make the analogy between the structures of the female body and mechanical structures. With the invention of the idea of interchangeable parts in the nineteenth century, fantasies of standardization and rationalization began to swirl around anatomy as well. Unfortunately, the human race persisted in throwing up a bewildering, and, to these scientists, occasionally frustrating variety of body types. This frustration reveals itself as early as 1841, the year in which F. H. Ramsbotham observed that:

Fortunate it would be indeed for childbearing women if they each possessed a pelvis of the figure and dimensions already given as standard. Such, however, is by no means the case; and this organ is subject to great varieties, as well in form as size. It would indeed be difficult to select from all the preserved specimens in existence any two which exactly resemble each other.[9]

This frustration recurs in the literature, as does annoyance at women for being poorly evolved in the first place, as is evidenced in Edward A. Schumann's article 'The Dynamics of the Female Pelvis; Its Evolution and Architecture with Respect to Function', a piece that was also his Fellowship Thesis in the American Gynaecological Society. In his 'consideration of the facts pertaining to the process of parturition in the human female', he makes the argument that women are reproductively inefficient due to the fundamental 'disharmonies of function and structure' that typify female pelvic anatomy.[10] Thus we see that, in much professional opinion, the pathological, or at least the inefficient, is the norm for the female body.

In an article appearing in the June 1899 number of *The American Journal of Obstetrics and Diseases of Women and Children*, Edward P. Davis estimates that some 32 per cent of American women have abnormal pelves.[11] It is useful to mention, at this point, the grossly unequal standards of living in the United States and Europe then and now, and the widespread incidences of diseases of malnutrition, especially rickets, observed by practitioners of pelvimetry. Eugenic considerations come into play here. Rickets was often seen as a disease of the half-starved, sunlight-deprived inhabitants of London, New York, and other Anglo-American metropoles. Additionally, fantasies of racial domination could cut both ways at this time. It was reasoned that as men (particularly white men) evolved bigger and bigger brains, the unimproved or even degenerating pelves of (especially white) women could not keep up with demand, particularly if those pelves were abnormally contracted or twisted due to the softening and deformation of the bones resulting from rickets or osteomalacia, the adult form of the disease. Thus, as A. L. Rongy writes in 1930, 'Obstetrics [becomes] largely a mechanical art. Every case of labor is an engineering problem. The obstetrician like the engineer must guide himself wholly in accordance with the principles which make a mechanical problem safe or unsafe, possible or impossible'.[12] Rongy's simile effects a wished-for identification with a prestigious profession; one rather like that of obstetrician.

So some obstetricians using pelvimetry in their practices, like Rongy, literally thought of themselves as social engineers working in the cause of streamlining and rendering society more efficient. But what kinds of mechanical means did pelvimetry use to solve the potentially unique structural and physical problems presented by each individual birth? A great deal of variety exists in the literature as to what measurements are the most important and how they should be taken. However, certain common practices and apparatuses emerge, and they find able exponents in the work of Julius Jarcho and Herbert Thoms, two American obstetricians who wrote definitive and often-referenced books on the subject. The goal of taking the various measurements by several means was to ascertain whether the pelvis was obstructed or abnormally contracted in any direction, and to determine the size, front to back and side to side, of the pelvic outlet so as to make informed decisions as to how to assist the laboring mother. If all hope was to be abandoned, as in the case of a deformed or stillborn child, measures could be taken to lessen the head and save the life of the mother. These important pelvic measurements were termed the anteroposterior, transverse, and the oblique diameters of the superior strait, or the upper part of the pelvis, and then the anteroposterior and transverse diameters of the outlet.[13]

The hand of the practitioner comprised the first pelvimeter. The hand as a piece of laboratory equipment has certain drawbacks, notably its variable and often uncomfortably larger size in the case of male practitioners. However, authorities in the field recommended 'touching' – and this advice remained current until the end of the period under review: 'when the obstetrician's hand is small and the vagina large and distensible, introduction of the entire hand may yield valuable information. It allows the most efficient palpation of the vaginal canal for various causes of obstruction, including bony prominences'.[14] Presumably, the sensitivity of the physician's fingertips argued for manual pelvimetry's continued utility. However, since rising standards of professional expertise demanded more exact measurements by mechanical means, new and improved designs for pelvimeters proliferated.

There were many different makes and models of pelvimeters on the market in the decades before roentgenography (X-rays) and ultrasound began to push efficient, medicalized pelvimetry away from graphic bodies and towards body graphics. The basic design, however, revolved around a set of calipers or measuring arms coupled with rulers or other measuring devices. Pelvimeters could also double as cephalometers, or devices used to measure the baby's head as it pressed against the mother's abdomen. The often-mentioned Skutsch pelvimeter/cephalometer was one of the first and the prototype that inventors measured their own efforts against, as may be seen in James B. Bullitt's article 'A New Pelvimeter', which appeared in *The American Journal of Obstetrics and Diseases of Women and Children* in 1893. Bullitt's improvement derives from 'ideas evolved by Skutsch', and involves replacing the more pliable lead arm of the Skutsch with a stiff arm that can press into the woman's flesh, reducing the margin of error of the doctor's measurements.[15] The pelvimeter could also be used to measure internal dimensions, such as the true conjugate, which Jarcho describes as 'the most important single diameter in obstetrics [...] [the] anteroposterior diameter of the pelvic brim'.[16] This diameter determined the chances of success of a natural labour when the child presented by the head. Fractions of centimetres were important in this context, and the information provided by the pelvimeter/cephalometer would influence decision-making as to how a labour should be conducted and for how long. Here we see desire for efficiency meeting humanity and common sense.

Yet talk of efficiency and compassion could work hand in glove with ideas of degeneration and strategies for white racial uplift that formed at least some part of the new, professional identity of the modern medical man. Obstetricians and gynaecologists had an observable tendency to see themselves as mechanized secular saints delivering the civilized white race from oblivion. In *Degeneration, Culture, and the Novel*, William Greenslade looks at the utilitarian tendencies of late Victorian and Edwardian social thought, particularly 'the need to regulate fecundity in the interest of racial progress [that] gathered force from the *fin-de-siècle*'.[17] A convergence of social forces helped to effect this change: 'The explanation lies in a complex realignment of scientific positivism, culture and politics at the turn of the century'.[18] The obstetric experts involved with advancing science as well as their own careers remained keen to influence women in ways they felt would dispel the common spectres of a supposedly differential birth rate that threatened possible race suicide of the eugenically sound.

Such considerations lead us to a thorny problem − an assessment of the ways in which social class determined pregnant women's access to pelvimetric techniques and just how much autonomy might be possessed by a working-class woman offering up her body as a medical illustration device in return for a doctor's care. How might her experience differ from that of a middle-class or upper-class woman with money and choice at her disposal? If we are dealing with an increasing medicalization of women's bodies, one in which women participated to a certain extent, how might the giving up of autonomy actually have seemed like the exercise of that agency at the time? We do not have the scope to analyse the necessary case studies and statistics here to answer these questions fully, but we might offer some tentative suggestions.

On the one hand, we do see a coercive undertow in the pelvimetry literature when it reports on the disciplining of the female bodies used as research subjects in the large hospitals of England and America. Wilson, the epilogue of whose work takes in the development of hospital-based research programmes of the late nineteenth and early twentieth centuries, observes that this overt medicalization of the lower-class female body was more institutionalized and programmatic in America.[19]

For an example of this tendency, we may turn to the work of Edward P. Davis, a Professor of Obstetrics at Jefferson Medical College in Philadelphia in the 1890s. His paper on how to conduct labour in the case of abnormal pelvic conformation is often cited in the literature. His patients were drawn from the poorer ranks of society, and, as such, were effectively under his authority. Their various 'diagnos[es] of abnormality of the pelvis...[were] made by pelvimetry, palpation, and vaginal examination'.[20] Davis's patients worked in the hospital to offset the cost of their care, which could include treatment decisions based on Davis's assessments of a woman's moral as well as physical fitness:

> In effecting delivery by abdominal section, the choice between celiohys-terotomy and celiohysterectomy must be made. In married women who do not request that the power of reproduction be removed, celiohysterotomy is to be preferred. Among those highly deformed, ill-developed mentally or bodily, and of uncertain morals, celiohysterectomy we believe to be indicated. Among the latter we have not found that an effort to solicit an intelligent choice from the patient is successful. Such women will choose craniometry upon the living fetus, having no sense of responsibility to the unborn child. If we heed at all the teachings of sociology, hope of improvement morally and physically in the mother is far less than the possibilities of evolution in the child.[21]

Here we have late Victorian utilitarianism at its worst.

However, other voices added differing perspectives to this debate, as is indicated in an article by Barton Cooke Hirst entitled 'The Newer Gynaecology', which appeared in *The American Journal of Obstetrics and Gynaecology* in 1924. Hirst writes with a sense of his own modernity as he articulates the state of obstetrics in the aftermath of the First World War and lays out the profession's goals for the future. These include the discovery of safe analgesics for use during labour, control over the use and abuse of birth control ('who is to limit the limitation of fecundity?'), and the succouring of women injured in childbirth.[22] Hirst also counters Davis when he reveals his sensitivity to the power dynamics inherent in the doctor-patient relationship. When discussing possible pitfalls that the profession may fall into, he writes 'We might stray into an error incidental to our special work. Let the feminist say what she will, the male dominates the female throughout Nature. Dealing with women alone as patients there is noticeable in some of us gynaecologists an autocratic manner, an inclination to individualistic thought and practice contrary to the cooperative trend of modern medicine'.[23] Hirst's argument for a more user-friendly gynaecology bears a resemblance to the new model of companionate marriage popularized in the 1920s: the man would still be the senior partner, but he would wear his authority more lightly. After all, as Hirst writes at the article's end, the doctor's role remains 'a privilege all our own, superintending the reproduction, the perpetuation and the improvement of the human race from generation to generation'.[24] The supremacy of the doctor remains intact.

And yet eugenic arguments did enable some women to conceive strategies of performance as successful medical professionals in their own right. We may observe the influence of discourses of maternalism in some of these professional position-takings. As the nineteenth century wound to a close, the nature of eugenic arguments began to shift. Whereas before scientists such as Broca had mobilized the forces at their disposal to prove the anatomical and intellectual superiority of the white man, now medical men and women became anxious to learn all they could from white competitors and the so-called savage races alike. In the context of pelvimetry, the superior status previously granted to the oval-shaped pelvis typical of the white woman was increasingly considered to have been a mistake, and the virtues of round, so-called 'savage' pelves began to be seen. This shift in emphasis owed much to a widespread fascination with the primitive that was certainly compatible with maternalism's valorization of the sacred earth mother figure. The oval, contracted, flattened pelvis began to be ascribed either to rickets or to constricting clothing, particularly the corset, as is seen in a 1936 paper entitled 'Is the Oval or Female Type Pelvis a Rachitic Manifestation?' Part of the paper reads:

> When alterations are considered in environment surrounding female infants and adolescent children during the past twenty-five years, changes brought about not only by a great difference in diet, but by such influences as outdoor exercise and life in the open, it must be admitted that the environment for this group has changed indeed during that period. When one further considers the sedentary habits, the type of clothing, the diet, and general restrictions that previously were a part of the life of female infants and children, may one not speculate as to the effect of such an environment on the adult form of the female pelvis?[25]

As we did in Hirst's article, we see a self-conscious modernity here, a sense that, yes, women could and should seek a certain amount of liberation as long as they stayed true to their biological (and hence social) imperatives.

But the larger point is that at least some women professionals parlayed allegiance to such arguments to professional success in their own right. We see this at work in Kathleen Vaughan's 1931 paper 'The Shape of the Pelvic Brim as the Determining Factor in Childbirth'. She adheres to the belief that women who work outside have easier labours than do the cosseted ladies of the British and American upper classes. We see the primitivist, maternalist elements in such ideas. Vaughan's paper enjoyed a great deal of success; it is referred to time and again, and is cited as late as 1956 in Thoms' book on pelvimetry. The one time superintendent of the fabulously named Diamond Jubilee Zenana Hospital of Srinagar, Vaughan recalls for her readers the easy labours of the 'field worker, the woman who lives out of doors tending the cattle, planting out crops often knee-deep in cold water in the rice-field', comparing them to the hard confinements and frequent deaths in childbirth of Indian city-dwelling women who live in purdah.[26] Closer to home, she cites the Carnegie Trust Report for 1917 in which 'we read of easy labours and large families among the Highland women who, bare-footed, haul in the nets with the men, follow the plough, and engage in field work [...] Strong contrast, this, to the maternal mortality rate and the infant death rate to be met with in cities such as Edinburgh and Glasgow'.[27] Vaughan published this paper in the *British Medical Journal*, a testament to the high esteem in which it – and she – were held by a medical establishment.

This period's overarching obsession with efficiency became the place where subsidiary fantasies of primitivism and mechanism could meet in a characteristically early twentieth-century synthesis. We see this tendency at work in more fields than just the obstetric; these urges motivated the development of the imaging technologies of pelvimetry, culminating in our period in the proliferation of roentgenography (X-rays) as a diagnostic and therapeutic tool. Lisa Cartwright writes of the 'paradoxically antivisual tendency' of turn-of-the-century medical imaging, tracing the lineage of early twentieth-century medical motion pictures, kymographs, etc., back to the calipers, craniometers, and, it may be added, the pelvimeters of nineteenth-century science.[28] Doctors found comfort and prestige in rendering down what was alien, whether it was the body of an animal or the complex physiology of the female reproductive system, into numbers and visuals. The worship of the mechanical fetish led to scientific practices in which 'the experimental apparatus both pervade[d] and incorporate[d] the body of the analyst as well as the analyzed subject'.[29]

Such a drive may be witnessed in Hugo Ehrenfest's article 'A Method of Determining the Internal Dimensions, Configuration and Inclination of the Female Pelvis', which appeared in *The American Journal of Obstetrics and Diseases of Women and Children* in 1903.[30] In his paper Ehrenfest debuts two new instruments called the Pelvigraph and the Kliseometer. The Pelvigraph came with a set of arms sized to reach the differing points of the pelvis; the round end contained a spirit level and a marker, which the doctor's assistant used to register points on a sheet of draughting paper attached to the examination table. The pelvimetrist then connected the dots to produce a graphic representation of the shape of the pelvis. The Kliseometer resembled the external pelvimeters that had been in use since the nineteenth century. It was used to ascertain the inclination of the pelvis. The reader is struck by the increasing tendency of the literature to relegate the woman's body to the background and to emphasize the apparatus, the new machines that stand to make their inventors famous and well respected.

However, Ehrenfest would find that he had patented a Zeppelin at the dawn of the age of the fighter plane. *The Historical Review of British Obstetrics and Gynaecology: 1800–1950* dismisses Ehrenfest's invention as 'impracticable'.[31] By the early twentieth century, more primitive pelvigraphs and kliseometers had given way to the X-ray, or to pelvic roentgenology, as it was first called. Budin, a Frenchman, and Albert, a German, are given credit for having the idea to use roentgen rays in pelvimetry in 1897 and 1899, respectively, and J. R. Riddell of Glasgow was one of the earliest, if not the first, person to write on the subject in English. He and his colleagues are lauded in the literature for giving 'exactness to pelvic mensuration'.[32]

The First World War served as a brutally efficient proving ground for many new medical technologies, surgical techniques as well as imaging technologies, as may be seen in a remark by Dr E. Seth Hirsch in the 1922 number of *The American Journal of Obstetrics and Gynaecology*. Hirsch notes that 'numerous methods of localizing foreign bodies developed by the war may be applied to the measuring of the pelvis. They are all more or less complicated, difficult and tedious, though many of them give very exact figures'.[33] The new technology's clarity, its exactness, was its selling point. In the context of the increasing professionalization of medicine, we can speculate that the reverence granted to the X-ray upon its discovery certainly would have made its possible use in the field all the more desirable for both doctor and patient.

Yet these great strides in efficiency were taken at a cost that is perhaps impossible to ascertain from this distance in time. The history of the X-ray is certainly littered with the shrivelled corpses of its devotees, including the scientists Marie Curie, Thomas Edison, and his assistant Clarence Dally; the latter two certainly knew that X-rays caused cancer long before 1903.[34] The fact is that the literature on X-ray pelvimetry and radium treatment of gynaecological conditions is riddled with uncertainty and debate over what constituted safe doses and whether using such therapies was safe in the first place. In his article 'The Contraindications To Radium In The Treatment Of Diseases Of The Female Pelvis', F. E. Keene makes the point that the

indiscriminate use of radium or the x-ray by those inexperienced in gynaecology [...] must inevitably be followed by dire consequences. Examples of these misdirected efforts have repeatedly come under our observation and, as a consequence, not only much discredit has fallen upon radium but, what is more important, actual harm has been done to the patients.[35]

Certainly, these women's physicians meant to heal them, not harm them; medicine is not always an exact science. However, in the face of evidence such as this, the reader wonders why the medical profession was so committed to the use of X-ray pelvimetry. We may surmise that, in many cases, doctors felt that X-ray pelvimetry was worth the risk.

Reuben Peterson, for example, typifies his pro-roentgenography peers in the benefits he lists as accruing to practitioners from employing the procedure in his 1924 article 'The Diagnosis of Early Pregnancy in Roentgenography', which appeared in *The American Journal of Obstetrics and Gynaecology*. Peterson dismisses any charges that exposure to radiation is harmful to the foetus or to its mother:

> Up to the present time, at least, the obstetrician has either neglected roentgenography altogether or has feared to use it in pregnant women on account of its effect upon the fetus. The last question has been answered practically by the results of thousands of diagnostic exposures where no appreciable harm resulted in either fetus or mother.[36]

We can appreciate the weight that word 'appreciable' is being made to bear in this context.

Peterson also cites the X-ray's ability to distinguish between kinds of masses in the woman's abdomen. Tumours could be differentiated from cysts and foetuses could be identified by their bones. Fantasies of control over the recalcitrant flesh are also attested to by visual images of differing X-ray techniques. Jarcho's and Thoms' standard texts on pelvimetry, published in 1933 and 1956, respectively, are particularly helpful in this context. In these manuals, we see the organic, physical body of the woman being absorbed into the workings of a machine, being eaten, as it were, by a new technology that can strip away her physicality and reveal that of the unborn child. As a result, the foetus began to become rather the senior partner in the dyad of mother and child, a process further facilitated by the technology of ultrasound, in which we are enabled to see the foetus moving, underscoring its 'status' as a living, separate being.

So we see that the history of pelvimetry in the period under review has its moments of comedy and pathos, of hope and horror. This essay has reminded us that medicine existed then and exists now as wheels within wheels, in which ethics recombine with the profit motive and desires for status and agency to produce some very strange bedfellows indeed.

NOTES

1. Anonymous, 'Unsigned Review', *Journal of Psychological Medicine and Mental Pathology* (1851): 17–20 (18–19).
2. Ornella Moscucci, *The Science of Woman: Gynaecology and Gender in England, 1800–1929* (Cambridge, UK: Cambridge University Press, 1990), p. 38.
3. Mary Poovey, '"Scenes of an Indelicate Character": The Medical "Treatment" of Victorian Women', *Representations*, 14 (Spring 1986): 137–68 (138).
4. Adrian Wilson, *The Making of Man-midwifery: Childbirth in England, 1660–1770* (Cambridge, MA: Harvard University Press, 1995), p. 187.
5. J. G. Garson, MD, 'Pelvimetry', *Journal of Anatomy and Physiology, Normal and Pathological*, 16 (1882): 106–136 (106).
6. Garson, 'Pelvimetry', p. 110.
7. Garson, 'Pelvimetry', p. 109.
8. Wilson, *The Making of Man-midwifery*, Chapter 2.
9. Herbert Thoms, MD, *Pelvimetry* (New York: Paul B. Hoeber Inc, 1956), p. 13.
10. Edward A. Schumann, MD, 'The Dynamics of the Female Pelvis; Its Evolution and Architecture with Respect to Function', *American Journal of Obstetrics and Diseases of Women and Children*, 81.1 (January 1915): 1–29 (1).
11. Edward P. Davis, MD, 'The Treatment of Labor in Abnormal Pelves', *American Journal of Obstetrics and Diseases of Women and Children*, 39.6 (June 1899): 721–28 (722).
12. Thoms, *Pelvimetry*, p. 13.
13. Julius Jarcho, *The Pelvis in Obstetrics: A Practical Manual of Pelvimetry and Cephalometry Including Chapters on Roentgenological Measurement* (New York: Paul B. Hoeber, 1933), p. 33.
14. Jarcho, *The Pelvis in Obstetrics*, p. 195.
15. James B. Bullitt, 'A New Pelvimeter', *The American Journal of Obstetrics and Diseases of Women and Children*, 38 (July–December 1893): 562–565 (562).
16. Jarcho, *The Pelvis in Obstetrics*, p. 189.
17. William Greenslade, *Degeneration, Culture and the Novel, 1880–1940* (Cambridge, UK: Cambridge University Press, 1994), p. 136.
18. Greenslade, *Degeneration*, p. 136.
19. Wilson, *The Making of Man-midwifery*, p. 202.
20. Davis, 'The Treatment of Labor', p. 721.
21. Davis, 'The Treatment of Labor', pp. 724–725.
22. Barton Cooke Hirst, MD, 'The Newer Gynaecology', *American Journal of Obstetrics and Gynaecology*, 8.1 (July 1924): 1–6 (5).
23. Hirst, 'The Newer Gynaecology', p. 4.
24. Hirst, 'The Newer Gynaecology', p. 6.
25. Herbert Thoms, MD, 'Is the Oval or Female Type Pelvis a Rachitic Manifestation?', *American Journal of Obstetrics and Gynaecology*, 31 (1936): 111–126 (111).
26. Kathleen Vaughan, 'The Shape of the Pelvic Brim as the Determining Factor in Childbirth', *British Medical Journal* (21 November 1931): 939–41 (940).
27. Vaughan, 'The Shape of the Pelvic Brim', p. 940.
28. Lisa Cartwright, *Screening the Body: Tracing Medicine's Visual Culture* (Minneapolis, MN: University of Minnesota Press, 1995, p. 23.

29. Cartwright, *Screening the Body*, p. 38.
30. Hugo Ehrenfest, MD, 'A Method of Determining the Internal Dimensions, Configuration and Inclination of the Female Pelvis', *American Journal of Obstetrics and Diseases of Women and Children*, 57.5 (May 1903): 577–90.
31. J. M. Munro Kerr, R. W. Johnstone and Miles H. Phillips (eds.), *Historical Review of British Obstetrics and Gynaecology, 1800–1950* (London: E. & S. Livingstone, 1954), p. 73.
32. Kerr, *Historical Review*, p. 73.
33. 'Discussion', *American Journal of Obstetrics and Gynaecology*, 4 (July–December 1922): 316–19 (318).
34. Cartwright, *Screening the Body*, p. 110.
35. F. E. Keene, MD, 'The Contraindications to Radium in the Treatment of Diseases of the Female Pelvis', *American Journal of Obstetrics and Gynaecology*, 8 (July–December 1924): 201–204 (201).
36. Reuben Peterson, MD, 'The Diagnosis of Early Pregnancy by Roentgenography', *American Journal of Obstetrics and Gynaecology*, 8 (July–December 1924): 770–78 (772).

10

'She read on more eagerly, almost breathlessly': Mary Elizabeth Braddon's Challenge to Medical Depictions of Female Masturbation in The Doctor's Wife

LAURIE GARRISON

In the early to mid-nineteenth century, medical accounts of female masturbation were strangely contradictory. In the many legitimate as well as quack
medical treatises on reproductive health that were in circulation in this
period, female masturbation was either utterly unimportant or it was a much
more devious vice than the same habit in men – and therefore a subject of the
utmost importance. Some texts argued that women had little to no sexual
feeling, as William Acton sought to establish in *Functions and Disorders
of the Reproductive Organs* (1857).[1] Some included discussion of women as
a minor and sidelined element of their work, as does George Drysdale in
Elements of Social Science (c. 1854–55).[2] Others saw female masturbation as the
temptation to a whole range of other forms of vice, as in Samuel La'Mert's
Self-Preservation (1841) and Tissot's *New Guide to Health and Long Life*
(1808).[3] In discussions of masturbation in each of these texts, examination
of the practice of male masturbation was dominant. Female masturbation
is only ever presented as an aside, subordinated to the much more pressing
issue of managing male indulgence in the practice. Though their titles
suggest a much more encompassing range of interests, it was not until the
later decades of the century that female masturbation came to be widely
studied in its own right.[4]

One of the striking similarities of all of these texts is that male masturbation was portrayed as an affront, in its wasteful inefficiency, to capitalist
ideology.[5] The male masturbator is continually described as wasted, dried,
and weak because seminal fluid is repeatedly expelled to no productive (or

reproductive) purpose. Curiously, though, these texts do not discuss the female orgasm in such determinedly physical terms. This was partly because many medical professionals assumed that women seldom masturbated. But it was also due to the fact that if no bodily fluids were repeatedly wasted, the female body would be less affected.[6] The discussion of female masturbation in these texts, when it appears, commences at a further remove from the body than discussions of male masturbation: more specifically, at the point of moral transgression. Texts that addressed the issue of female masturbation were less concerned with the immediate physical effects on the masturbator's body and more concerned with the idea that masturbation was the top of a slippery slope that could lead to prostitution or adultery. This relative silence on the physical effects of female masturbation, bounded on one side by indifference and on the other by paranoia about dire consequences, left a void that could be filled by other forms of popular culture.

Mary Elizabeth Braddon's *The Doctor's Wife* (1864) is one such form of popular culture.[7] First published as a serial in Temple Bar, then quickly followed by a triple-decker edition, *The Doctor's Wife* was Braddon's 'literary' novel for 1864. Braddon is well known for her massive literary output and her strategy of writing more than one novel at the same time, usually a sensation novel and a more artistic work. There are some sensational incidents in *The Doctor's Wife*. In one fast-paced sequence of events, the heroine Isabel's criminal father violently murders the object of her affections just before he escapes arrest for forgery by boarding a ship bound for New York. However, the novel's ambitions towards literary status are also very clear. The text abounds with erudite references to the novelists Walter Scott, Edward Bulwer-Lytton, Charles Dickens, and William Thackeray; the poets Byron, Shelley, and L.E.L.; and a whole range of historical incidents and political figures. Braddon does not use these references strictly as an advertisement for her worldliness and education. Rather, in her characteristically playful manner she creates a heroine who is addicted to pleasuring herself with fantasies about these figures, a strategy that is at times quite comical. Isabel exhibits many of the symptoms of the masturbator as described in the medical literature. She is also surrounded by scientific figures who attempt unsuccessfully to treat her, which is presumably a deliberate attack on the medical profession that produced these treatises. Her fantasies easily shift from man to man and from woman to woman, mimicking some of the moral transgressions alleged against female masturbators. Where the medical literature offers little more than silence on how, when, and where the act of female masturbation was carried out, Braddon provides a whole range of fantasies, incidents, and consequences that undermine medical and social surveillance of female self-pleasuring and female sexuality more generally.

A comparison between some of the symptoms of the masturbator and various characteristics of the heroine suggests that Braddon may have deliberately drawn on the literature of masturbation in constructing her heroine. Medical treatises on masturbation – termed the 'solitary vice' by many of the writers on the subject – deal with the isolation that was both a cause and a symptom of the practice. Braddon places her intelligent young heroine in isolating domestic settings that do not offer her ample mental exertion. First in her family home, then in a role as a governess, and finally in a sorely uneventful married life, Isabel is left alone with her books and her daydreams. Indeed, the narrator informs us that Isabel lives 'as much alone as if she had resided in a balloon, for ever suspended in mid air, and never coming down in serious earnest to the common joys and sorrows of the vulgar life about her' (p. 29). In *Elements of Social Science*, Drysdale writes that the masturbator suffers from '[i]ncapacity for study or any mental exertion' and the same idea is reiterated in the works of Acton, Smith, and Tissot.[8] Isabel attempts to take up useful occupations, including the writing of novels and poetry, but the result is that 'she began a great many undertakings, and grew tired of them, and gave them up in despair' (p. 231).

La'Mert argues that in the masturbator '[a]ll the intellectual faculties are weakened; the man becomes a coward, apprehensive of a thousand ideal dangers, or sinks into the effeminate timidity of womanhood'.[9] Isabel also exhibits timidity; the nobleman she comes to have a platonic affair with, Roland Lansdell, remembers her after their first meeting as 'a pretty automaton, who had simpered and blushed when he spoke to her, and stammered shyly when she was called upon to answer him' (p. 154). Much more accustomed to solitude than social interaction, like the masturbator, Isabel has difficulty communicating with nearly every other character in the novel. All the major works on masturbation identify self-love as one of its major symptoms. La'Mert claims that the masturbator is guilty of 'Waywardness, stubborn self-love, selfishness in every modification, or that form of it which requires and would attract the anxiety and attention of others too exclusively upon himself'.[10] Though she lacks the confidence necessary for effective social interaction, there are many scenes where Isabel lovingly contemplates her own reflection in the mirror. In one of these scenes, she 'looked at her reflection in the glass, and saw that she was pretty. Was it only prettiness or was it something more, even in spite of the brown dress?' (p. 105). Isabel is unmistakably isolated and desirous of isolation. She is also timid and occasionally guilty of self-love or selfishness, particularly when her relationship with Roland Lansdell commences. However, the narrator also suggests that Isabel turns to fantasies because her husband neglects her. Significantly, no children are produced from Isabel's marriage. Some readers might therefore infer that she turns to pleasurable fantasies due to her husband's neglect, or, in the more extreme interpretation, Isabel may have lost interest in sex with her husband because she prefers masturbation – a complication of the habit discussed by Acton.

It would not have been unusual for Braddon or her readers to be familiar with these treatises on masturbation. The earliest and most famous of these was the anonymously published *Onania*, which was continuously circulated and published in a number of different editions throughout the eighteenth century. The sensation caused by *Onania* led to a slew of imitations, which continued to appear at least up to the 1850s.[11] One of these was the aforementioned *A New Guide to Health and Long Life* by Tissot.[12] La'Mert's *Self-Preservation* and Henry Smith's *The Private Medical Friend* serve as two examples verifiably in circulation in the 1850s.[13] However, these texts are more ephemeral in form and their pronouncements on health are much more sensational in tone. These texts would presumably have been cheap as well as accessible for a large number of readers. Textbooks like Acton's *Functions and Disorders of the Reproductive Organs* and Drysdale's *Elements of Social Science* are much more tempered in their medical and moral views.[14] These volumes were likely to have been written partly as alternatives to their ephemeral competitors and eighteenth-century predecessors. Drysdale deplores 'the degrading advertisements for "silent friends", and "cures for certain diseases", arguing that such works, presumably including La'Mert's text, frighten the victim much more than necessary.[15] Acton also devotes an entire section of *Functions and Disorders of the Reproductive System* to debunking such works. However, evidence suggests that virtually all of these texts had a wide circulation: books by Acton and by Drysdale went into new editions for decades, with the thirteenth edition of *Elements of Social Science* issued in 1875. The circulation of ephemera is more difficult to judge, but La'Mert's *Self-Preservation* claims to be in its 64th edition by the 1850s.

Furthermore, one of the conventions of these texts was a documented interaction between their authors and readers, whether real or imaginary. The treatises of Acton, La'Mert and Smith each includes a collection of letters written by sufferers requesting advice, appended to the main body of the text. In the case of La'Mert and Smith, these letters usually thank the author for his advice and for his unnamed form of medicine that subdued the desire, leading to a successful cure. As is suggested by the publishing histories of the works described above, those who wrote about masturbation often enjoyed a successful publishing record, though the idea that this was because these texts cured the readers of their desire seems questionable. Rather, this interaction between the reader and the supposedly scholarly author was part of a larger trend of exchange between readers and texts that played on readers' and writers' desires in a variety of ways. In his massive work, *Solitary Sex*, Thomas Laqueur proposes the possibility that such writings served to inspire desire in their readers, as well as the medical professionals themselves. Laqueur argues that the rise in medical attention to masturbation was accompanied by a developing industry of pornography, as well as a subset of 'medical soft-core porn', identifying Bienville's *Nymphomania*[16] and Tissot's *New Guide to Health and Long Life* as examples of the genre.[17] Laqueur argues that due to the rise of these genres, a seemingly natural alliance between masturbation and reading came to be formed: 'Sexual desire and curiosity were magnified and embedded in reading; masturbation was intensely textual'.[18] Furthermore, the status of the woman reader was particularly at stake in this market: 'the woman reader was the gold standard of the moral corruption latent in all fiction. She was the misguided reader par excellence, the enthralled reader, the prototypical victim of imaginative excess'.[19] Indeed, Laqueur states that many pornographic images from the late seventeenth century onward represent women masturbating with a book in hand or displayed nearby.[20] Braddon's novel about a young woman who becomes addicted to weaving erotic fantasies with the events and characters in her books might therefore be said to be a late manifestation of this trend.

The most substantial discussions of female masturbation in nineteenth-century medical treatises generally deal with the larger social consequences of the practice in women. In *Functions and Disorders of the Reproductive Organs*, Acton devotes a section of his book to discussing the female lack of sexual feeling as an apparent cause of impotence in the male. In these passages, Acton constructs a very long scale, with the vast majority of women who exhibit no sexual feeling placed on one side, and a small deviant minority who experience excessive sexual feeling placed on the distant opposite. Acton writes:

> I admit, of course, the existence of sexual excitement terminating even in nymphomania, a form of insanity that those accustomed to visit lunatic asylums must be fully conversant with; but, with these sad exceptions, there can be no doubt that sexual feeling in the female is in the majority of cases in abeyance, and that it requires positive and considerable excitement to be roused at all: and even if roused (which in many instances it never can be) it is very moderate compared with that of the male.[21]

The very wording of this sentence – continually perforated with clauses, commas, colons, and semicolons – suggests hesitation, perhaps insecurity, in Acton's thinking and the strength of his arguments. The use of the term 'abeyance' in particular indicates that there is feeling to be stimulated; it is simply dormant. However, Acton undermines this idea by qualifying it with the claims that 'considerable excitement' is necessary for arousal, which is not guaranteed and will be 'moderate compared with that of the male'. As much as Acton may seek to support a notion of a Victorian woman who is entirely lacking in problematic or dangerous desire, he cannot help but undercut his own arguments in discussing the sexuality of this type of female.

The section that immediately follows the passages on want of sexual feeling in the female deals with 'Perversion of Sexual Feeling'. However, the only perversion Acton examines (in a book about male reproductive health) is female masturbation – and he only provides two paragraphs on this perversion. The bulk of these passages consist of an anecdote about a man who comes to Acton for advice after having read a previous edition of *Functions and Disorders*. The man, whose complaint is that his wife seems to evince no sexual feeling, candidly tells Acton:

> I am led to think that my wife's want of sexual feeling may arise, if you can affirm to me that such a thing is possible, from self-abuse. She has confessed to me that at a boarding school, in perfect ignorance of any injurious effects, she early acquired the habit. This practice still gives her gratification; not so connection, which she views with positive aversion, although it gives her no pains.[22]

Again, Acton's reasoning behind his assessment of this case seems to contain contradictory urges. He writes: 'If the unnatural excesses of masturbation take place early in life, before the subjects who commit them have arrived at maturity, it is not surprising that we meet with women whose sexual feelings, if they ever existed, become prematurely worn out'.[23] Again, there is something contradictory about this argument: if women who masturbate manage to 'wear out' their sexual feelings, then why do they continue to masturbate? Where the male masturbator possibly irrevocably damages his health and drains his body of life, the female masturbator drains her body of sexual feeling. At another point in the passage, Acton equates male and female masturbation as being equally dire in consequences: 'So ruinous is the practice of solitary vice, both in the one and the other sex, so difficult is it to give it up, that I fear it may be carried on even in married life [...] and may actually come to be preferred to the natural excitement'.[24] There are two issues that seem to continually haunt Acton and to undermine his arguments. First, he cannot quite reconcile his moral beliefs with the idea that women may experience sexual desire, and secondly, he cannot quite conceive of masturbation as a sexual act, one that signifies sexual desire.

Acton was considered the leading expert on reproductive disorders for decades in the nineteenth century, but a whole range of other opinions circulated during this time. The birth control advocate George Drysdale offered a very different point of view in *Elements of Social Science*, one that is much less pessimistic than Acton's. Drysdale writes that 'probably few men have not done more or less' than to 'for a while indulge in the practice [...]

yet soon relinquish it, for the more natural and infinitely more desirable sexual intercourse, and thus any injury they may have done themselves is soon corrected'.[25] For Drysdale, masturbation is not particularly deviant and, as long as the practice is not overindulged, resulting symptoms will completely and quickly disappear. In fact, Drysdale recommends 'sexual intercourse' as 'the main part of the treatment', even if this meant indulging in extramarital sex.[26] Furthermore, his views on the state of social codes of sexual practice fly in the face of Acton's traditional positioning of women as moral superiors to their desirous male counterparts. Drysdale argues that

> As long as the present rigorous sexual code continues, so long will the whole of our youth of both sexes be liable to this disease [masturbation] [...] Were [sexual intercourse] readily attainable without the danger of disease and the degradation of illicit intercourse, masturbation would rarely if ever be resorted to, and one of the most fearful and prevalent causes of disease, moral and physical, eradicated.[27]

Here, as in Acton's work, masturbation is a 'cause of disease', not a sexual act, but what Drysdale proposes is much more revolutionary than Acton's arguments. For Drysdale, the real solution to the social problem of masturbation – in both sexes – is an entirely new structuring of social codes where extra-marital sex would not be subject to such moral censure. Not surprisingly, it is difficult to find another such text that offers such a severe criticism of Victorian sexual mores. Contemporaneously with the height of circulation of Acton's and Drysdale's texts, Henry Maudsley was beginning to self-consciously fashion himself as a leader of the medical and psychological professions, a stance partly bolstered with extreme and gloomy observations about insanity caused by masturbation. As *The British Medical Journal* reports, Maudsley believed it was 'entirely unjustifiable to recommend marriage to the confirmed masturbator', asserting that recovery was not likely 'when once his mind was affected by this vice'.[28] For Maudsley, reproduction by a masturbator would surely result in the production of more masturbators and so recommending sexual intercourse was a risky method of treatment in any case. Maudsley's agenda, however, was to claim the masturbator for the study of his developing field of psychiatry, justifying the field's claim to be a serious medical subspecialty.

In the more ephemeral texts, there is just as much disagreement on the issue of female masturbation. Henry Smith most determinedly dismisses female masturbation. In *The Private Medical Friend* he argues that it is not necessary to substantially address the problem of female masturbation because, due to 'the delicacy and purity of the sex generally', 'this filthy habit is only to a partial extent practised amongst them'.[29] La'Mert takes a different view entirely, which is delivered in his characteristically exaggerated rhetoric.

When under the influence of 'nature roused by repeated and fruitless efforts [...] the unfortunate female falls a prey to some vile seducer [...] her offence is not altogether without palliation, and the husband may well, yet painfully, accuse himself, as the cause of her unhappy deviation'.[30] For La'Mert, masturbation in women is potentially an impetus to adultery. As in Acton's and Drysdale's texts, masturbation simultaneously leads to sex but does not exactly function as a sex act. Significantly, the female masturbator is 'roused by repeated and fruitless efforts', suggesting that orgasm, as well as any sort of gratification, are not possible.

One of the anxieties surrounding masturbation in both sexes was that the habit was learned from schoolmates or servants.[31] Acton, for example, does not straightforwardly conceptualize this problem in terms of the engagement in a sex act with one or more members of the same or the opposite sex. Indeed, the detail about learning to masturbate at a public school in the husband's story of his self-abusing wife is glossed over by Acton. La'Mert, however, unflinchingly tackles the issue, noting that a 'depraved servant, or playmate' generally introduces the child to the practice. Schools are 'foci and hotbeds of contagion, where destructive immorality assumes a thousand protean aspects, and where obscenity, is instilled by every device of example, persuasion and menace'.[32] Once introduced to the practice of masturbation, the child becomes an additional 'instructor in evil'.[33] As in the more weighty medical tomes by Acton and Drysdale, masturbation is considered a disease; it is spread like a 'contagion'. But the extreme manner in which La'Mert conceptualizes the teaching of masturbation to be 'obscenity', 'persuasion', and 'menace' suggests that there is something especially unnerving about the act itself. Furthermore, once a child has been introduced to the practice, innocence cannot be recaptured. The only possible result seems to be that the child suffers a moral fall comparable to that of the fallen woman, becoming an 'instructor in evil'.

The most detailed view on the issue of engaging in masturbation with others or teaching the habit to others appears in Tissot's *New Guide to Health and Long Life*. For Tissot, female masturbation and sexual acts among women are virtually indistinguishable. The text seamlessly shifts from discussion of masturbation to lesbianism:

> another kind of pollution, which may be called *clitoral*, the known origin of which is to be traced so far back as the time of the second Sappho [...] And which was so much too common amongst the Roman women, at the time when all morality was lost, that it was more than once the subject for the epigrammists and satirists of that age.[34]

By referencing the supposed free licence of Roman society, Tissot creates a space that allows him to discuss sexual acts among women in much more direct terms. Although the question of whether teaching others to masturbate is a sexual act is debated in other texts, here, masturbation quite clearly leads to experimentation with different forms of sexuality.[35] Furthermore, the mention of these acts as 'the subject for the epigrammists and satirists of that age' almost self-referentially reveals the source of Tissot's information. Ancient texts describe such acts with the dual intention of entertaining and stimulating the reader. Such intentions surely must also be on Tissot's agenda, no matter how convincing his stance as a scientific observer may be, and, as I will show, such intentions may have been on Braddon's mind as well. Like Drysdale, Tissot also discusses an overthrow of the current social order, but he describes this overthrow in drastically negative terms. Tissot writes:

> Nature has been pleased to give some women a semi-resemblance to man; this has, upon slight inquiry, given rise to the chimera, which has prevailed for some centuries, of hermaphrodites [...]. Some women who were thus imperfect, glorying, perhaps, in this kind of resemblance, seized upon the functions of virility [...] it is frequently practiced at present, and it would be easy to find more than one Laufella, or a single Medullina, who, like those Roman females, so much esteem the gifts of nature, as to think they ought to abolish the arbitrary distinction of birth.[36]

Here, Tissot creates a slippery slope that begins with women masturbating and ends with masculine women seizing political power. The attempt to 'abolish the arbitrary distinction of birth' suggests not only that masturbating women or otherwise sexually abnormal women may seek sexual partnerships with other women, but also that if this occurs the whole moral order may be under threat. If women create sexual partnerships with other women, then male sexual partners may well become unnecessary and male roles in society may be taken over by women. As in other discussions of female masturbation, Tissot's analysis of 'clitoral pollution', as he terms it, takes social consequences for this practice as his central concern. Where discussions of male masturbation are centrally concerned with the immediate and local treatment of the male body, discussions of female masturbation are always much more focused on consequences at a societal level. Masturbation in both sexes, however, posed a threat to the procreative family unit in that it offered alternative sexual practices that were often accompanied by alternative social practices.

If *The Doctor's Wife* might be said to take part in these debates about masturbation, its contribution is to provide an everyday example of how a woman might generate her own erotic fantasies. We see Isabel repeatedly 'dreaming over her books, weaving wonderful romances in which she was to be the heroine, and the hero − ?' (p. 74). Isabel's favourite novels by Bulwer,

Dickens, and Thackeray offer plots that culminate in the attainment of marriage and sexual maturity for the central female character. But even more scandalously, part of the pleasure she derives from fantasizing about being in the place of her favourite heroines is through constant interchange of different partners. In her fantasies the

> hero was the veriest chameleon, inasmuch as he took his colour from the last book Miss Sleaford had been reading. Sometimes he was Ernest Maltravers, the exquisite young aristocrat, with violet eyes and silken hair. Sometimes he was Eugene Aram, dark, gloomy and intellectual [...]. At another time he was Steerforth, selfish, haughty and elegant. (p. 74)

This overt and continual exchange of desire for one man, then another and another, is tempered with suggestions that Isabel is not entirely aware of the implications. Significantly, Isabel is most interested in dangerous male literary figures, especially villains and Byronic heroes. When the canny sensation novelist Sigismund Smith questions Isabel about her reading, he tells her that her favourite books are '[d]angerously beautiful [...] beautiful sweet-meats, with opium inside the sugar' (p. 24). The alignment of Isabel's favourite books with opium, a consciousness-altering and addictive drug, relieves her of some of the responsibility for her susceptibility to scandalous levels of fantasy based on them. However, Sigismund asks her, 'These books don't make you happy, do they, Izzie?' and her reply makes the base level of her enjoyment of them clear (p. 24). '"No, they make me unhappy; but" – she hesitated a little, and then blushed as she said – "I like that sort of unhappiness. It's better than eating and drinking and sleeping, and being happy that way"' (p. 24). Isabel's blush at Sigismund's recognition of the type of enjoyment her books offer her, as well as her bashful admission that she enjoys 'that sort of unhappiness', suggests that there is a clandestine undertone to this conversation. Reading for Isabel is on the one hand classed with the bodily satisfactions of 'eating and drinking, and sleeping' as though it is a physical act, and on the other with much more intensely pleasurable physical satisfactions, potentially ones that are sexual or masturbatory. The pleasurable 'sort of unhappiness' that Isabel describes – where one is continually waiting for a resolution to the plot, continually slightly dissatisfied, continually developing more and more anxiety – sounds suspiciously reminiscent of La'Mert's depiction of an 'unfortunate female' who, 'roused by repeated and fruitless efforts', is at risk of becoming 'a prey to some vile seducer'.[37] It is in this manner that references to Isabel's reading become a code for discussing her frustrated and over-stimulated sexual desire.

As in the work by some of the more moralistic medical writers such as Acton, La'Mert, and Tissot, Isabel's fantasies sometimes seem to descend a slippery slope of greater and greater transgression. After her marriage to

George Gilbert, the doctor of the title, Isabel makes the acquaintance of two local aristocrats, Roland Lansdell and his cousin Gwendoline Pomphrey. She occasionally meets them socially through her connection as former governess to the local amateur scientist and philosopher Mr Raymond. Isabel encounters these minor nobles with awe, never really hoping that the acquaintance will progress, but her interactions with them provide her with plenty – and more exciting – material to inspire her fantasies. This, for Isabel, 'was better than reading'; she decides that her novel-based fantasies are 'quite a tame thing after these reveries' (p. 183, p. 134). In fact, there is something climactic about Isabel's meeting with Roland Lansdell. To Isabel, he is

> the incarnation of all the dreams of her life; he was Byron alive again, and come home from Missolonghi. He was Napoleon the First, restored to the faithful soldiers who had never believed that fiction of perfidious England, the asserted death of the immortal hero. He was all this; he was a shadowy and divine creature, amenable to no earthly laws. (p. 139)

Isabel does engage in a flirtatious relationship with Roland Lansdell, but what is curious about her association with him is that it always remains, to a large extent, in the realm of the imaginary; the relationship is never consummated. Like the masturbator who turns with disgust from the sexual act, Isabel does not seem to desire a physical relationship with Roland or her husband. Roland is no different, no more human or concrete, than the fictional heroes she has so often fantasized about. In fact, Isabel can only understand him in terms of the variety of types she has encountered in her books: Byron, Napoleon, Maltravers, Aram, Steerforth. This continual circulation of different fantasies, different 'heroes' and living people that Isabel fantasizes about is just the sort of detail a fictional writer such as Braddon can provide to illuminate the issue of women's erotic fantasies. Such detail would have been virtually impossible to include in medical texts on masturbation (whether they are legitimate or quack) if the author was seeking to appeal to an audience that wanted reliable information rather than 'medical soft-core porn', as termed by Thomas Laqueur.[38] Where the medical texts remained largely reticent on the details of female masturbation, Braddon can provide a fictional account of a vast array of desire-inspiring fantasies.

Furthermore, *The Doctor's Wife* has the liberty of placing this representation of the fantasizing heroine into larger and multiple contexts of cultural and social debate. Not only is Isabel enchanted by her novels and her own fantasies about their contents but she is also thrown into the same enthralled and obsessive state due to her contact with Roland's expensive and plentiful collections of possessions. When Isabel is in Roland's presence and when she fantasizes about him, her thoughts merely touch on him as subject, then instantly shift to the things that surround him in his home. When Isabel visits Roland's house for dinner, her appreciation of Roland's appearance in 'his loose black-velvet morning coat' with 'a waxen-looking hothouse flower in his button-hole' is contrasted with a more brilliant focus on his 'assets' (p. 172). For Isabel,

> It was all a confusion of brightness and colour, which was almost too much for her poor sentimental brain. It was all a splendid chaos, in which antique oak cabinets, and buhl and marqueterie, and carved ebony chairs, and filigree work and ivory, old Chelsea, Battersea, Copenhagen, Vienna, Dresden, Sèvres, Derby, and Salopian china, Majolica and Palissy ware, pictures and painted windows, revolved like the figures in a kaleidoscope. (p. 172)

Isabel's addictions are multiple and interchangeable; her obsessions with novel-reading, erotic fantasy, Roland Lansdell, and the things he owns all seem to be the effects of the same indulgence. The narrator's manner of describing this 'confusion of brightness and colour' that seems to overwhelm Isabel's 'poor sentimental brain', creates a sense that Isabel is not at this moment capable of rational thought. She does not appear to be in a rational state of consciousness when she reads her novels, when she fantasizes about Roland, or when she gazes on Roland's possessions. Her altered psychological state, similar to that of the daydreaming, occupation-less masturbator as depicted in the medical literature, seems to facilitate this anxious shifting from one object of fantasy to the next. There is also a similarity with the medical depictions of masturbators here, in that desires are easily transferable: there is no fidelity to partners or possessions. In the medical literature, a woman begins by masturbating, then moves on to illicit sex, then sometimes to sex with other women.

Isabel indeed also flirts with this final step. On her first visit to Roland's castle, Isabel's attention is first and primarily absorbed by Gwendoline rather than Roland:

> She looked longer and more earnestly at Lady Gwendoline than at Roland Lansdell, for in this elegant being she saw the image of herself, as she had fancied herself so often [...]. A faint perfume of jasmine and orange-blossom floated towards her from Lady Gwendoline's handkerchief, and she seemed to see the fair-haired lady who smiled at her, and the dark-haired gentleman who had risen at her approach, through an odorous mist that confused her senses. (p. 129)

Transferrable desires are here paired with transferrable sensual stimulation. Isabel's vision and her sense of smell are confused to the point that she comes to see through rather than smell 'an odorous mist'. But this synesthesia signifies more than Isabel's confused and altered consciousness. The intermingling of the senses is complemented by an intermingling of Isabel and Gwendoline, at least in Isabel's mind. Gwendoline is the woman Isabel 'had fancied herself'. Isabel desires not only to *be* this woman, but to possess her, and to consume her, as she desires to consume Roland's assets. In Isabel's state of heightened sensation, senses share stimulation and female bodies become interchangeable – capable of intermingling like Isabel's confused senses of smell and sight. The desires to possess and consume objects and people therefore become coloured with an intensity that is erotic. In a more overt example of Isabel's interest in Gwendoline, she indulges in an intense scrutiny of the latter in the dressing room:

> Lady Gwendoline removed her bonnet – another marvellous bonnet – and drew off the tightest coffee-with-plenty-of-milk-in-it-coloured gloves, and revealed long white hands, luminous with opals and diamonds. The Doctor's Wife had time to contemplate Lady Gwendoline's silk dress – that exquisitely fitting dress [...] and the tiny embroidered collar, fitting closely to the long slender throat. (p. 173)

In this semblance of a striptease, Gwendoline's body in particular is fetishized as an object of beauty. Isabel revels in her view of Gwendoline's tightly fitting gloves, the whiteness of the skin revealed when they are removed, the perfect fit of her dress and the manner in which her collar enhances the beauty of her slender throat. Here Gwendoline's expensive adornments of her body are so closely aligned with her body itself that the text seems to insistently suggest that the desire for one is the equivalent to the desire for the other, a formulation that makes Isabel's desire appear covetous, intense, and erotic.

Part of the reason that the most detailed description of female erotic fantasies appears in a novel rather than a medical text is that, in the early to mid-nineteenth century, there was pressure on medical professionals not to indulge in the racy rhetoric of earlier, and quack, treatises on masturbation. Surgeons and physicians were vying against each other for the legitimation that expertise in treating masturbation would afford them as individuals and as professional groups. In the 1840s, debates carried out in *The Lancet* fought particularly fiercely in favour of surgeons.[39] As is noted above, Maudsley also used the 'disease' of masturbation as a platform to claim a rightful domain of the developing field of psychiatry. Identification of certain texts as quack treatises might lead to stigmatization of the individual and of his professional group. La'Mert was in fact taken off the medical register for publishing an 'indecent and unprofessional treatise';[40] this publication was almost surely *Self-Preservation*. Though it was still likely to have been in circulation at mid-century, Tissot's *New Guide to Health and Long Life* simply would not have been written by a medical professional intending to pursue a career. To portray a masturbator – especially a female masturbator – was therefore a challenging task at mid century. Braddon negotiates these limitations by creating a discourse of sexual fantasy that depends on a continually shifting repertoire of associations between masturbation and other forms of addiction, hence the constant exchange of one obsession for another, of men for women and people for things. This discourse of sexual fantasy does not dwell on a single object long enough for it to be condemned as encouraging a particular scandalous behaviour or illicit desire.

Furthermore, it is no accident that Sigismund Smith compares Isabel's novels to 'beautiful sweet-meats, with opium inside the sugar' (p. 24). Frequent references to Isabel's obsessions and her mental state suggest that her ailment is similar to opium addiction. A similar professional conflict over the right to treat opium addicts, in this case involving physicians, surgeons, and chemists, was also particularly intense in the 1860s, culminating in the 1868 Pharmacy Act.[41] Fierce debates about the ready availability of various preparations of laudanum regularly appeared in *The British Medical Journal*, *The Lancet* and other professional publications throughout the 1860s.[42] Some argued that irresponsible chemists who recklessly administered laudanum ought to be held responsible for facilitating what seemed to be an increasing number of poisonings and suicides. Others argued that a larger moral question was at stake, since opium was used to quiet working-class children while their parents worked, often resulting in children of a very young age becoming addicted. Furthermore, opium was supposedly used to placate the ill in workhouses, again resulting in addiction or poisoning. Addiction to opium, like masturbation, had become a useful arena for carrying out territorial battles that would lend legitimacy to the branch of the medical profession that succeeded in claiming it. As in the medical texts on masturbation, medical depictions of opium addiction sought to suppress all mention of the vivid dreams and visions one might enjoy through the use of opium. In *The Doctor's Wife*, the alignment of Isabel's ailment with addiction to opium is much more openly stated than the alignment with masturbation. Indeed, this deliberate construction of Isabel as a sufferer of something like opium addiction accounts for her frequent confusion and disorientation. We are directly informed at one point that Isabel wastes away her time 'as an opium eater beguiles his listless days with the splendid visions that glorify his besotted stupor' (p. 232). The dual connotation of 'besotted' (inebriated and infatuated) is particularly relevant here. Isabel is at once in love – with a variety of men, women, fictions, and things – and she is drunk with the pleasure of fantasies about them. Isabel's pleasurable disorientation, a characteristic entirely missing from the medical accounts of masturbation, functions partly as a device that allows Braddon to place her heroine in such compromised situations and to attribute such questionable desires to her. It also allows her to solidify the connection between Isabel's symptoms and various forms of addiction that references to the behaviour of masturbators simply cannot openly achieve.

However, novels are firmly positioned as the most fruitful sources of addictive fantasy in *The Doctor's Wife*. They are the catalyst that commences the process of Isabel's shifting obsessions with characters, plots, and people. Braddon deliberately creates a very recognizable type of woman reader in Isabel; she is the silly lady reader who was continually in danger of literature that did not adhere to recognized moral standards. Henry Mansel's often quoted review of novels by Braddon and other sensation novelists for *The Quarterly Review* condemns such literature for its varied and devious means of corrupting 'unsuspecting ladies'.[43] Readers such as Mansel were likely to have recognized Isabel as one of this easily influenced type. One reviewer claims that Isabel 'is but a deeply shaded sketch of hundreds around us'.[44] The symptom of these 'hundreds' is 'that mixture of reverie, sympathy, sentimentality, and discontent, which novel-reading is apt to produce among imaginative girls'.[45] Isabel's mental state could presumably be explained away as an addiction to novel-reading, but what Braddon suggests is that this addiction to novels is also easily aligned with other, more transgressive addictions such as masturbation and opium-eating. Although the medical texts I discuss in this chapter deal only with masturbation, Braddon's novel, as a text written for a more mainstream arena, can deal with the larger cultural refiguring of addiction that was at its most intense point in the mid-nineteenth century. Addictions to various things (masturbation, opium, novels) had become useful to the medical profession and were therefore addressed more and more as part of their rightful domain of study. The result was a prioritization of the developing medical – as opposed to moral – conception of addiction. In addition, by aligning masturbation with reading in this novel, Braddon is very directly raising the question of whether women's reading ought to be considered an addiction, or an impetus to an addiction to masturbation. Braddon also questions whether reading or other distinctly female addictions ought to be monitored by the male medical profession. Her conclusion in this novel is not in the medical profession's favour.

The Doctor's Wife in fact presents a harsh critique of the medical profession that appoints itself to carry out this surveillance of women's habits. During a portion of the novel, Isabel acts as a governess to the two orphan nieces of one of the scientific figures of the novel, Charles Raymond, 'the kindly phrenologist' and the 'philosopher of Coventford' (pp. 82–83). He does not hesitate to set to work diagnosing the wayward Isabel and planning her future. His assessment of her is that the 'weak unhappy child is perishing for want of some duty to perform upon this earth; some necessary task to keep her busy from day to day' (p. 210). Acknowledging that she is intellectually gifted, though poorly educated, Raymond insistently muses that a domestic existence for Isabel '*is* the best', as '[s]ociety wants commonplace people' and might 'comfortably dispense with those gifted beings, who are perpetually running about with flaring torches men call genius' (p. 83). According to Raymond, the 'highest fate' to which Isabel might aspire is 'to share the home of a simple-hearted country surgeon, and rear his children to be honest men and virtuous women' (p. 82). Raymond does not condemn her to the deviant end of a moral trajectory, as other members of the medical profession condemned the female masturbator, and his course of treatment for her focuses on gentle moral training, marriage, and useful occupation. Significantly, Raymond does not identify Isabel as a masturbator or as a young lady reader addicted to novels, which suggests that Braddon did not intend to argue that female masturbation or novel-reading were dire ailments in desperate need of attention. However, Raymond's treatment is also unsuccessful. As is so typical of Braddon's novels, she broadly critiques the male social circles that sought to diagnose, treat, and control middle-class women in a variety of ways. And, as is also so typical of her work, this critique is playful and gentle, never completely condemning the medical professionals and never completely taking up the part of her imperfect heroine.

At Raymond's urging, then, Isabel marries the country surgeon, George Gilbert, the second medical professional of the novel and a man whom the narrator constructs as Isabel's inferior in all ways but for the possession of wealth. Isabel's motivation for marrying him is evident to everyone except George. He in turn sets out to diagnose and treat Isabel's wayward ways, hoping to mould her into the ideal wife 'by means of that moral flat-iron called common-sense' (p. 116). George's course of treatment for Isabel also includes moral and domestic training. He

> took upon himself to lecture Isabel, on sundry occasions, with regard to her love of novel-reading, her neglect of plain needlework, and her appalling ignorance on the subject of puddings. He turned over her leaves, and found her places in her hymn-book at church [...] and he frowned at her sternly when he caught her eyes wandering to distant bonnets during the sermon. (p. 101)

George's various diagnoses of Isabel at different points in the novel are sorely inadequate and comical in their inaccuracy. Following Isabel's disappointment over the impossibility of a relationship with Roland Lansdell, for instance, George diagnoses her as 'bilious' from having eaten lobster salad (p. 224). The narrator informs us that he 'had not the faintest suspicion of any mental ailment lurking at the root of these physical derangements' (p. 227). Isabel's dreamy spells of disorientation are suggested to be similar to the symptoms of the masturbator, but her unconsummated relationship with Roland Lansdell causes her more intense dissatisfaction. Before her husband's death, Isabel longs for a more satisfying romantic relationship with Roland, but after his death, she is plagued with feelings of guilt and regret because of her neglect of him. Significantly, these circumstances are entirely lost on the scientific figures in the novel. Braddon also teasingly and purposely sets up Isabel's progression from one addiction to another in order to suggest that she will commit adultery, like the frustrated female masturbator of the medical texts. Indeed, *The Doctor's Wife* was a rewrite of *Madame Bovary*, where the dreamy heroine fully indulges in an adulterous relationship and finally commits suicide – significantly – with an overdose of opium. Isabel's namesake in *East Lynne*, though she is less of a dreamer than Braddon's heroine, also succumbs to adulterous temptation in order to escape a life of boredom and neglect, eventually suffering a tragic death. However, Braddon trumps this slippery slope trajectory by presenting a heroine who follows every step of the moral decline, but at the last minute turns down her lover's offer to elope. In fact, Isabel's biggest disappointment is her discovery that Roland's love for her is 'only the vulgar everyday wish to run away with another man's wife' (p. 271). Indeed, *The Spectator* reviewer admired the originality in this turn of events: we 'confess when we came to this incident we expected the ordinary routine, – the silly woman beguiled into elopement with her idol, [but Isabel] makes her weaknesses her preservative'.[46] It is as though Isabel's preference for fantasy over adultery has saved her from the clichéd fate of becoming a runaway wife and fallen woman.

Whereas quack and legitimate medical treatises on masturbation maintain silence on the elements of fantasy, longing and desire involved in female masturbation, *The Doctor's Wife* takes this imaginary, fictional realm as its central subject. Writing in a much less constrained genre, Braddon appropriates some of the ideas and discourses of the medical texts and constructs a vivid, racy picture of how, when, and where women might be tempted to indulge in such fantasy. She also places her depiction of the female fantasist in a wider cultural context, drawing ideas from medical discourses of masturbation as well as other forms of addiction. The convenience of the similarities and interchangeableness of these addictions was not lost on Braddon, as both scientific figures in the novel attempt to assert their power over Isabel by diagnosing and treating her dreamy disorientation. The results are comical in their inaccuracy and this is one of the ways Braddon challenges medical discourses of female sexuality. Most daringly, she writes off all the medical texts' dire warnings about the drastic social consequences of female masturbation, as well as addictions to reading and daydreaming. Her heroine flirts with all of the worst consequences of these practices, but emerges unscathed from her imaginary sexual adventures.

NOTES

1. William Acton, *Functions and Disorders of the Reproductive Organs in Youth, Adult Age and Advanced Life*, 5th ed. (London: Churchill, 1871; first published 1857).

2. George Drysdale, *Elements of Social Science*, 13th ed. (London: Truelove, 1875; first published c. 1854–55).

3. Samuel La'Mert, *Self-Preservation: A Medical Treatise on Nervous and Physical Debility, Spermatorrhoea, Impotence and Sterility*, 64th ed. (London: The author, c. 1854–59; first published 1841). M. Tissot, *A New Guide to Health and Long Life; or, Advice to Families* (London: The translator, 1808). For each of these publications, I have listed the earliest date of publication I can identify. The publication history of each of these works is either very difficult to trace or complicated with multiple editions and printings and, therefore, also difficult to pin down. In some cases, this was probably partly due to the nature of the subject.

4. In Eve Sedgwick's article, 'Jane Austen and the Masturbating Girl', she argues that the anxieties over female masturbation 'contributed more to the emergence of gynecology, through an accumulated expertise in and demand for genital surgery; of such identities as that of the hysteric; and of such confession-inducing disciplinary discourses as psychoanalysis'; see Eve Kosofsky Sedgwick, 'Jane Austen and the Masturbating Girl', in *Solitary Pleasures: The Historical, Literary, and Artistic Discourses of Autoeroticism*, ed. Paula Bennett and Vernon A. Rosario II (London: Routledge, 1995), pp. 133–53 (p. 140). This may have been true of the latter half of the nineteenth century, but in the medical literature of the early decades of the nineteenth century, female masturbation simply was not examined nearly as often as male masturbation, and, more generally, these texts assumed masturbation to be a primarily male ailment. Sedgwick's assessment of Austen's work in this context may therefore be somewhat anachronistic, since it suggests a more linear progression of thought on the issue of female masturbation across the entire nineteenth century than seems likely. This is not to say that female masturbation did not figure in scientific debates; the Isaac Baker Brown clitoridectomy scandal, which reached its height in the year leading up to his expulsion from the Obstetrical Society in 1867, briefly placed female masturbation at the centre of public and medical attention (see Ann Dally, *Women Under the Knife: A History of Surgery* (London: Hutchinson Radius, 1991), pp. 168–80). This article, however, is concerned with medical and quack texts published before these significant events of the late 1860s, events which were likely to have had a large influence on the developments Sedgwick describes in the ensuing years.

5. For a full discussion of the way male sexuality came to be increasingly scrutinized via monitoring or prevention of masturbation, see Ed Cohen, *Talk on the Wilde Side, Toward a Genealogy of a Discourse on Male Sexualities* (London: Routledge, 1993), which deals with male masturbation in virtually all the same texts I discuss in this article with reference to female masturbation. Cohen uses these texts as evidence to argue that 'once they reached puberty (if not even before), middle-class male bodies would be continually subjected to a wide array of institutional gazes that sought to give precise (sexual) meanings to their minute behavioral patterns' (p. 35). In *Solitary Sex, A Cultural History of Masturbation* (New York: ZoneBooks, 2003), Thomas Laqueur substantially deals with the

way in which male masturbation disrupts middle-class capitalist morality and work ethic.

6. Although Laqueur's account is probably somewhat overstated, he presents a similar argument about female masturbation: 'masturbating women made the most perfect onanistic tropes because they literally produced desire and only desire in their solitary reveries. Loss of substance is simply irrelevant'. Laqueur, *Solitary Sex*, p. 203.

7. Mary Elizabeth Braddon, *The Doctor's Wife*, ed. Lynn Pykett (Oxford: Oxford University Press, 1998). Although criticism of *Lady Audley's Secret* (1862) is ample and continues to be produced, work on *The Doctor's Wife* remains scant. Kate Flint, in her massive work *The Woman Reader: 1837–1914* (Oxford: Clarendon Press, 1993, p. 288), has read *The Doctor's Wife* as 'the most sustained investigation of reading in relation to sensation fiction'. Flint reads sensation novels and writing about sensation novels, such as *The Doctor's Wife*, as literary forms that 'invite their readers to join in a process which involves the active construction of meaning, rather than its revelation' (p. 292). For Flint, the 'overall stance of [The Doctor's Wife] is encapsulated in the views of Sigismund Smith', who, as Flint observes, claims that novels are only dangerous for those who mistake their contents for reality (p. 289). Pamela. K. Gilbert, in *Disease, Desire, and the Body in Victorian Women's Popular Novels* (Cambridge, UK: Cambridge University Press, 1997, p. 112) argues that the 'familiar tropes' of *The Doctor's Wife* ('reading as a kind of foreplay; reading as a drug; novels as seducers') are components of a Derrida-esque kind of play where '[t]he novel defines itself by references to the thing that it is supposedly not; in fact it is created out of webs of those referents'. In *Culture and Adultery*, Barbara Leckie continually reiterates that 'the adultery does not happen' (see Barbara Leckie, *Culture and Adultery: The Novel, the Newspaper, and the Law, 1857–1914* (Philadelphia, PA: University of Pennsylvania Press, 1999), p. 142). For Leckie 'Braddon conflates adultery and reading and focuses her considerable narrative energies on an indictment of reading' (p. 142). Leckie also argues, 'Isabel's reading is her greatest crime against the family in *The Doctor's Wife*; it competes with her husband's tedious dinner-table talk and compromises her role as a wife' (p. 147). This reading seems difficult to support, however, when we consider how concerned Braddon was with her position as an author who wrote popular novels for what was often assumed to be a largely female audience.

8. Drysdale, *Elements*, p. 88.

9. La'Mert, *Self-Preservation*, p. 130.

10. La'Mert, *Self-Preservation*, p. 130

11. I have chosen to look at a range of legitimate and quack medical texts that I have been able to confirm as being in circulation at least in the early nineteenth century and preferably in active circulation in the years leading up to the publication of *The Doctor's Wife* in 1864. Based on the holdings of the Wellcome Library, it appears that *Onania* was no longer being printed by the nineteenth century.

12. I have been unable to establish the history of circulation of Tissot's *New Guide to Health and Long Life*, but Thomas Laqueur identifies it as the most famous and widely circulated text on masturbation after *Onania*; see Laqueur, *Solitary Sex*, p. 333. The edition I have used, held at The Wellcome Library, was published in 1808, but I would assume this is not the first edition.

13. Henry Smith, *The Private Medical Friend, or a Warning Voice to Young Men* (Newcastle, UK: The author, 1857). It is difficult to speculate about the first appearance and exact publication history of the La'Mert or the Smith texts. Each was published by the author rather than a known publisher. La'Mert's text claims to be in its 64th edition by the 1850s, while Smith's appears to be in its first edition in 1857. The date associated with La'Mert's publication is taken from the Wellcome Library catalogue. Mason identifies a Henry Smith as one of the 'Holywell Street purveyors of *risqué* works' and editor of the 'semi pornographic weekly the *Exquisite*', and though it seems likely, I can only speculate that this may have been the same person (see Michael Mason, *The Making of Victorian Sexual Attitudes* (Oxford: Oxford University Press, 1994), p. 187).

14. Mason documents that *Elements of Social Science* seems to have first appeared under the title *'Physical, Sexual and Natural Religion'* in 1855, but that later editions suggest that the original publication date was 1854 (see Mason, *Sexual Attitudes*, p. 193). The title *Elements of Social Science* was adopted in 1856 and the book continued to appear in successive editions for the following 50 years, though Drysdale was not named on the title page until 1904 (see Mason, *Sexual Attitudes*, p. 193).

15. Drysdale, *Elements*, p. 88.

16. *Nymphomania* was translated into English by Edward Sloane Wilmot in 1775 (see M. D. T. Bienville, *Nymphomania*, trans. Edward Sloane Wilmot (London: Bew, 1775)). Again, as in the case of Tissot's *New Guide to Health and Long Life*, it is likely that earlier editions were in circulation, particularly since a reading knowledge of French would not have been unusual for the literate in the eighteenth century.

17. Laqueur, *Solitary Sex*, p. 333.

18. Laqueur, *Solitary Sex*, p. 336.

19. Laqueur, *Solitary Sex*, p. 340.

20. Laqueur, *Solitary Sex*, p. 341.

21. Acton, *Functions*, p. 115.

22. Acton, *Functions*, p. 118.

23. Acton, *Functions*, p. 119.

24. Acton, *Functions*, p. 119.

25. Drysdale, *Elements*, p. 87.

26. Drysdale, *Elements*, p. 91.

27. Drysdale, *Elements*, p. 90.

28. 'Reports of Societies'. [Harveian Society of London, 5 Mar 1868.] *The British Medical Journal* (18 April 1868): 386–90 (387).

29. Smith, *The Private Medical Friend*, p. 48. S. Pancoast, author of the American work *The Ladies' Medical Guide* (Philadelphia, PA: Potter, c.1875) also argues that women are not as susceptible to the pressures of sexual desire: 'In general, they bear more easily both the excesses and privations of sexual love; yet, when these privations are not voluntary on their part, they have generally for women, especially those who are solitary and unemployed, inconveniences and miseries unknown to the nature of man' (pp. 231–32). Pancoast argues that it is these women who are susceptible to masturbation and will suffer a 'languid existence', 'prey to hysteric and nervous affections' (p. 232).

30. La'Mert, *Self-Preservation*, p. 107.

31. A number of historians have noted that the practice of masturbation was often assumed to lead to sexual exploration with members of the same sex. See Laqueur,

Solitary Sex; see also Jean Stengers and Anne Van Neck, *Masturbation: The History of a Great Terror,* trans. Kathryn A. Hoffman (Basingstoke, UK: Palgrave, 2001).

32. La'Mert, *Self-Preservation,* p. 66.
33. La'Mert, *Self-Preservation,* p. 66.
34. Tissot, *New Guide to Health and Long Life,* p. 50.
35. Alan Hunt also argues that masturbation occupies 'a problematic location between heterosexuality and homosexuality' (see 'The Great Masturbation Panic and the Discourses of Moral Regulation in Nineteenth- and Early Twentieth-Century Britain', *Journal of the History of Sexuality,* 8.4 (1998): 575–615 (587)). Ellen Bayuk Rosenman claims that the spermatorrhea debates that many of these texts took part in were actually a 'kind of alias for homoerotic activity' (see Ellen Bayuk Rosenman, 'Body Doubles: The Spermatorrhea Panic', *Journal of the History of Sexuality,* 12.3 (2003): 365–99 (398)).
36. Tissot, *New Guide to Health and Long Life,* pp. 50–51.
37. La'Mert, *Self-Preservation,* p. 107.
38. Laqueur, *Solitary Sex,* p. 333.
39. For a more detailed discussion of the debates in *The Lancet,* see Ellen Bayuk Rosenman's article 'Body Doubles'.
40. Rosenman, 'Body Doubles', p. 340.
41. This Act required that patent preparations of laudanum be labelled as poisons. Therefore this was not considered a particularly meaningful victory for surgeons or physicians.
42. See, for example, 'A Case of Opium Poisoning', *The Lancet* (4 February 1871): 164; William Cochran, 'Horrors of Opium: Part 1', *The Food Journal,* 4.37 (1874): 2–6; Alexander Fleming, 'Clinical Lecture on the Treatment of the Habit of Opium Eating', *The British Medical Journal* (15 February 1868): 137–39.
43. Henry Mansel, 'Sensation Novels', *Quarterly Review,* 113 (1863): 481–514 (486).
44. Anon, 'Miss Braddon's New Novel', *The Spectator* (22 October 1864): 1214–15 (1215).
45. Anon, 'Miss Braddon's New Novel', p. 1214.
46. Anon, 'Miss Braddon's New Novel', p. 1215.

11

Mrs Robinson's 'Day-book of Iniquity': Reading Bodies of/and Evidence in the Context of the 1858 Medical Reform Act

JANICE M. ALLAN

Through the summer months of 1858, the newspaper-reading public was both shocked and tantalized by the ubiquitous and detailed reporting of the Robinson v. Robinson and Lane divorce case. Despite the fact that this case was deemed, by the Lord Chief Justice no less, to be nothing short of 'remarkable in its character and circumstances',[1] few modern readers appear aware of its existence, let alone its import. Thus this chapter is, in part, an act of essential recuperation. For as was recognized, even at the time, the Robinson divorce case involved 'large social interests [...] which have a much wider range than the petty and personal issues among the individuals immediately implicated or concerned'.[2] Coming before the public at a pivotal moment in the professionalization of medicine – the passing of the 1858 Medical Reform Act – the case directed the nation's attention towards a singularly important encounter between physician and patient. As we shall see, the 'large social interests' arising from this seemingly 'petty and personal' encounter involved nothing less than the collective authority and status of the medical profession.

Opening their copy of *The Times* on 15 June 1858, readers encountered the following narrative about the marriage and divorce of Mr and Mrs Robinson. The petitioner, Mr Henry Robinson, a civil engineer, married the respondent, Isabella Elizabeth Robinson, then a widow with an independent income, in 1844. For more than a dozen years they seemed, to all outward appearances, to be a respectable, if not altogether happy, married couple. In 1857, however, Mrs Robinson became ill and, as was reported in *The Daily News*, 'in consequence of some hints which she let fall while she was in a delirious state her husband took possession of her diary'.[3] Like the latest novel from Mudie's, the diary extended to the requisite three volumes and covered a period of five years between 1850 and 1855. Among the entries for 1854 were certain passages that appeared to suggest that the author had engaged in an adulterous affair with a trusted family friend, Dr Edward Lane. Lane was the proprietor of a well-known hydropathic establishment and a respected young physician who had married into the peerage and counted Charles Darwin among his patients. Armed with his wife's diary and evidence obtained from one of Lane's groomsmen, Mr Robinson initiated, in December 1857, a successful suit for a divorce *à menso et thoro* (a divorce from bed and board) through the Ecclesiastical Courts. Not satisfied with this half-measure, he then initiated proceedings for an absolute divorce (divorce *à vinculo*) in the new civil Divorce Court that opened in January 1858.

As many readers are doubtless aware, the steady flow of information from the Divorce Court to the dining table – via the daily papers – literally brought home the alleged infidelities of English wives. What distinguished the Robinson case from myriad others was, in the words of Darwin himself, 'the unparalleled fact of a woman detailing her own adultery'.[4] The case was rendered even more remarkable when, the groom's testimony quickly discredited, the diary became the sole evidence on which the Court could base its decision. While condemning it as 'a confession of filth' and 'a day-book of iniquity',[5] the papers reprinted its contents, verbatim and at length, for all their readers to peruse.[6] Brought before the public as a body of evidence and as evidence of female bodily passion, Mrs Robinson's diary became the site of conflicting legal, medical and moral readings that pitted the word of a sexual woman against that of her respected physician.

Although these two constructions of the diary are related, I will treat them separately, starting with the diary as evidence of a woman's bodily passions and desires. Consider the following entries introduced by the Council for the petitioner:

> *7th (October, Moor Park).–* [H]e led me away and alone to our favourite haunts, taking a wider range and a more secluded path. At last I asked to rest, and we sat on plaid and read 'Athenaeums', chatting meanwhile. *There was something unusual in his manner, something softer than usual in his tone and eye; but I knew not what it proceeded from, and chatted gaily*, leading the conversation in talking of Goethe, of women's dress, and of what was becoming or suitable. We walked on and again seated ourselves in a glade of surpassing beauty. The sun shone warmly down upon us; the fern, yellow and brown, was stretched away beneath us; fine old trees in groups adorned the near ground; and far away gleamed the blue hills. *I gave myself up to enjoyment; I leaned back against some firm dry heather bushes, and laughed and remarked as I rarely did in that presence. All at once, just as I was joking my companion on his want of memory, he leaned over me and exclaimed, 'If*

*you say that again, I will kiss you'. You may believe I made no opposition, for
had I not dreamed of him and of this full many a time before. What followed,
I hardly remember; – passionate kisses, whispered words, confessions of the past.
Oh, God! I had never hoped to see this hour, or to have my part of love returned!
Yet so it was. He was nervous, and confused, and eager as myself. At last we
roused ourselves and walked on; happy, fearful, almost silent, we sauntered, not
heeding where, to a grove of pines, and there looked over another view beautiful
as that on this side, but wilder. In descending, we had seen the Browns, and now
thought it necessary slowly to join them. They had observed nothing; we were
safe. Constraining ourselves to converse, we succeeded in disarming all suspicion,
and reached the house together, but late for dinner.*[7]

10th. – *We drove off, Alfred [Mrs Robinson's son] soon taking place on the
box. I never spent so blessed an hour as the one that followed, full of such bliss
that I could willingly have died not to wake out of it again …. I remembered
him of my lines from 'Paul and Virginia', and owned they were addressed to
him. I shall not relate ALL that passed; suffice it to say that I leaned back
at last in silent joy in those arms I had so often dreamed of, and kissed the
curls and smooth face so radiant with beauty that had dazzled my outward
and inward vision since the first interview, 15th November, 1850. He had
always known I had liked him, but not the full extent of the feeling, and
owned it had never been indelicately expressed; this relieved me. Heaven
itself could not be more blessed than those moments; while life itself shall
endure their remembrance will not pass away from a memory charged with
much suffering and little bliss; how gentle, how gentlemanly he was – how
little selfish!*[8]

14th (*Ditto*). – [T]he Dr after talking some little time appeared to return
to his former kind feeling for me, caressed and tempted me, and finally,
after some delay, we adjourned to the next room *and spent a quarter of
an hour in blissful excitement.* I became nearly helpless with the effects of
his presence and could hardly let him depart, *wept when he bade me try
to obviate consequences,* and finally bade him a passionate farewell. I was
alone, passion wasted, and sorrowful, sleep was far from me that night;
I tossed and dreamed and burned till morning, too weary and weak to
rise.[9]

Elsewhere in the diary, its author complains of the 'preponderance of
amativeness' in her own character,[10] and confesses to finding it 'impossible
to love where I ought, or to keep from loving where I ought not'.[11]

As entries such as these made all too clear to the nation's readers, Mrs
Robinson was driven by sexual desires well in excess of those attributed to
a 'normal' middle-class woman.[12] She appeared, moreover, to derive great
and unapologetic pleasure from her intimate physical encounters with Lane.
Anticipating the sensational heroines of the following decade, she represents

herself as one of a new breed of women who, according to Margaret Oliphant, 'give and receive burning kisses and frantic embraces, and live in a voluptuous dream, either waiting for or brooding over the inevitable love'.[13] Thus it is hardly surprising that the diary was seen to embody and, through its publication, unleash an unruly, transgressive – and hence dangerous – female sexuality. Confronted by such a threat, journalists, lawyers, and doctors joined forces to contain and defuse it by effectively rewriting desire as disease.[14]

It was Mrs Robinson's own defence counsel who took the lead in this process of reconstruction. Appearing for the respondent, Dr Phillimore, QC, stated in his opening address: 'He should contend that the passages relied on for the petitioner were written under the influence of a uterine disease, which had the effect of producing the most extraordinary delusions in the mind of the patient, and frequently caused them to accuse themselves of crimes of the most horrible kind'.[15] To sustain this proposition, Phillimore called first upon Dr Joseph Kidd, Mrs Robinson's medical attendant, who testified that he had previously treated her for a 'disease of the womb'.[16] Phillimore then examined three further medical experts: Dr Forbes Winslow, Sir Charles Locock and Dr James Henry Bennet. As the question of a doctor's professional status and reputation is at the heart of this case, it is worth noting that Winslow was considered one of the pre-eminent alienists of his time, while Locock was physician-accoucheur to the Queen. A well-established London obstetrician, Dr Bennet had also achieved considerable fame as an advocate for the use of the speculum in gynaecological examinations.

Although the exact details of their testimony are not available – as it was universally deemed 'not of a fit nature for a detailed report'[17] – we do know that these witnesses considered, in addition to the possibility of uterine disease, the role of both nymphomania and erotomania in 'producing extraordinary delusions in the mind of the patient'. Indeed, 'instances were mentioned by them of ladies, while affected by one or other of the[se conditions], accusing themselves, without the slightest foundation, of the most flagrant acts of unchastity'.[18] As part of his own defence, an issue considered below, Dr Lane argued that Mrs Robinson 'had been labouring under a disease peculiar to women' and, more precisely, menopause.[19]

One might think that the sheer vagueness of this medical testimony (the use of the catch-all term 'uterine disease') and the lack of consistency in diagnosis (was Mrs Robinson suffering from nymphomania (a physical condition), erotomania (a psychological condition), or simply going through the menopause?) would undermine its credibility. Dr Kidd, for example, was 'not prepared to state that [Mrs Robinson] ha[d] suffered from "nymphomania" or "erotomania"',[20] while Edward Tilt, author of *The Change of Life* (the only full-length contemporary monograph devoted to the subject of the menopause) insisted that erotomania 'is very rare at the change of life'.[21] What we must recognize, however, is that any gaps or inconsistencies in this testimony were more than compensated for by the prevailing belief in its single underlying assumption that all women were, from puberty through menopause, ruled and governed by a 'uterine economy'.[22] According to the logic of this economy, there was an irresistible connection between a woman's reproductive organs and the rest of her body, including her brain and nervous system. In the words of John Millingen, woman 'is less under the influence of the brain than the uterine system, the plexi of abdominal nerves, and irritation of the spinal cord'.[23] Charles Meigs, in turn, asks his fellow physicians to consider 'whether such an organ can be of little influence in the constitution of the woman; whether *she* was not made in order that *it* should be made, and whether it may not on occasion become a disturbing radiator in her economy'.[24] As such it was widely, if not universally, believed that any disturbance or irritation of the uterine functions, especially the catamenia, might result in a corresponding disturbance in mental health.[25] We need look no further than Mrs Robinson's own medical experts for a salient example of this logic at work. Commenting on the effects of uterine inflammation on the brain, Dr Bennet argues in his study of the subject that:

> The aberration of the mind often follows a uterine direction, and a previously modest and moral female will depart strangely from the tenor of her previous life, both in words and actions. Such, however, is not always the case. I have known homicidal and suicidal mania, melancholy, hallucinations of the senses and delusions, evidently to originate in this cause, as proved by the complete restoration of the mind following the cure of the uterine disease. It is worthy of remark, that the period of the cessation of the menses in females is a critical one in this sense. I have repeatedly known the reason to give way under the combined influence of the meno-pause and of uterine disease.[26]

Within the court room, the weight and authority of such beliefs carried the day and Mrs Robinson's diary was discredited as 'the insane delusions of a diseased mind'.[27]

It is worth noting that none of the three medical experts ever met or examined Mrs Robinson; rather, their diagnoses were based solely on the reading of her diary, which, in the words of *The Saturday Review*, 'stands self-convicted of insanity'.[28] Even Dr Kidd, who treated Mrs Robinson for seven years, was forced to admit, under cross-examination, that 'he only drew the inference that she had been suffering under that malady after reading the passages in the journal'.[29] This unquestioning conflation of Mrs Robinson's body with Mrs Robinson's text – the former put into public circulation through the latter – is, in itself, evidence of how, during this period, 'the balance of power shifted away from the patient and towards the doctor' as medicine became increasingly 'object-' rather than 'person-oriented'.[30] At the same time, the strategic reduction of Mrs Robinson from sexual subject to pathologized object effectively normalized this shift by constructing the female as an inherently unstable body in need of expert interpretation and superintendence.

In one of the few modern critical readings of the case, Barbara Leckie argues that 'despite her age [...] Mrs Robinson becomes a case study [...] of the vulnerable "young" woman [as j]ournalists, legal professionals, and doctors alike participate in a mass diagnosis that reads Mrs Robinson's account of her adultery as an illness specific to women'.[31] While this is certainly true when the diary is considered as evidence of bodily passion, a very different picture emerges when we consider it as a body of evidence and, more specifically, a body of evidence against Dr Lane. Consider the following editorial comments from *The Daily News*:

> [Mrs Robinson] filled her diary with raving entries which, if taken literally (an absurd process to apply to such emanations of frenzy), undoubtedly seemed compatible with no other theory than that she had at last persecuted Dr Lane into consenting to the gratifications of her passions. [....] *Now comes the important part of the case.* This diary – these self-accusations of this romantic woman – these incoherent rhapsodies in which she had gratified a loose imagination by substituting dreams for realities – formed literally all the evidence against Dr Lane. [....] The court was asked to ruin the rising prospects of this young and meritorious man, – to wreck the home, and brand the name, and poison the existence of this affectionate husband – solely because a crazy woman, not far off fifty, had chosen to fall in love with him.[32]

In much the same way, *The Times* asserts that it is 'somewhat hard upon a respectable, hard-working professional man to be travestied into an Abelard without any fault of his own. [...] Dr Lane's position is a most painful and a most trying one. He has been dragged before the public in a way that is calculated to ruin his professional prospects'.[33] Finally, *The Saturday Review* complains that Mrs Robinson 'selects for her literary paramour a young and married gentleman to whom she owed the confidence, and who gave her the confidence, of his profession. She selects her physician as the partner of her impenitent transgressions, and he is bearing the terrible consequences of her skill in the art of depicting the circumstances of an ideal adultery'.[34]

Seen in these terms, Mrs Robinson is anything but a 'vulnerable "young" woman'. Indeed, this is the role assumed by Dr Lane, her 'persecuted' and hapless victim who, like the proverbial fly, is unable to 'break through the extraordinary web which the fancy of Mrs Robinson has woven around him'.[35] Nor is it without significance that Mrs Robinson is consistently compared to a range of male writers, including Pope, Shelley, and, most tellingly, Rousseau. In the wake of the 1857 Obscene Publications Act, such comparisons received an additional charge. Significantly, *The Saturday Review* deemed the diary to be 'perhaps as filthy [a] composition as ever proceeded from any human pen' (note the use of the word 'human' rather than 'female') and explicitly likened it to the pornographic wares of Holywell Street.[36] Closely echoing Lord Campbell's rationale for the Obscene Publications Act, this article then proceeded to describe the diary as 'one of those unspeakably filthy curiosities which it is the duty of any one who is so unfortunate as to find them to put and to keep out of the way of those who are likely to be injured by them'.[37] As the individual most directly injured by the diary, Dr Lane is implicitly aligned to that group of vulnerable bodies whom the Act was designed to protect: women, children, and the feeble-minded. Conversely, the power of corruption attributed to Mrs Robinson, as the author of the diary, is decidedly gendered as masculine. Considered as a body of evidence, it thus appears that Mrs Robinson's diary inverts the accepted organization and distribution of power, not simply between men and women but, more crucially, between a doctor and his patient.

Building on the work of Michel Foucault, Roberta McGarth has argued that the nineteenth century witnessed a profound shift in the doctor/patient relationship as 'listening *to*, a reciprocal process of giving and taking meaning, was replaced by looking *at*, in which the object to be known is cut off from the knowing subject'.[38] This process, she continues, reflects a new epistemological paradigm concerned with 'power, transcendence and control':

> Knowledge is masterful, powerful and punishing: it interrogates, penetrates, extends, creates. It is not a knowledge born of love, but a defensive knowledge born of fear. It is a means not to comprehend or understand the world but to control its meanings and master its material. It is, in short, a discourse of domination.[39]

To extend this argument one step further, I would suggest that the most apposite symbol of how this new conception of knowledge and/as power was exercised within the specifically gendered encounter between female patient and male physician was the speculum. Indeed for those who, like Humphry Davy, viewed the man of science as one who interrogated nature 'not simply as a scholar, passive and seeking only to understand her operations, but rather as a master, active with his own instruments',[40] the speculum might be said to represent the acme of a 'penetrative gaze' that simultaneously enacted and extended the power of a male physician over his female patient.[41]

Within the inverted relationship under consideration, however, it was Mrs Robinson rather than Dr Lane who was in possession of the instrument of power: the diary itself. In its effects, moreover, this diary bears more than a passing resemblance to the speculum. If examination by speculum involved 'the exposure and instrumental penetration of parts that were defined as "private" and, moreover, permanently damaged the integrity of those subjected to its use',[42] so too did examination by Mrs Robinson's diary. Like the prostitutes of continental Europe, Dr Lane had been 'dragged before the public', his private life and intimate relationships exposed to the shame and degradation of a public examination.[43] And while the *British Medical Journal* remained confident that 'the public will acquit him', they still 'question[ed] very much if his prospects [...] will not suffer in consequence'.[44]

If such an analogy appears exaggerated, I would argue that it is more than justified by the immediate context of the case: specifically the fraught atmosphere associated with the Medical Reform Act.[45] By establishing the General Medical Council to oversee standards of medical education and professional conduct, as well as the Medical Register, this Act was designed to draw clear and unequivocal boundaries between legitimate qualified practitioners and unqualified 'quacks'. In so doing, it can be read as an attempt to cement the public reputation and public standing of the profession as a whole.[46] Within this particular climate, it should not come as a surprise that, for some, the 'large social interests' on trial in the Robinson case centred upon a woman's ability to impeach the authority and reputation of her doctor. According to the *British Medical Journal*, for example, the case 'affords an extraordinary example of the dangers to which medical men above all others are exposed'.[47] Indeed, so significant was the 'danger' posed by this woman's accusations that professional squabbles were cast aside in order to concentrate on protecting the reputation and elite status of the profession as a whole:

> Of course we cannot be expected to sympathise with hydropaths particularly, but his case may be our own any day. Any of our associates with 'curls and smooth face', and less favoured ones, for that matter, may some day find themselves plunged from domestic happiness and pecuniary prosperity into utter ruin, unless the public sympathy is unmistakably shown in order to support them whist undergoing such an ordeal.[48]

A writer for *The Times* was less partisan, arguing that 'the case might happen to any of us. We really know of no reason why Mrs Robinson should not have selected the Archbishop of Canterbury [...] as the hero of her romance'. As this writer goes on to suggest:

It is a mere question of credibility on either side. Now, in the present instance, every particular of Dr Lane's position, both socially and professionally, is calculated to negative the hypothesis of improper conduct on his part. On the other hand, every act of Mrs Robinson's leaves us nothing but the choice between two conclusions, – either she is as foul and abandoned a creature as ever wore woman's shape, or she is mad. In either case her testimony is worthless.[49]

The 'question of credibility' was, however, rendered problematic by the fact that Dr Lane was debarred from taking the stand in his own defence.[50] Unable to exhibit and exercise the authority of his profession and gender, he was reduced to a passive and implicitly feminized object to be looked *at* rather than listened *to*. As the first step towards reinstating Lane as an active and professional 'knowing subject', it was imperative that he be enabled to testify and Lane's counsel insisted that he be dismissed from the suit in order to qualify as a witness. In seeming recognition of all that was at stake, the case was adjourned to allow an Act of Parliament to be passed that would allow the Court to dismiss any respondent or co-respondent from a suit, 'if it shall think there is not sufficient evidence against him or her'.[51] Significantly, no consideration was ever given to dismissing Mrs Robinson.

When the case was reconvened on 26 November 1858, Dr Lane was duly dismissed from the suit. The impact on his professional standing was immediate and twofold. In the first place, his dismissal entailed a complete rejection of Mrs Robinson's diary as evidence against him. This decision sent out an unequivocal message about a woman's right to imperil the reputation of her doctor. At the same time, Lane's dismissal granted him, at long last, the 'opportunity of vindicating his character, a character doubly valuable to him as a professional man'.[52] Taking the stand, he stated simply: 'I have seen the statements in the diaries. They are utterly and absolutely false – a tissue of romances from beginning to end'.[53] The importance of this testimony, which constituted little more than a simple denial, lay in its expression of knowledge and/as power: it was 'a means not to comprehend or understand the world but to control its meanings and master its material'.[54] In performing his authority, the traditional distribution of power was restored. Needless to say, Dr Lane was not cross-examined.

Lane's acquittal resulted in an unprecedented legal anomaly. As Mrs Robinson's counsel pointed out to the Court: 'Dr Lane had now been acquitted of the charge of adultery, and, notwithstanding that acquittal, it must be contended on the other side that Mr Robinson was entitled to a divorce on the ground of his wife's adultery with Dr Lane'. Astonishingly, Sir Cresswell dismissed this most fundamental of solecisms as 'merely a technical matter'.[55]

Thus it appears that the status of Mrs Robinson's diary was entirely dependent upon the person to whom it was directed as a body of evidence. Significantly, once the case against Lane had been quashed, the Court went as far as to question the evidence of the medical experts; in the words of the Lord Chief Justice, they could find 'nothing in this case which would warrant us in concluding that the scenes narrated by Mrs Robinson were the delusions of a disordered mind'.[56] In the end, the judgement came to rest, not on the state of Mrs Robinson's mind and nerves, but upon the absence of any 'clear and unequivocal admission of adultery having taken place'.[57] The case for the petitioner was dismissed and so ended the case of *Robinson v. Robinson and Lane*. Writing from Moor Park in February 1859, Darwin interrupted his work on *The Origin of Species* to inform a correspondent that 'we are a very pleasant party here and very comfortable and I am glad to say that not one of Dr Lane's patients has given him up & he gets a few fresh ones pretty regularly'.[58] What happened to Mrs Robinson and her diary is unknown.

NOTES

1. 'Court for Divorce and Matrimonial Causes', *The Times* (3 March 1859): 10.
2. 'Ladies' Letters and Ladies' Confessions', *The Saturday Review* (26 June 1858): 655–56 (655).
3. 'Court for Divorce and Matrimonial Causes', *The Daily News* (27 November 1858): 6–7 (6).
4. Cited in Ralph Colp, Jr., 'Charles Darwin, Dr Edward Lane, and the "Singular Trial" of *Robinson v. Robinson and Lane*', *Journal of the History of Medicine and Allied Sciences*, 36.2 (1981): 205–13 (205). Darwin's comment reflects the contemporary belief that women were endowed with a more highly developed sense of modesty than men. Consider the following, particularly apt, comment by James Foster: '[God], I say, in the case of the woman, has been pleased to implant, and temper with her very constitution, an ingenuous modesty, that is shocked at the thought of all indecent freedoms and gross impurities; [...] And from this root it is, that she feels more bitter agonies of confusion and remorse, in the first prospect of being publicly exposed, than are generally found to spring either from the principle of honour, or the passion of shame, in men' (*The Duties of the Married State* (London: Frederick Lover, and Ward and Co, 1843), pp. 74–75).
5. Untitled report, *The Times* (6 July 1858): 8–9 (8).
6. In this respect the Robinson case is reminiscent of the 1857 trial of Madeleine Smith for the murder of her lover Emile L'Angelier. Accused of administering a dose of arsenic in his cocoa, Madeleine's letters to the victim formed the crux of the prosecution's case and although they were, like Mrs Robinson's diary, deemed unfit for publication, they were still widely reprinted. Together with the Yelverton bigamy trial, these two cases suggest that at mid-century, female authorial and female erotic agency were seen to go hand in hand. For a discussion of this issue, see Ellen Bayuk Rosenman, *Unauthorized Pleasures: Accounts of Victorian Erotic Experience* (Ithaca, NY, and London: Cornell University Press, 2003), pp. 124–66.
7. M. C. Swabey and Thomas Tristram Hutchinson, *Reports of Cases Decided in*

the Court of Probate and the Court for Divorce and Matrimonial Causes (London: Butterworths, 1860), pp. 374–75. Italics appear in the original and were used to designate passages that Mr Robinson's counsel felt to be particularly germane to his case.

8. Swabey and Hutchinson, *Reports*, p. 376.
9. Swabey and Hutchinson, *Reports*, p. 378.
10. 'A Married Woman's Diary: Extraordinary Case in the Divorce Court', *Liverpool Mercury* (18 June 1858), n. pag.
11. Swabey and Hutchinson, *Reports*, p. 367.
12. Most readers are familiar with William Acton's often quoted assertion that 'the majority of women (happily for them) are not very much troubled with sexual feeling of any kind'. *The Functions and Disorders of the Reproductive Organs*, 1857, 3rd ed. (London: John Churchill, 1862), p. 101.
13. Margaret Oliphant, 'Novels', *Blackwood's Edinburgh Magazine*, 102 (September 1867): 257–80 (259).
14. For a discussion of this strategy, see Pamela K. Gilbert, *Disease, Desire and the Body in Victorian Women's Popular Novels* (Cambridge, UK: Cambridge University Press, 1997).
15. Swabey and Hutchinson, *Reports*, p. 381.
16. 'A Married Woman's Diary', *Liverpool Mercury*, n. pag.
17. 'Court for Divorce and Matrimonial Causes', *The Times* (16 June 1858): 11.
18. Swabey and Hutchinson, *Reports*, p. 382.
19. 'Court for Divorce and Matrimonial Causes', *The Times* (27 November 1858): 10–11 (11).
20. Swabey and Hutchinson, *Reports*, p. 382.
21. Edward J. Tilt, *The Change of Life, in Health and Disease*, 1857, 4th ed. (Philadelphia, PA: P. Blakiston, Son & Co., 1882), p. 125.
22. Sally Shuttleworth, 'Female Circulation: Medical Discourse and Popular Advertising in the Mid-Victorian Era', *Body/Politics: Women and the Discourses of Science*, ed. Mary Jacobus, Evelyn Fox Keller and Sally Shuttleworth (London: Routledge, 1989), pp. 47–68 (p. 64).
23. John Gideon Millingen, *The Passions: or, Mind and Matter*, 2nd ed. (London: John and Daniel A. Darling, 1848), p. 157.
24. Charles Delucena Meigs, *Woman; Her Diseases and Remedies: A Series of Letters to His Class*, 1850, 2nd ed. (Philadelphia, PA: Lea and Blanchard, 1851), p. 58.
25. For a recent discussion of the relationship between uterine functions and mental health, see Andrew Mangham, *Violent Women and Sensation Fiction: Crime, Medicine and Victorian Popular Culture* (Houndsmill, Basingstoke, UK: Palgrave Macmillan, 2007).
26. James Henry Bennet, *A Practical Treatise on Inflammation of the Uterus, its Cervix, & Appendages, and on its Connexion with Uterine Disease*, 1845, 3rd ed. (London: John Churchill, 1852), p. 112.
27. Swabey and Hutchinson, *Reports*, p. 397.
28. 'Ladies' Letters', p. 656.
29. 'Court for Divorce and Matrimonial Causes', *The Times* (27 November 1858): 10–11 (11).
30. Ivan Waddington, *The Medical Profession in the Industrial Revolution* (Dublin: Gill and Macmillan, 1984), pp. 199, 224.

31. Barbara Leckie, *Culture and Adultery: The Novel, the Newspaper, and the Law 1857–1914* (Philadelphia, PA: University of Pennsylvania Press, 1999), p. 56.

32. Untitled report, *The Daily News* (23 June 1858): 4–5 (5). My italics.

33. Untitled report, *The Times* (6 July 1858): 8–9 (8). Claims that female patients sought sexual or amatory gratification from medical examination were not uncommon and played a prominent role in both the chloroform and the speculum debates of mid-century. See Mary Poovey, *Uneven Developments: The Ideological Work of Gender in Mid-Victorian England* (Chicago, Ill: The University of Chicago Press, 1988), pp. 24–50; and Ornella Moscucci, *The Science of Woman: Gynaecology and Gender in England 1800–1929* (Cambridge, UK: Cambridge University Press, 1993), pp. 112–27.

34. 'Ladies' Letters', p. 656.

35. 'Robinson v. Robinson and Lane', *British Medical Journal*, 1.80 (10 July 1858): 561–62 (561).

36. 'The Purity of the Press', *The Saturday Review* (26 June 1858): 656–57 (657).

37. 'Purity', p. 657.

38. Roberta McGrath, *Seeing Her Sex: Medical Archives and the Female Body* (Manchester, UK: Manchester University Press, 2002), p. 11.

39. McGrath, *Seeing Her Sex*, p. 12.

40. Cited in McGrath, *Seeing Her Sex*, p. 12.

41. For a discussion of the 'penetrative gaze' and its role in policing (same sex) desire, see Max Fincher, *Queering the Gothic in the Romantic Age: The Penetrating Eye* (Houndsmill, Basingstoke, UK: Palgrave Macmillan, 2007).

42. Moscucci, *The Science of Woman*, p. 114.

43. Charged descriptions of the public examinations that took place in continental Europe formed part of the arsenal adopted by opponents of the speculum. Robert Lee, for example, describes how Parisian prostitutes were compelled by the police to attend examinations: '[O]ne by one in succession they took their places upon their backs, with their knees drawn up and separated, on a kind of bed or table, [...] had the speculum introduced into the vagina, and the parts publicly explored by the medical officers of the institution before students and strangers from foreign countries'. 'On the Use of the Speculum in the Diagnosis and Treatment of Uterine Disease', *Medico-Chirurgical Transactions*, 33 (1850): 261–78 (265).

44. 'Robinson v. Robinson and Lane', p. 561.

45. Cowper's Bill, first introduced in March 1858, came before the Commons and the Lords in July before finally receiving Royal Assent on 2 August 1858. For a discussion of the complex history of the Act, see Waddington, *The Medical Profession*, pp. 96–132.

46. In the words of Dr Isaac Ashe, author of *Medical Education and Medical Interests* (1868), 'the question is evidently not in what light do we look upon ourselves or upon each other but in what light are we looked upon by the external world'. Cited in Noel Parry and José Parry, *The Rise of the Medical Profession: A Study of Collective Social Mobility* (London: Croom Helm, 1976), p. 132.

47. 'Robinson v. Robinson and Lane', p. 561.

48. 'Robinson v. Robinson and Lane', p. 561.

49. Untitled report, *The Times* (6 July 1858): 8–9 (8).

50. Parties to a suit initiated in consequence of adultery were not deemed to be competent witnesses and hence were not allowed to speak in their own defence.

51. Swabey and Hutchinson, *Reports*, p. 388.
52. Untitled report, *The Daily News* (23 June 1858): 4–5 (5).
53. 'Court for Divorce and Matrimonial Causes', *The Times* (27 November 1858): 10–11 (11).
54. McGrath, *Seeing Her Sex*, p. 12.
55. 'Court for Divorce and Matrimonial Causes', *The Times* (27 November 1858): 10–11 (11).
56. Swabey and Hutchinson, *Reports*, p. 397. Reporting on the outcome of the case, *The Journal of Psychological Medicine and Mental Health*, edited by Winslow himself, questioned 'by what process his lordship can satisfy himself respecting the soundness of the medical dicta he has laid down, and yet reject the highest medical testimony'. 'Robinson v. Robinson and Lane', *The Journal of Psychological Medicine and Mental Health*, 12 (1 January 1859): xxvi–xxviii (xxviii).
57. Swabey and Hutchinson, *Reports*, p. 398.
58. Cited in Colp, 'Singular Trial', p. 213.

12

Rebecca's Womb:
Irony and Gynaecology in
Rebecca

MADELEINE K. DAVIES

Daphne du Maurier's *Rebecca* (1938) radiates contempt for most 'types' and for both sexes, but it seems to reserve particularly harsh judgement for women. Like its literary antecedent *Jane Eyre*, the fairytale heroine triumphs at the expense of every other woman in the novel.[1] These women are at best caricatured and at worst condemned, often aligned with sinister, perverse connotation. From the loathsome vulgarian Mrs Van Hopper to the hideous Mrs Danvers, female presence is regarded in this novel as a threat, a dangerous encounter requiring ruthless counter-tactics and survival strategies. In no character is this dangerous horror surrounding femaleness more acutely realized than in the snake-like, subversive Rebecca, and her danger is echoed in nuanced terms in the voice of the storytelling narrator herself.[2]

The question is, though, why would a female novelist write women in this way? So frequently dismissed as a Gothic 'romance', that death knell to literary pretension in women's writing, *Rebecca* is, as feminist critics have been constantly aware, a rather more complex affair in its occupation of liminal territories relating to psycho-sexual desire and patriarchal relationships, and in its narrative tactics that call into question issues of subjectivity, identity, and readerly tactics. Less emphasized in critical discussion, but no less crucial to this text's meaning, is the comment passed within it on an old order in its death throes. Written in 1938 on the eve of war, but set in 1931, *Rebecca* is a 'memory text' that expresses nostalgia for a world of class privilege, excess, and splendour, but that also celebrates its demise. In this sense, the Manderley estate is a 'monument' to a past recalled, but its foundation is insecure and the beautiful façade is fissured by flawed masculinist values, acts of bad faith, and shabby moral corruption. This less discussed current in *Rebecca* is, this essay argues, fundamentally implicated in the expression of misogynistic animus that chiefly concerns the debate here, since it is central to the ironic conversion of the female body into a site of dis/ease, and into a carrier of ideological meaning, and in coded signification gathering around questions of 'transgressive' sexual desire. In drawing the female body, and specifically the womb, into a metaphorical relationship with property as a symbol of patriarchal inheritance, *Rebecca* invites interrogation of a range of encoded meanings generated by traditional literary, medical, and cultural models.

As Judith Fetterley observes, female readers are used to a world view demonizing femaleness from their reading of canonical male-authored texts: in such texts, 'as readers and teachers and scholars, women are taught to think as men, to identify with a male point of view, and to accept as normal and legitimate a male system of values, one of whose central principles is misogyny'.[3] Certainly, *Rebecca* quite deliberately offers its readers ample opportunity to 'construct oppositional narrative positions within the text from which to challenge its dominant values and gender assumptions', but the question of how these 'values' and 'assumptions' are generated (together with the question of authorial motive) remains crucial and, I would argue, proves to be intimately related to loaded questions gathered around cultural representations of sexuality and the female body.[4]

Rebecca offers a direct challenge to interpretation in that for every reading, there is a counter-reading. The result is that readers and critics are trapped within the novel's own ambivalence, unable to decide whether du Maurier's apparent endorsement of representations of women as angels or demons actually constitutes an ironic and deeply subversive challenge to patriarchal modes of thinking and writing. In seeming to encourage readers 'to read women as men read them, accepting men's visions of the feminine as their own', is du Maurier actually gesturing towards complex questions relating to representation, consumption, and cultural codings of the female body?[5] [6]

The female bodies most in question here are, of course, those of the narrator, Mrs Danvers and Rebecca herself. Other female bodies feature, but chiefly as carriers of malevolent humour. Of the bodies that most sustain our interest, that of the narrator seems the least suggestive: draped in shapeless clothes, this body is 'flat' and 'dull'.[7] Its desires and needs are underplayed to the extent that du Maurier presents a sexless, anorexic cipher whose body signifies the acted upon rather than the active. This under-needy body is clearly what attracts the Bluebeard figure Maxim de Winter, who responds positively to the boy-like doormat he meets in Monte Carlo. Without curves and thus without the sexual danger implied by them, without apparent appetite and thus without the lure towards excess implied by that, the narrator appears asexually passive.[8] Were Maxim more sophisticated in his reading of the apparently need-less body, he would understand that self-abnegation potentially encodes a pathological desire for excess. The narrator's autophagic and masochistic behaviour, rather than contrasting her to her predecessor, actually aligns her with the lushly excessive Rebecca: the only difference lies in the level of denial and repression achieved.

I would suggest that Maxim himself is no stranger to self-denial, as repressed homosexual instinct attaches itself to him throughout the text. That he has married a bisexual woman as his first wife and a sexless, appetite-free, boy substitute as his second wife makes his choices begin to look very much like displaced homosexual desire. However, both relationships appear remarkably sexless, so it seems that the repression of his natural desires (which he would deem transgressive) disrupts the façade of normative sexuality he so ruthlessly maintains. But in Maxim's world of 'law' and class-bound patriarchal authority, sexual desire, and certainly sexual 'transgression' (perhaps one and the same thing in this world view) *should* be suppressed. That Rebecca felt no need to do so (quite the opposite) is one of the things he most detests in her, and perhaps it is this about which he is, as Mrs Danvers and Jack Favell cryptically and consistently suggest, 'jealous'. Rather than suffer from cuckolded ire, Maxim may instead have envied Rebecca's sheer lack of sexual guilt. All this may account for the reason why Maxim's relationship with the narrator seems so frigid at all but times of sharpest crisis, and his second marriage to another surrogate boy seems likely to be as wintrily unproductive as his first.

It is also of interest that a girl whose beloved father has recently died almost instantly attaches herself to a man old enough to be her father; a girl who is bizarrely accepting of the father-daughter, employer/employee marital relationship imposed by Maxim and arguably implicitly encouraged and endorsed by her. If, finally, she begs Maxim to allow her to be 'your friend and your companion, a sort of boy', insisting that 'I don't ever want more than that' (p. 297), it is as if she may have finally understood not only her own and Rebecca's 'tastes' but also, vitally, those of her ruthlessly repressed husband.

Instant understanding is clearly not this narrator's strength, and her inability to perceive that yet another intimate relationship in which she is involved is similarly marked with repressed desire provides an ironic echo to her blindness in respect of her husband. Initially terrified by the spectral and obscurely threatening Mrs Danvers, Rebecca's lieutenant is also surrounded by suggestive connotation hinting at taboo recesses of experience and desire. The connotations of lesbianism that enshroud her are combined with her gothic characteristics, rendering her a liminal and deeply paradoxical figure in every respect. The only 'mother' in this novel of absent or thwarted maternity, since she nurtures Rebecca from childhood and is thus represented (and self-constructed) as a maternal surrogate, she is a curious carrier of quasi-incestuous lesbian signification. Physically, she is hideous: the narrator's introduction to her sets her up as a spectral, lurking presence. She is dressed in black and her face is dominated by 'prominent cheek-bones and great, hollow eyes' which produces the effect of 'a skull's face, parchment-white, set on a skeleton's frame' (p. 74). The text allows little opportunity here to read sexual sub/version in any but disturbed terms, actively encouraging the reader to position it on the sinister hinterland between 'known' and 'other' (the forbidden), and thus implicating the reader in a world view which endorses the value of 'normative' patriarchal codes. The sexual coding of the female body is once again here centrally involved in the 'values' and 'assumptions' of a text that seems to side rather too firmly with a world view it at other times actively contests. Its base note of parodic revulsion later connects with questions of ironic inflection within a narrative that strategically challenges literary representations of transgressive desire.

It is Mrs Danvers who first articulates the taboo of 'forbidden' desire to the virginal narrator, who is predictably embarrassed and deeply confused at this glimpse of a hidden world: 'it was as though she had spoken words that were forbidden' (p. 81). In fact, Mrs Danvers is only building upon the narrator's prior 'awakening' to this realm, initiated immediately upon her arrival at the corrupt 'fairyland' where a Conradian drive through the heart of darkness ('penetrating even deeper to the very heart surely of the forest itself', p. 72) climaxes in a wall of brazen rhododendrons which produce in her a discombobulating and entirely alien sensuous response. The narrator is breathless as she describes 'a wall of colour, blood-red' which she recalls finding 'bewildering, even shocking' in its 'slaughterous red, luscious and fantastic' profusion. These are not the 'homely, domestic thing, strictly conventional, mauve or pink in colour, standing one beside the other in a neat round bed'. Instead, she concludes, they are 'monsters' (p. 72). The passage reveals much about the narrator, about Manderley, but perhaps most of all about the positioning within the text of signs of female desire and sexuality, together with signification gathering around the secret spaces of the female body. The rhododendrons are as surely a sign of Rebecca as is her signature and they indicate the abundance and anarchy of her desire, while providing an early metaphor for her interior space in their 'blood-red wall'. Suggested here is danger and menstrual blood, while a glimpse of sinister profusion similarly connotes the unchartable recesses of the womb. No wonder the narrator is 'bewildered' and 'breathless', for she is catching a glimpse of the unseen, the unknown, the repressed, where beds are not 'neat', desire is not pastel, and where excess defies rule-bound authority.[9] This is as close to coitus as the narrator has clearly managed to get, married to the frigid Maxim, and it is the closest she can possibly be – despite her desire, performances, and imaginings – to Rebecca's internal body.[10]

It is, of course, around the eponymous absence that all questions gather. For the duration of this novel, Rebecca is a remarkably corporeal spirit; while the reader may have difficulty in evolving a clear idea of what the narrator looks like (other than being oddly similar to Joan Fontaine, but that is another story), no such problem is encountered with the gloriously lush Rebecca herself. We are told, many times, of her physical loveliness and provided with detail endorsing her mother-in-law's description of Rebecca's 'breeding, brains, and beauty' (p. 304). Similarly, we are constantly reminded that Rebecca is tall, slim, dark-haired, white-skinned, athletic, and extraordinarily beautiful, a modern Diana. She seems to materialize before the reader as she does to the unconvincingly 'innocent' narrator herself. Clearly the true 'heroine' of the novel, Rebecca is witty, clever, cultured, organized, and active, and we are told that she is frightened of nothing. Further, she seems loved by all, except by the 'jealous' Maxim, who dismisses her charm and ability to generate adoration and approval as nothing more than a 'damnably clever' performance (p. 304).

In fact, Rebecca, even in memory, offers the female reader a clear focus for identification, a template of action, dominance, free-ranging sexuality and liberty more usually inscribed into representations of maleness. An established critical viewpoint in Film Theory offers a way of thinking about the female reader's positioning within this text: Laura Mulvey argues that the female cinema viewer has traditionally been coerced into either surrendering the pleasure of identificatory desire when viewing films, since there have been so few female models embodying the set of values she longs to endorse, or identifying with a male character who embodies freedom, action, and effectiveness.[11] Although Hitchcock's film adaptation of this text does all it can to avoid coercing the female viewer, *Rebecca*, as a text, appears to enforce it.[12] When a woman reader encounters Rebecca, she potentially meets a version of her fantasy embodiment; here is a woman who is fearless in the face of authority, who defies the rule of patriarchal law, who resists the traditionally 'feminine' code of nurturing and selflessness, and who is physically splendid into the bargain – but physically diseased too, and herein lies the problem.

Rebecca, it transpires, is 'sick'. Further, Maxim is sick of this active, educated, strong and sexual wife who outshines him in every way. Her punishment is a chain of clichéd, patriarchal labels signifying the female demonic ('devil', 'damnable', 'filthy', and so on), and a lethal bullet to the abdomen before cancer ate her away. The reader, who has found ample space for resistant interpellation in this nuanced, sardonic text, must note the crude nature of despatch and feel both perplexed and cheated by it. In short, even the unresisting reader must resist at this point.[13]

Enforcing this sense of near-betrayal is the fact that du Maurier offers us competing versions of Rebecca's death, both of which lead to the same thing. Firstly, that there is more than one version of 'what killed Rebecca' situates each as a sub/version of the other, thus destabilizing not only the text but also the reader's orientation within it.[14] Secondly, both of these 'versions' relate directly to the specifics of a radically shattered female gynaecology. In the chilly Maxim's version, he reveals that he may have shot Rebecca in her occupied womb; then, in the text's resolution, we are informed that Rebecca was suffering from some type of gynaecological cancer. Du Maurier remains coyly unspecific here, but we are given sufficient information to deduce what Rebecca's disease may have been. Doctor Baker tells us that 'Mrs. Danvers' had presented complaining of 'certain symptoms' and that an X-ray had revealed an inoperable, 'deep-rooted' 'growth'. Incidentally, he also reveals that 'the x-rays showed a certain malfunction of the uterus [...] which meant she could never have had a child; but that was quite apart, it had nothing to do with the disease' (pp. 412–13). Since Rebecca's uterine deformation is a separate issue entirely, and since it is also a wholly unnecessary detail in terms of the plot, its inclusion screams out for attention. Maxim, it seems, had been right after all: Rebecca was 'not even normal' (p. 304). Her anatomical arrangement disrupts her female biology rendering her infertile: she is not a 'real' woman, then, because she cannot give Maxim an heir. (The question of whether Maxim is capable of reproduction is not considered.) Rebecca is 'miscarrying' her own womb within a novel twice-begun and once-aborted as a 'literary miscarriage'.[15]

Though Rebecca's faulty womb had nothing to do with her 'growth', that death rather than life nestles in her abdomen is necessarily loaded with negative implication. When the odious Favell subsequently enquires, 'This cancer business [...] does anyone know if it's contagious?', the reader is encouraged both to condemn his ignorance, and also to understand that venereal disease may be implied (p. 415). Infertile, internally deformed (but externally perfect so that the malformed uterus suggests a secret mark of Cain), promiscuous, and bisexual, the narrative seems to condemn Rebecca more fatally than even Maxim's bullet.

In either version of her death, then, Rebecca's womb is responsible for killing her, and this seems to be a curiously clichéd 'punishment' for the 'dangerous' Rebecca, one we would usually attribute to the moral judgements, values, and assumptions traditionally associated with the male-authored canon with its 'persistent plot pattern' dealing out 'suffering and death' as 'the inevitable fate of sexually transgressive heroines'.[16] The question as to why Rebecca requires punishment, and why du Maurier decided to inflict this via her gynaecology, deserves attention. The answer, I would argue, clearly resides in the realm of ironic inflection and ideological generation of meaning.

Rebecca successfully 'dis/eases' Maxim, opening up some searching questions concerning the 'rule' and 'authority' he represents. These are gestured towards (though not fully explored) by John Sutherland when he investigates the set of riddles threading *Rebecca*, including the deceptively playful question, 'Where was Rebecca shot?'[17] Sutherland's question raises something uncomfortably ambiguous right at the heart of this novel that leads us to ask whether Maxim's crime encodes connections between patriarchal inheritance and the female body and thus represents less a crime of passion than a crime of property. In this set of debates, du Maurier's selection of Rebecca's death sentence increasingly becomes loaded with ironic implication.

As Sutherland notes in discussing the fatal bullet, for it to have left no mark on any bone for the coroner to find when Rebecca's body is finally recovered, Maxim must have shot her in the abdomen. The systems of textual signification here, however, suggest that Maxim in fact shoots Rebecca in her uterus; further, the implication is clearly that this is not a 'missed' shot at Rebecca's duplicitous heart (as Maxim claims) but sharp-shooting at its most deadly. In anatomical terms, the soft flesh of the belly is positioned above the womb, which nestles within the pelvis, but because the occupied womb moves upwards as it expands and swells the central section of the body, the abdominal area culturally, if inaccurately, represents the fertile centre of femaleness. Had Maxim actually shot Rebecca in her womb then the bullet would have scraped the pelvis and left evidence (thus scuppering the latter stages of the narrative), but in shooting Rebecca in the abdomen, he metaphorically shoots the core of female biology *and* leaves no trace.

This matter is of such acute significance, as Sutherland recognizes, because Rebecca has just told Max that occupying her womb, later to be revealed as diseased, is the illegitimate heir to her husband's patriarchal signifier of permanence, inheritance and ownership, Manderley. We are significantly informed, early in the novel, that the estate has been 'in his family's possession since the Conquest', thus establishing a male history of property and class rights, and yet another echo of *Jane Eyre*, where Thornfield Hall is also coded in terms of male inheritance (p. 16). Upon hearing Rebecca's news, Maxim loses control, and breaks his own wintry code of conduct, because Rebecca has broken one rule too many. Moreover, it is the 'rule' that lies at the 'heart' (Maxim's declared target) of patriarchal authority. In so magnificently shattering the 'feminine' rule of chastity, Rebecca has ruptured the patrilineal line of inheritance, disrupting the male-defined basis of capitalist logic into the bargain. Maxim has already indicated that he always puts Manderley first, and Rebecca has already indicated that the estate is entailed (what an odd comment for Maxim to remember about his last conversation with his wife if it were not significant), so the idea that it will be inherited by the illegitimate product of Rebecca's womb pushes him over the edge of reason. Rebecca has already, in Maxim's reading, insinuated herself into his world of privilege and patriarchal order, but to disrupt and taint his blood-line and its rightful 'space' at Manderley with that supposedly growing in the 'space' of Rebecca's transgressive body, is simply going too far. Thus, Rebecca is killed for crimes of trespass and contamination.[18]

Thus the murder of his wife which, as Sutherland establishes, looks solidly premeditated, is a crime generated by Maxim's insistence upon the 'rules' of female chastity, inheritance, family blood, and a pile of stones.[19] Ironically, Maxim need not have bothered, since Rebecca is going to die anyway; she has, Maxim insists, premeditated her own murder with typically snake-like cunning, thus saving herself from a lingering death. Further, she has subjected Maxim to one final, glorious snub, stabbing at the heart of his entire world view into the bargain.

It is surely this world view that is condemned here, and in far less ironic and ambivalent terms than the judgement passed on Rebecca. Maxim's first wife has been in permanent rebellion against androcentric power, 'laughing' at men, as well as appropriating their possessions and destabilizing their assumed control. Her subversive tactics have been uncontested by Maxim because his wife has taken all the bullets. She knows he fears exposure, rumour, and gossip, and that he over-values social prestige and authority; thus, there is nothing he can do to expose Rebecca since he would also risk exposing himself (see p. 306). One hundred years on from Brontë's account of Rochester's trouble-shooting tactics, Maxim does not even have a handy attic in which to store his sexual, taboo-busting wife, and Rebecca is far too visible and vocal a presence for this fate anyway. As an updated Grace Poole, Mrs Danvers also extends our understanding of how patriarchal tactics have been more delicately contested in the intervening hundred years, since she is the opposite of a proxy warden, operating instead as a transgressive co-conspirator and accomplice. Thus, with no attic and with no tactics, Maxim himself updates the notion of a secret prison and buries Rebecca in the cabin of her boat, under water. Rebecca, he claims, drove him to it, but the energy surrounding the corpse recovered from the uterine tomb (or watery attic) and instantly re-encrypted, tells another story.

Maxim attempts a spectacular piece of special pleading in exempting himself morally from the crime he commits. The narrator instantly and rather too gleefully enters into complicity with her 'wronged' husband ('I too had killed Rebecca', p. 319), and both spend the rest of the novel scurrying around attempting to conceal Maxim's crime.[20] That the narrator enters so easily into this business would cause us serious concern unless Maxim's story is largely credible, but without the narrator's sympathy, the suspense of the final stages of the text could not be generated. Thus, the narrator is convinced that Maxim's account is honest, but the reader who has been attuned to the shadows of his characterization up until this point may well be less confident. The narrator has much at stake herself in buying the demonic construction of her predecessor offered by Maxim, not least the promised fairytale prince and his lovely castle. Her utter lack of sympathy for Rebecca's fate obviously echoes Jane's unfeeling response to that of Bertha in the earlier novel, but it leaves a nasty taste in the mouth nevertheless. Responding in part to this inflection, the reader spends the latter stages of the text in a schizophrenic position, half willing the narrator and Maxim to emerge scot-free, but half wondering whether they deserve to succeed in their cover-up. Breathless, we emerge from the narrative still unsure as to whether justice has been served and we may remember that the concept is traditionally emblematized via the motif of a blindfold.

Maxim and the narrator are, of course, 'punished' at the last gasp (and at the first, given where we enter the novel) by the loss of Manderley: 'just deserts' have been apportioned after all, and this goes some way towards diffusing the sense of having been cheated out of a more genuine payback for the cover-up and for Maxim's self-serving demonization of Rebecca. She, the reader senses, has been given a very raw deal indeed. Du Maurier has made it clear that several of Rebecca's actions spring from an insistence upon autonomy and upon the rights of a self-authored set of 'rules' as an alternative to those imposed by her frigid husband and by the patriarchy whose system he upholds. Her upkeep of a cottage on the beach and a flat in London, for example, may have nothing to do with providing venues for promiscuous encounters, but more to do with carving out physical and imaginative 'rooms' of her own. In her London flat, Rebecca can evade Maxim's controlling gaze and it may be this refusal of dependence, as much as anything else, that Maxim cannot bear, so significantly shooting her at the cottage, a no-man's-land between freedom and constraint, but significantly owned and policed by him. Maxim's presence is suffocating and his gaze is as surveillant as that of the 'Gentleman Unknown', whose 'eyes followed one from the dusky frame' (p. 15). Rebecca can hardly be blamed by anyone except her husband for seeking liberation from both. So when Maxim and his accomplice drift around Europe, existing through days of un-Rebecca-like boredom, with the narrator as a nurse/companion/surrogate mother, the text works its last trick in causing us to realize that where Rebecca's double punishment via murder and disease may have been ironic, that of Maxim and the narrator is nothing of the kind.

A further detail, 'hidden' in the text due to early placement, confirms this sense that the wrong transgressor has, with conscious irony, been (twice) 'punished'. The narrator is in Monte Carlo, disconsolate because her day with Maxim is at an end; bored, she reads a volume of poetry lent to her by Maxim that had been given to him by Rebecca. The volume falls open 'at what must be a much-frequented page', and the connotations of what she reads are intriguing:

> I fled Him, down the nights and down the days;
> I fled Him, down the arches of the years;
> I fled Him, down the labyrinthine ways
> Of my own mind; and in the midst of tears
> I hid from Him, and under running laughter.
> Up vistaed slopes I sped
> And shot, precipitated
> Adown Titanic glooms of chasmed fears,
> From those strong feet that followed, followed after. (p. 35)

Within the context of the story that follows, revisiting Francis Thompson's poem carries unsettling meaning.[21] Who 'fled' whom in the marital relationship described by Maxim, and why? The speaker is chased, hounded psychologically and physically, unable to break away or hide because the 'strong' feet inevitably 'follow'. Further, when the full text of the poem is explored, a subsequent line, 'All things betray thee, who betrayest Me' offers clear direction to the reader regarding textual interpretation. Encoded here is not a warning against Rebecca (with Maxim the pursued and suffering subject), but a sinister warning against Maxim delivered from beyond the grave. Typically, the narrator notes only the signature on the title page and closes the volume, but the reader may have a longer memory of the ambiguous tone struck by the lines and by the ambivalent chain of meanings triggered by them. This early in the narrative, the inclusion of these lines offers a deep-lying clue as to the 'true' situation of this relationship, far more significant and far less overt than all the other textual clues so liberally scattered and so consistently destabilized.

There are a great many clues and secrets in this novel of riddles that remain ambiguous and concealed: we never, for example, learn for sure where Rebecca was shot and whether her murder speaks less of a loss of control (literally and metaphorically), or whether it was the premeditated action of an outraged cuckold in defence of his world view.[22] All of this militates against any simple reading of the text as a 'little' Gothic romance, an interesting though finally insignificant 'novelette'. Rather, it is a text that opens up spaces for dissent and interrogation in our reading not only of *Jane Eyre* but also in the genre to which it belongs. Certainly, *Rebecca* can be read in entirely conventional ways, but it more clearly invites us to read it as a narrative stab at the heart of the 'rule of law' embedded in Maxim's name, analysing the basis and practice of male authority and the 'winter' it creates around it, and exploring meanings implicit in female sexuality and, through the conventional literary punishments for it, in the ideological resonances it connotes.

Carrying disease and signifying dis/ease, Rebecca is finally 'shut up', but in fact just as she is twice-murdered, so also is she twice-silenced. To impose muteness upon a subject is, of course, an expression of power; that Maxim flexes his patriarchal muscles in such a way is of no surprise, and his re-presentation of the demon's words, and indeed of her entire being, is an ideological appropriation we are used to seeing in canonical literature.[23] Converting the noisy rebel into a silent space allows the dominant grouping to rewrite the terms of protest and to reinflect their meaning. But that both the narrator, snipping Rebecca's striking signature from a title page, and du Maurier herself silence Rebecca, prior to killing her twice, again indicates ambivalence and irony at the core of the text. Maxim insists that Rebecca's vocabulary is as 'filthy' as her sexual behaviour (both are situated as infected in a continuation of the disease and contamination emphases he attaches to Rebecca) and, as it turns out, as her gynaecology. That so many riddles remain in this novel of secrets suggests that what we have here is a 'partial' story in both dominant senses: Rebecca's story is not wholly given and what is left of it is filtered through a biased and self-serving witness. Rebecca's words have been taken from her and a significant narrative gap emerges as a result. That this gap is so pointed suggests that the missing sub/version of Maxim's 'authorized' version indicates some anxiety to open up questions around female silencing. Later, writers such as Jean Rhys in *The Wide Sargasso Sea* (1966), Sally Beauman in *Rebecca's Tale* and Susan Hill in *Mrs de Winter*, will extend the implications of this silencing, understanding that as a potent carrier of ideological resonance, it is beaten solely by the metaphor of the twice-inflicted womb.

As the forces of law and order surround Maxim to protect one of their own, a reader must surely side with the dead Rebecca, twice murdered via her womb, twice silenced, and twice encrypted. Rebecca, we have been told, despised men and laughed at them: it is a philosophy echoed in the bleakly ironic heart of this narrative and etched into the secret space of Rebecca's mortified gynaecology. To murder the heroine via her womb once is condemnation, but to murder the heroine via her womb *twice* is surely the ironic over-fulfilment of just deserts. The final implication of this disturbing narrative may well be that Rebecca's tumour expresses not du Maurier's moral judgement, but a challenge to male forms of representation. It is to this that *Rebecca* 'talks back' in a subversive act of ironic literary larceny; rather than feel 'figuratively crippled by the debilitating alternatives her culture offers her' in its insistence upon polarized female models of 'angel' or 'monster', du Maurier instead cripples the models and opens up questions about how and why this culture represents female sexuality and defiance in terms of the pathologized gynaecological body.[24]

NOTES

1. See Ruth Robbins, *Literary Feminisms* (Hampshire, UK: Palgrave, 2000). The relationship between *Jane Eyre* and *Rebecca* is usefully explored in several critical essays, but particularly productively by Patsy Stoneman in *Brontë Transformations: The Cultural Dissemination of Jane Eyre and Wuthering Heights* (London: Prentice Hall/Harvester Wheatsheaf, 1996). The process of revisionism within a feminist context is discussed in full by Pam Morris in *Literature and Feminism* (Oxford: Blackwell, 1993), pp. 13–36, but Adrienne Rich's thumbnail definition of revisionism as a potent feminist literary tactic remains the most useful and flexible: 'Re-vision – the act of looking back, of seeing with fresh eyes, of entering an old text from a new critical direction…an act of survival', quoted in Sandra M. Gilbert and Susan Gubar, 'Infection in the Sentence: The Woman Writer and the Anxiety of Authorship', in *Feminisms: An Anthology of Literary Theory and Criticism*, ed. Robyn R. Warhol and Diane Price Herndl (New Brunswick, NJ: Rutgers University Press, 1991), p. 292.
2. As E. L. Doctorow cannily reminds us, 'there is no one more dangerous than the storyteller', quoted in Margaret Atwood, *Negotiating with the Dead: A Writer on Writing* (London: Virago, 2003), p. 34. In the case of *Rebecca*, the namelessness of the narrator should certainly not connote blamelessness and, just as the reader asks some searching questions about Jane's testimony in the revisioned novel, so also are we made continuously aware here of the potential duplicity of du Maurier's storyteller.
3. Judith Fetterley, quoted in Morris, *Literature and Feminism*, pp. 28–29
4. Morris, Literature and Feminism, p. 29
5. Morris, *Literature and Feminism*, p. 15. There is an opportunity here to investigate the issue of female reading practice but, within the discussion I present, there is a risk of digression. However, this important and certainly related issue is particularly cogently outlined in Jonathan Culler, 'Reading as a Woman', in *On Deconstruction* (1982), in Warhol and Price Herndl (eds.), *Anthology*, pp. 509–25. Culler here offers a distilled overview of questions circulating round feminist readings of the female reader.
6. Another interpretation may be that du Maurier herself shares what Dorothy Dinnerstein terms, 'men's anti-female feelings – usually in a mitigated form, but deeply nevertheless' (quoted in Culler, 'Reading as a Woman', p. 515). Although evidence to support this view could be rallied from this text, the energies and systems of meaning generated in the novel as a whole militate against it.
7. Daphne du Maurier, *Rebecca* (1938; London: Virago, 2003), p. 235. Future references to this text will appear in the main body of the text.
8. The narrator's lack of appetite and neurotic under-consumption are given regular and peculiar emphasis throughout the text: she repeatedly mentions missing meals, eating very little, or nothing at all, as on p. 342: 'I did not want anything to eat. I could not swallow'. That this is so consistently emphasized (only once is she 'ravenous', following the visit to Dr Baker on p. 420) is surely significant. Gilbert

and Gubar point out that both Charlotte and Emily Brontë 'depict the travails of starved or starving anorexic heroines', so du Maurier may, at least in part, be gesturing towards a female tradition of self-representation in including this emphasis ('Infection in the Sentence', p. 298).

9. The knotted drive through the forest, together with the anarchic burst in which it 'climaxes' also, of course, suggests a journey into the unconscious and a glimpse of Rebecca's id. The tangled, dark disorder of the drive is echoed in the out-of-control pathway that leads down to Rebecca's beach.

10. Early foreshadowing of Rebecca's gynaecological disease is provided via the rhododendrons on p. 150 when the narrator notes that they have begun to fade and their petals have begun to drop: 'Theirs was a brief beauty. Not lasting very long'. Their status as a metaphor for Rebecca's womb and, by extension, her sexuality is thus made clear.

11. This question of the female cinema spectator's focus of identification is explored in several critical discussions, including Laura Mulvey's seminal essay, 'Visual Pleasure and Narrative Cinema' (1975), in *Feminism and Film Theory*, ed. Constance Penley (London: BFI Publishing, 1988), pp. 57–68.

12. Alfred Hitchcock's film adaptation of *Rebecca* was released in 1940: the novel was set nine years earlier and the wartime adaptation fully exploits the source text's nostalgic recollection of a lost Eden-England. However, Hitchcock's film arguably found less wrong with this vanished world view than did du Maurier's novel. This seems supported by the fact that the 'adaptation' process involved a complete ideological reinflection of the source text. Starring Joan Fontaine fresh from her role as a cinematic Jane Eyre (thus bestowing intertextual resonance), and Laurence Olivier at the height of his heartthrob fame, Hitchcock appears to view Rebecca as a demonic force who thoroughly deserved her fate. In line with this, he represents the circumstances of her death completely so that Rebecca dies as the result of a fall, not of a bullet fired by Maxim; the latter emerges as the wronged hero and the narrator as his faithful, right-thinking wife, and the chain of meanings to do with patriarchal ownership as triggered by the fatal bullet to the abdomen are lost. Possibly, the energies of the source text may have proved too ambiguous for the more literal medium of cinema so the story was 'clarified' (notably, in line with patriarchal sympathies) for this different format and audience. That the film emerges as a less nuanced and suggestive document than the text indicates the crucial nature of du Maurier's choice of female punishment.

13. This ascription of 'resistance' derives from Morris, *Literature and Feminism*, p. 29.

14. This question of versions and subversions obviously connects with the issue of doubleness and duality within the modern Gothic novel. In one clear example, Rebecca and the narrator are 'doubled' (most obviously in the scene involving the fancy dress ball, which also invites questions around female insinuation into the 'male' domain of class privilege and inherited 'pedigree'), and Sally Beauman speculates whether the apparently opposing characters represent two sides of du Maurier herself and articulate the author's dual responses to her own sexuality ('Introduction' to du Maurier, *Rebecca*, p. vi). See also Martyn Shawcross, *The Private World of Daphne du Maurier* (London: Robson Books, 1991). A second example involves the doubling necessarily generated by the revisionary project and gestures towards the complex relationship between this text and *Jane Eyre*.

15. Daphne du Maurier quoted by Beauman, 'Introduction', p. vi.

16. Morris, Literature and Feminism, p. 31.

17. John Sutherland, *Where was Rebecca Shot?: Puzzles, Curiosities and Conundrums in Modern Fiction* (London: Weidenfeld and Nicolson, 1998), pp. 49–56. This is the title question of Chapter 10.

18. Rebecca's 'trespass' into and 'contamination' of Manderley is made explicit in the description of another of Rebecca's private spaces, this one within Manderley itself. The morning room belongs to Rebecca and it is crammed with all the finest treasures Manderley has to offer. She has looted the storage rooms, 'ignoring the second-rate, the mediocre, laying her hand with sure certain instinct only upon the best'. The language used here plainly suggests that Rebecca's appropriation is a greedy one. Further, 'her' rhododendrons invade the rooms, crowding the windows, bursting from vases, and filling the room with 'glow' and 'brilliance'. Sexuality invades this Aladdin's Cave, but that it is 'vividly alive' rather than 'musty' suggests that it is condemned less surely than it initially seems (p. 93).

19. *Rebecca* has not only been adapted to cinema and television but has also been twice revisioned in Sally Beauman's *Rebecca's Tale* (2001), and Susan Hill's *Mrs de Winter* (1993). In the latter, the author avoids the whole issue of Rebecca's shooting, subsequently stating, 'I was very careful not to get mixed up in it'. Hill also adds that Maxim's version of the fatal night 'doesn't hold water' (quoted in Sutherland, *Where was Rebecca Shot?*, p. 196).

20. It should be noted that not even for a second does Maxim seem to consider confessing his crime to the police; instead, he does not even pause before concealing the evidence of the murder and covering his tracks. Maxim appears to think he is above the law and, given the subsequent patriarchal cover-up led by Colonel Julyan, the narrative suggests that he is not mistaken.

21. 'The Hound of Heaven' by Francis Thompson (1859–1907). The title of the poem is indicated when the narrator, having read the poem, asks, 'What hound of heaven had driven him [Maxim] to the high hills this afternoon?' Again, the narrator may have misidentified the oxymoronic 'hound' here (p. 35).

22. One riddle Sutherland overlooks involves the mystery of the locked cabin: if Maxim bolted the door as he left the cabin, why did no investigator into the 'accident' note that for the door to be locked from the outside, someone other than Rebecca must have drawn the bolt? That this logistical flaw goes unnoticed may be yet another example of neglectful policing in a novel that consistently interrogates the machinery and the patriarchal sympathies of 'the law'. Alternatively, of course, it may simply be a case of authorial oversight.

23. When, for example, he reports his post-wedding conversation with Rebecca in which she 'told me about herself, told me things I shall never repeat to a living soul', Maxim not only silences her but also leaves it to the listener's imagination to re-write Rebecca's statement in the most lurid terms (p. 305). In fact, it would not take much to shock the frigid and curiously naïve Maxim.

24. Gilbert and Gubar, 'Infection in the Sentence', p. 297.

13

Representations of Illegal Abortionists in England, 1900–1967

EMMA L. JONES

The abortionist is a shadowy figure in the history of British gynaecology in the twentieth century. Before the 1967 Abortion Act, which for doctors, provided a legal defence for performing abortions, those accused, tried, and convicted of carrying out terminations were often demonized. The medical profession, the legal system, and the media regularly expressed shock and horror at the violent injury and death sustained by those women who placed themselves under the care of the untrained and unskilled. An important focus of contemporary allegations rested on the methods used to procure abortions, and the gynaecological knowledge and skills of those employing them. Estimates of the annual number of illegal abortions always greatly exceeded the number of deaths attributed to the crime. Yet medical literature, popular culture, and journalistic exposés did much to preserve the more shocking elements of abortion practices. Analogously, popular histories have leaned towards sensationalist accounts of individual abortionists.[1] This essay provides an analysis of the parallels and contradictions between the available empirical evidence and contemporary representations of abortionists and their methods. It explores early to mid-twentieth century (mis)perceptions in relation to medical professionalization, and scientific and cultural ideas on health and hygiene.

The following assessment draws upon a sample of abortionists extracted from criminal investigations and trials conducted in England between 1900 and 1967.[2] Many were tried under the Offences Against the Person Act of 1861.[3] Sections 58 and 59 of this statute made it a criminal offence for a woman to abort herself and for others to supply or procure any poison, noxious thing, or instrument with the intention of using it to procure a miscarriage unlawfully.[4] This offence was punishable by imprisonment from three years to life. When an abortion ended in the death of a woman, an accused might also face the charge of murder or manslaughter. By definition, an abortionist was anyone who performed the operation. For present purposes, women who induced their own abortions, as well as those men who procured the abortions of their wives and lovers, are excluded. Not only is the evidence of both phenomena statistically negligible when measured against that for other categories of abortionists but contemporaries also viewed these offenders quite differently.[5]

Legal records are only representative of those cases which came to the notice of the authorities. Thus, any sample, however large, can provide only a partial glimpse of the sorts of individuals involved in abortion practices. The 116 women and 51 men whose criminal activities are described in the legal records consulted for this study do, nevertheless, come from a range of occupational backgrounds. Housewives and widows, mostly working class and middle-aged, are over-represented. Thus the sample is overwhelmingly 'lay' in character. Only ten women had received, or claimed to have received, nursing or midwifery training, or had worked in other medical settings, namely, in pharmacies or as hospital orderlies.

In contrast, men swelled the ranks of those whose legitimate occupation was in some form of medical care or advice; over three times as many as among females accused. There are some notable absences from the legal records, however. Our knowledge of those working in the upper tier of the abortion marketplace remains hazy and relies heavily on fictionalized and (auto)biographical accounts.[6] The fewer numbers of general practitioners (there were seven among the sample), as well as the lack of appearance of West End physicians in the sources, reflects both the selective nature of abortion policing and prosecution and the fact that professional and financial resources kept many of them beyond the grasp of the law. In the absence of a therapeutic proviso in the abortion legislation, the medical profession accepted the induction of abortion by their own members according to an expanding number of health, eugenic, and economic indications, so long as practitioners abided by professional ethics and sought the consultation of their fellow professionals.[7] The absence of female doctors from the official records surely corresponds with their proportionately lower numbers within the profession as a whole, while a desire to establish and maintain what was already an ambiguous status perhaps made them less likely to court suspicion by participating in abortion.[8]

For a miscarriage to take place, a foetus has to be disturbed, whether through external trauma, dilation of the cervix, irritation of the uterine cavity, or perforation of the uterus. The contents of the uterus have to then be expelled or physically removed. The method of choice among the lay abortionists, as well as some doctors in my sample was that of an enema of boiled water mixed with flakes of anti-septic soap (for example, 'Lifebuoy', 'Sunlight', 'Family Health') passed through the cervix via a rudimentary syringe or catheter. Alongside syringing with soapy water were listed soda water, vinegar, branded disinfectants, and antiseptics such as 'Dettol' and 'TCP', phenol (carbolic acid), camphor, and quinine.[9] Use was also apparently made of applications to the genital area of salts, ergot (used medically to produce uterine contractions), and the purgative aloe.[10] The use of pill emmenagogues and ecbolics (designed to contract the uterine muscle and induce menstrual flow),[11] as well as the injection of abortifacient pastes, such as Utus paste, between the uterine wall and the foetal membranes, were also evident.[12] These latter technologies were increasingly used in therapeutic abortion by the medical profession after World War II.[13] Many of the more basic instruments and applications were, however, familiar domestic objects and could be easily purchased at chemists and pharmacies. It was customary, for example, for women to possess syringes, such as the Higginson Syringe (a household name), for self-douching, while many of the medicaments listed in police reports were those commonly used in 'ordinary family medicine'.[14]

Medical instruments such as male catheters, catheter rods, and specula make some very rare appearances in those criminal trials sampled,[15] as do other objects found in the possession of suspected abortionists such as slippery elm bark, Cornish elm bark, crochet hooks, and knitting needles.[16] Manual internal manipulation and external trauma via stomach massage or punching of the stomach were also referred to in a few cases.[17]

However, it was the array of more sinister instruments and methods, together with exercises such as rigorous dancing or throwing oneself downstairs, and the taking of abortifacient pills, potions, and hot baths and gin that were sensationalized in popular fiction, memoirs, and oral testimonies, both of the period and later.[18] This sensationalization further widened the gap in popular perception between the back-street abortionist and the qualified obstetrical surgeon, who used the comparatively safer dilatation of the cervix and curettage of the uterus, or 'D and C' as it became popularly known.

Another method was electricity. In 1926, E. Blackwell of the City of London Police wrote to Sir Bernard Henry Spilsbury, the Chief Medical Officer to the Home Office and expert medical witness for the Crown, to express his concern about rumours of 'a new means of procuring abortion by some sort of application of electricity, and that young society women are now resorting to this means to get rid of pregnancy'.[19] Spilsbury replied that he too had 'received information from several sources [namely doctors who had received the information from their patients] that electrical methods are employed for procuring abortion'.[20] He went on to describe the method, which involved the placing of electrodes in the abdominal wall and inside the vagina, after which a current passing through the body would shock the foetus and lead to its expulsion. Spilsbury had also heard of two related methods. The first, employed in America, involved the guiding of a pair of electrodes along the neck of the uterus until they transfixed the foetus. The current, when passed, electrocuted the foetus, whose death would then bring on an abortion. The second related method involved exposure to X-rays.[21] Commenting on the level of danger involved, Spilsbury wrote: 'Such methods as these, if employed carefully and skilfully, should be free from most of the risk attendant upon procuring of abortion, with the exception of fatal shock, which is a rare event. If a fatality should occur it might be impossible by post-mortem examination to elucidate the cause of death'.[22]

The voicing of these rumours is significant on a number of levels. It represents a classic statement on modernity, merging the evolution of new technologies with contemporary fears of rebellious womanhood. In this period, concerns over abortion were tied to fears over Britain's declining birth rate, a decline believed to be prevalent among the healthier and racially superior middle classes. Young, wealthy, and emancipated middle-class women were accused of avoiding motherhood for purely selfish reasons of convenience. Abortion narratives in misogynistic novels of the 1910s and 1920s see women punished for their absence from the family home and neglect of their reproductive duties.[23] Electrotherapeutics, meanwhile, was developed over the nineteenth century to establish moral order and discipline over bodies that could not cope with the stresses of modern civilization, found most prolifically in the sexually incontinent.[24] The use of electrotherapy to procure abortion was a potential misuse of this technology, threatening to invert the moral order it was supposed to exert over miscreant bodies. As Spilsbury's above comment suggests, medical authorities were also alarmed, perhaps, by the possibility that abortion by means of electricity might elude forensic detection.[25]

The fears of the Metropolitan Police were partially realized two years later when Charles Jackson Palmer was convicted at the Old Bailey of the abortion and manslaughter of Elsie Goldsmith, the nineteen-year old wife of a former naval officer, and sentenced to seven years' penal servitude. Palmer was found guilty of applying electrical methods before having 'recourse to other well-known means', in this case a syringe and soapy water, to procure the abortion of Mrs Goldsmith's pregnancy.[26] Spilsbury testified against the defence's claim that Mrs Goldsmith had died of shock from the passing of alternating currents through the body at a low voltage. Instead, he and another expert witness drew upon post-mortem findings that had revealed an abrasion, suggesting the use of a syringe and the presence of soapy water that had been recently injected.[27] Palmer, who possessed no medical qualification, was a Mayfair medical electrician tending to the minor ailments and injuries of the hunting and sporting world. Elsie fitted the description of a young society woman 'afraid of having a child'.[28]

Although this incident is historically contingent, it neatly illustrates how contemporary representations of abortion technologies were related to the politics of abortion more generally. Cases of abortion reflected wider cultural anxieties concerning medical knowledge, social class, sexuality, and race.[29] Over time, trials for abortion unearthed baby farms, prostitution, late-night drinking dens, and police corruption.[30] Abortion trials were always about much more than the physical criminal act. For example, in 1930, Ivy Braham, a cabaret dancer in London's West End, accused Neil Walker, a music-hall comedian, of being the father of her unborn child and of arranging to terminate the pregnancy. The police apprehended Walker before the operation took place. Braham later told a court how, under the influence of alcohol, she had been seduced by Walker, and coerced into agreeing to an abortion. Walker denied paternity, and portrayed Braham as a 'troublesome' girl accustomed to 'improper relations', who had been 'insistent' on pursuing the illegal operation despite the risks.[31] Walker was acquitted of all charges, although Braham later successfully applied for an affiliation order against Walker in support of the child.[32] It does appear, however, that it was Braham's work as a dancer that left her vulnerable to sexual innuendo both in and out of court. In his closing speech, which was reprinted in the press, the Court Recorder insinuated that Braham might have lied to the court. Moreover, the case, he argued, had shown the dangers that young women exposed themselves to when they followed the calling of 'public dancer'. Adding that he did not refer to Walker in this instance, the Recorder continued: 'If that is not white slave traffic, I do not know what is'.[33] Those women who contemplated abortion and lived to tell their stories in court could easily lose the chivalrous protection of the law if their character was found wanting. Braham had solicited risk, as well as an illegitimate pregnancy, and according to the court, she had only herself to blame. Thus, abortion trials permitted a range of voices to comment on the dangers of modern urban life.

Medical and forensic evidence presented at trials indicated that instruments were capable of entering the uterine cavity, causing irritation of the uterus or rupturing of the amniotic sac or membranes, and that women undergoing these procedures genuinely risked internal injury, long-term morbidity, and death. Death could either be immediate, via an air embolism (most commonly caused by the use of the syringe and pump method), haemorrhage, or shock,[34] or painfully delayed for hours and often days in the case of ensuing sepsis and peritonitis. According to medical expertise provided at criminal trials and in the medical jurisprudence literature, instrumental abortion required considerable skill as 'the pregnant womb is soft and it is very easy to perforate',[35] thereby carrying a high risk of injury and infection. However, even when pathologists could not establish the root cause of an infection or septic abortion, such uncertainty was qualified unequivocally: 'for an infection to complicate an ordinary miscarriage is extraordinarily rare [...]. Without instrumental interference there would be nothing to cause the septicaemia to appear'.[36] When instrumental abortion gave rise to injury and death, it was first and foremost attributed to a lack of skill: 'When the services of a skilled abortionist are obtained, probably an instrument is successfully passed through the os [extra-ovular space between the cervix and the uterus] into the uterus, and, as a rule, abortion follows without complication'.[37]

The risks associated with an abortion evidently depended on the medical expertise of the respective abortionist, but even qualified physicians could make mistakes.[38] Haste was believed to be a cause of injury, and a sure sign that an operation had been performed illicitly: 'When such second person is a medical man, the very fact of injuries being found argues want of skill, or secrecy and haste, and suggests an evil intent, though such must not be taken for granted, for when the operation is legitimately undertaken slight lacerations may occur'.[39] This textbook on medical jurisprudence went on to suggest that signs of criminal violence would be stronger in cases where the operation had been performed by a 'quack', showing 'a total lack of knowledge of the proper methods, and forbid[ding] even the supposition of justifiable attempts at a relief'.[40] Medical experts confirmed such views during criminal trials, asserting that the 'absence of injury might indicate skill, or good management',[41] and that signs of injury might imply that an 'operation was done hurriedly and with undue force'.[42] Jurors were often reminded by expert medical witnesses that there was 'no lawful purpose for which to insert soapy water into a pregnant uterus', and that 'a woman douching herself [...] could not unintentionally get it into the uterus'.[43]

There is some evidence which suggests that abortion could in fact be a relatively safe procedure. Anecdotal accounts attest to the proficiency and skill of abortionists. Giving evidence to the National Birth Rate Commission in 1914, for example, Mrs Ring from the Industrial Law Committee testified that she had seen knitting needles used 'very effectively by women of quite moderate midwifery knowledge'.[44] Meanwhile, the Registrar General's figures show that there were on average around 500 maternal deaths a year attributable to or associated with criminal abortion between 1928 and 1933.[45] Contemporary estimates of the number of illegal abortions taking place annually in the British Isles varied, but they inevitably exceeded the number of deaths attributed to the crime. For instance, the Interdepartmental Committee on Abortion, which reported in 1939, approximated that between 110,000 and 115,000 abortions took place annually, of which around 40 per cent were due to criminal interference.[46]

Incidences of abortion usually came to the notice of the authorities precisely because they had ended in the hospitalization or death of a pregnant woman. Conversely, an illegal abortion performed in secrecy could go undetected if a woman miscarried with no medical complications. Legal records are therefore no yardstick for the number of attempted, successful, or failed abortions. Police prosecutions and maternal mortality data provided the only official statistical measure of abortion, but even these are unreliable. The clandestine nature of abortion and the reticence of witnesses are understood to have led to large discrepancies between the number of actual incidences, cases known to the police, and prosecution rates.[47] Maternal mortality figures were notoriously problematic, with much confusion over the terminology used and the classification of maternal deaths.[48] Medical Officer of Health reports recorded few cases of intentionally induced abortion, while the records of hospitals and maternity units rarely specified a distinction between spontaneous and induced abortions among admitted patients.[49]

The 130 investigations and trials consulted for this study included indictments relating to 90 fatalities resulting from induced abortion. Strikingly, indictments also related to 93 non-fatal cases, although we cannot be sure whether these ever resulted in a successful abortion. The abortionists in the sample often claimed they had performed a number of successful terminations prior to their arrest, none of which had resulted in injury and, henceforth, detection. Previous clients of an abortionist might take the stand to testify they had undergone an abortion with no lasting damage. Acclaimed success may have been a defence tactic in court, but it might also imply competence on the part of at least some of these particular abortionists.

A high proportion of fatal abortions encountered in my research were procured via the syringing method at or beyond the third month of pregnancy.[50] As the stage of pregnancy advances, the risk of complications following an abortion increases.[51] This ultimately has implications for abortionists' knowledge of the attendant dangers. Some lay abortionists in the sample were not ignorant of gestation periods and the elevated risks, appearing to refuse compliance with requests from women who were too far advanced in their pregnancies, or who were unsure whether they were pregnant at all.[52] There is little evidence that sheds light on how lay abortionists learned to procure miscarriages or began to practise in the first place. We can therefore only surmise that such individuals, many of whom were mothers and grandmothers, were embedded in communities, and called upon to deal with these problems as they arose, much like the local handywomen who delivered babies and laid out the dead.[53] Especially in an era before hospital births became the norm, childbirth was an everyday neighbourhood event in which local women attended and participated.

This may have given some of them access to rudimentary knowledge of the pregnant body.

Medical authorities might take experience among lay abortionists as indication of obstetrical competence, turning this to their advantage in court. In January 1945, Violet Sprigens, a housewife from London, was sentenced to five years' imprisonment for the manslaughter of Elizabeth Moore. In a statement to the police, Sprigens admitted receiving Moore into her home. With Moore kneeling over a bowl, holding one leg up, Sprigens had administered a syringe of hot soapy water. Moore collapsed almost immediately. Unable to revive her, Sprigens waited with the body until her partner returned home and persuaded her to go to the police. A post-mortem examination, conducted by Spilsbury, revealed that Moore had been six months pregnant, not three and a half months as Sprigens protested. Police records revealed that the latter had been suspected of being an active abortionist for many years, first coming to their attention in 1934. A note to counsel, reporting on the evidence of Spilsbury, declared 'it is obvious that an abortionist of such long experience as the prisoner must have known that the deceased woman had been pregnant for longer than three months'.[54] Despite the evidence to suggest that Moore had died instantly, Sprigens was also condemned for leaving her 'uncovered on a cold stone floor for several hours without attempting to obtain any medical assistance, which was in itself more than likely to cause death or grievous bodily harm'.[55]

The health risks associated with the means of abortion were an important part of the state's armoury in its struggle against illegal operations, even though the number of attempted abortions, or injuries or deaths resulting from abortion attempts could not be measured statistically with any accuracy.[56] We have already seen how the estimated number of offences committed far exceeded the number of deaths attributed to abortion. Abortionists, especially the untrained, were condemned as unskilled and dangerous. The safer abortion was assumed to be the reserve of the qualified, medical practitioner, a view supported in fictional portrayals. Surprisingly few women die as a result of abortion in novels and films of the period. Indeed, an abortion death was even perceived as '*clichéd* and sentimental' in literary circles.[57] However, women who suffer badly do so at the hands of unqualified 'shady-looking', 'nameless' characters who perform 'blackguarrd [*sic*] work'.[58] Those women who do come away relatively unscathed overwhelmingly obtain help from doctors in private practice; their narrative conforms to the dominant discourse.

Since the 1800s, the medical profession had played a key role in shaping the legal regulation of abortion largely to suit their professional self-interests.[59] Successive abortion laws, culminating in the 1967 Abortion Act, delineated the field of competence for health practitioners, ensuring that abortion was brought under medical control and was not made available on an open market. Following the enactment of the 1861 legislation, The Infant Life (Preservation) Act (1929) prohibited the destruction of a child 'capable of being born alive', except for the purpose of saving the mother's life. According to the law, foetus viability was established at 28 weeks' gestation, and the abortion had to be performed in 'good faith' for the sole purpose of preserving the life of the mother. The Act simply extended the therapeutic proviso to the abortion law, outlined the circumstances under which a person would avoid criminal liability for destroying a child, and thereby provided a further defence of what was already taking place within the profession.[60]

Approval of therapeutic abortion was expressly confirmed from the bench during the trial and acquittal of Dr Aleck Bourne in 1938. Bourne had procured the abortion of a fourteen-year old girl who had been raped.[61] However, tacit sanctioning of the practice of abortion by medical professionals had been given long before. In 1920, Bernard Spilsbury announced at coroner's court: 'Operations for the removal of the products of pregnancy are under certain conditions necessary and justifiable. The conditions that necessitate them is that the life of the mother should be saved. Such an operation should never be performed by a respectable practitioner without consultation. That is a rule of the medical profession'.[62] Speaking here at the inquest into the death from abortion of Elsie Maud, Spilsbury drew on the double standard that characterized the medical profession's relationship with abortion, exposing the key loophole in the abortion law, and making a fellow professional appear to be an 'unrespectable' practitioner. Abortion was a legitimate, non-criminal operation if carried out by a qualified doctor, in consultation with other qualified doctors, and only then in order to save the life of the mother. Anyone performing outside these professional and ethical boundaries was classed a criminal. The doctor in this case, Paudit Devi Dayal Sasun, had not consulted a second opinion and had even attempted to conceal what he had done by dumping the dead woman's body on the street before alerting the police.[63] Dr Sasun had, on a number of occasions, been strongly suspected of procuring abortion. After his arrest, police found 400 names and addresses at his home in Southend-on-Sea, of which 116 were traced to incidents of criminal abortion.[64] A panel doctor in a poor district of the East End of London, Dr Sasun appears typical of those medical practitioners who came to the notice of the authorities, shunned by their social superiors because they 'lacked the professional and social skills to make a success of medical practice among patients with more than sixpence in their pockets'.[65] The legal records reveal a host of professional outcasts across the period – men of 'weak' or foreign medical credentials, foreign nationality, or ethnic minority.[66] On the fringes of the profession, these 'mavericks' did not enjoy collegial support.[67]

The medical profession defended their autonomy alongside their professional and scientific prestige through the courts and, in particular, through their role as expert witnesses at abortion trials. The use of 'expert' medical witnesses in criminal trials flourished in the late nineteenth and twentieth centuries. These 'experts' participated in the 'construction of facticity' and contributed 'to the apparent immutability of legal verdicts'.[68] Their opinion, generally supported by forensic proof, was often enough to cast doubt over the evidence of defendants and other witnesses, and to convince a jury of felonious intent. In providing evidence against irregular competition and 'quacks', such as in the case against the medical electrician Charles Jackson Palmer or the housewife Violet Sprigens, as well as against 'errant' members of their profession such as Dr Sasun, medical men constructed and reaffirmed medico-legal control over this sensitive and contested area of body politics.

The evidence of infection was key to establishing that an abortion had been procured illegally, with the use of instruments, under unsanitary conditions. Medical experts were again central to the stereotyping of lay abortionists. They were constructed as dirty, unhygienic, and life threatening – characteristics that were diametrically opposed to the sterile, hygienic, and safe standards exacted of the qualified doctor. As pathologist Keith Simpson expressed in court in 1941, 'the development of infection after abortion arouses suspicion that it was brought about instrumentally under unclean conditions'.[69] The labelling of abortionists as dirty, and as carriers of infection, reflected not only growing twentieth-century concerns of public health but it also associated the lack of cleanliness with dubious morals. The British Medical Association summarized attitudes of elite doctors when it called those 'unskilled' abortionists 'dirty in their person and careless in their method'.[70] Similar anxieties were at work in the state regulation of midwifery at the beginning of the twentieth century, where the desire to eradicate the Dickensian Sarah Gamp figure associated with maternal death, infanticide, and abortion stimulated the cleaning up and professionalizing of the service, the use of antiseptic procedures, and the restriction of midwives to 'normal' deliveries.[71] The trial and conviction of midwives for procuring abortion played a small but significant part in this process.[72]

It is unclear how individuals themselves interpreted the risks involved in procuring a miscarriage. Barbara Brookes argues that women knew from experience that abortion was relatively safe, despite what the medical profession said. Abortion, she argues, was 'the acceptable option and one far preferable to scandal, unemployment, or family poverty'.[73] Women may have also perceived the degree of risk differently to contemporary commentators, especially at a time when carrying a child to term brought its own very real threat of mortality.[74] Evidence certainly suggests, however, that exaggerated ideas relating to the unsanitary abortionist filtered through to popular perception. In an oral history study of abortion in South Wales, Kate Fisher found that individuals viewed a visit to an abortionist, as opposed to self-induced methods such as drugs or instruments, as the most risky method of inducing a miscarriage. This distinction, Fisher suggests, might partly be due to the fact that any resulting tragedy involving a third party was more likely to come to the public's attention through prosecutions and press reports of trials.[75] Furthermore, those in search of an abortionist sometimes refused to seek the help of those they perceived as 'dirty', either in terms of hygiene or morals. In the 1960s, for example, women wrote to the Abortion Law Reform Association of their determination not to resort to the sordid and dangerous back-street abortionist.[76] Correspondents instead asked for the names and addresses of reputable doctors who could help them out of their predicament, and others requested information relating to self-induced methods.[77]

Expressed awareness of the 'dangers' of back-street abortions may also bear the influence of broader improvements in medicine, health, and hygiene. The twentieth century witnessed major advances in medical knowledge and technologies, especially in the treatment of bacteria and disease. With the emergence of antibiotics, and the proliferation of products designed to rid the home of all traces of undesirable microbes, the fear and anxiety of dirt and disease was significantly lessened for those generations growing up after the Second World War.[78] If individuals could now feel a greater sense of control over their health and environmental conditions, they may have been more wary of procedures performed without these safeguards.

While remnants of the Sarah Gamp figure lingered on in popular fiction (the character of Winny in Nell Dunn's *Up the Junction* (1963) being a notable example), it was also common to find abortionists portrayed as observing the necessary hygiene, if not for entirely selfless motives.[79] In F. Tennyson-Jesse's *A Pin to See the Peepshow* (1934), the abortionist Mrs Humble 'at least, first scrubbed her hands, gnarled, but clean-looking hands, with carbolic soap and hot water'.[80] It is she who reminds the protagonist, Julia Almond, to keep herself clean: '[T]ake care of yourself', she says. 'Antiseptics, and all that. I'm careful myself. I've boiled everything, and I expect my patients to be careful too. It's hard on me when they ain't, see?'[81] Despite the cleanliness of her methods, an air of immorality and sordidness hangs over the activities of Mrs Humble. The illegal operations are performed above her little newspaper shop, which sits on a 'dark, irregular street with dingy little yellow-brick houses', and 'seemed more sinister than an ordinary house would have done'.[82]

While literary depictions perhaps owe more to the build-up of tension in abortion scenes than to accuracy, there is evidence in the legal records to support a claim that some abortionists took precautions to prevent sepsis, or at the very least understood that this was what might have been expected of them. A statement made to police in 1944 by Ethel Gibbons, a 57-year old married woman living in London arrested on suspicion of procuring the miscarriages of at least four women in an eight-month period, illustrates this point:

I have always used the syringe which was found by the Police under the mattress on the bed in my back bedroom on the first floor. I have used this with warm water and Lifebuoy soap and a drop of Dettol in it. The bowl the Police found I used to mix the soap and water and the penholder they also found I used to stir up the soap. This was so that I would not touch it with my hands.[83]

What is important here is Gibbons' use of antiseptic disinfectant and her attempt to hygienically prepare the syringe.

The notion that lay abortionists in particular posed a hazard permeated all levels of the investigative procedure. The standard police instruction book, issued in 1911, told officers investigating a possible case of abortion to perform a careful search for 'instruments or bottles which contain or have contained medicines or pills', as well as 'for instruments which may have been used'.[84] Here, abortion is situated within the realm of the doctor's surgery or the pharmacist's counter. However, Home Office proposals for a new instruction book, revealed in 1937, removed abortion from its medical setting and placed it firmly within domestic environs:

When making enquiry into a suspicious death, or when you have some other reason for thinking a crime of this nature has been committed, you should make a thorough search for anything which may have been used. Do not confine your search to looking for surgical or other special instruments, but remember that many simple domestic articles are often used for the purpose. The act is generally performed on the woman while she is in a recumbent position, and careful note should be taken of any article of furniture which offers an opportunity of being used as a medical couch. Innocent looking things such as crochet needles and wax tapers, accompanied by antiseptic douching, or even a wad of cotton wool smeared with an irritating substance applied internally, simply with the finger, are sometimes used. It is most important, therefore, that an exhaustive search for bottles or boxes which contain or have contained medicine, fluid of any kind, drugs, powders, pills or ointments; for instruments, douches, syringes, absorbents; for stains of any kind on beds, couches, armchairs, etc., and for any suspicious features that would indicate the commission of the crime. As certain traces of the crime are generally burned by the offender, a careful search should be made of firegrates and ashbins for deposits which might usefully be submitted to the analyst for examination.[85]

The above passage is evocative of the sort of discourse that guided prosecutions by the early decades of the twentieth century, when the non-medical practitioner was increasingly the target of law enforcers.[86] By positioning abortion within the home, involving everyday items like 'crochet needles and wax tapers', a firm distinction is drawn between medical and lay abortionists. The criminal suspect may not simply be the physician, surgeon, or chemist, but might also be the housewife. At the same time, the domestic environment metamorphoses into a clandestine surgery, equipped with its makeshift medical couch. However, the use of less advanced instruments, such as needles and douches, a lack of hygiene and anaesthetics, and the insertion of fingers into women's bodies marks a distinction, as Cornelie Usborne suggests in a study of abortionists in Weimar Germany, between the predominantly female, lay practitioners who act 'empirically relying on their senses', and the superior methods of the qualified, predominantly male, medics who are 'anti-empirical and indirect'.[87] The bogus surgery thus becomes an unskilled, dangerous place. The home is disturbed, stained by the offender's actions. Even the family hearth is not safe from the polluting touch of the abortionist. It is only when the domestic is sanitized by science, and when the evidence is submitted to forensic examination and analysis, that order can be restored.

While Home Office experts defined abortion as unclean using modern, pathogenic terms of bacterial transmission and hygiene, the operation's association with dirt and danger reflected enduring popular beliefs concerning the pollutant capabilities of the female body and its reproductive substances, particularly its 'decomposing matter' such as menstrual or postnatal blood.[88] In anthropological terms, Mary Douglas refers to dirt, the polluting matter, as 'a matter out of place', being 'the by-product of a systematic ordering and classification of matter'.[89] Stains were not in themselves unusual. Beds, couches, and armchairs were everyday items that furnished the setting of many sullying and polluting abortions, as practised by the unskilled and the unsanitary.

This study has illuminated several ways in which stereotypes of 'the abortionist' were created, reinforced, and occasionally challenged, with particular reference to the abortionist's method, skill, competence, and standard of hygiene. Furthermore, I have explored some of the rationales that sustained such typecasting. Thus, in twentieth-century English culture, the illegal abortionist was most often associated with the sphere of the low social class, the unskilled, the unclean, and the morally suspect. Moreover, on a methodological level the case study discussed here suggests that historical research does not exhaust itself in uncovering and representing empirical data. This is especially so when such data is itself likely to be incomplete and unrepresentative, as in the case of the criminalized act of abortion. Instead, only in a contextual analysis of various texts – medical, legal, oral, and literary – can we begin to discern why specific characterizations or labels were assigned in a specific context. These varied sources provide several interweaving and competing realities of the illegal abortionist that together make up the social and cultural history of this issue; and it is a history that continues to be retold. In 2004, *Vera Drake*, a film about a working-class housewife-abortionist in 1950s London, was released to critical and popular success.[90] *Vera Drake* perhaps offered the least sensationalized, fictional representation of a lay practitioner to date, and one most commensurate to the criminal trial evidence I have examined. Praised for its gritty realism and for 'stemming the flow of nostalgia',[91] the film was also criticized for being 'widely inaccurate' in terms of the method used by Vera (an injection of soapy water into the uterus), and for promoting 'the idea that abortion is easy – quick, clean, painless and successful'.[92] Thus, even today, when abortion can be practised legally up to the twenty-fourth week of pregnancy with medical approval, it seems that the illegal abortionist continues to hold a place in the popular imagination.[93]

NOTES

1. This has been more so the case for the United States; see Lucy Freeman, *The Abortionist by Dr X as told to Lucy Freeman* (London: Victor Gollancz, 1962); Allan Keller, *Scandalous Lady. The Life and Times of Madame Restell: New York's Most Notorious Abortionist* (New York: Atheneum, 1981); Clifford Browder, *The Wickedest Woman in New York: Madame Restell, the Abortionist* (Hamden, CT: Archon Books, 1988). For a more scholarly approach to a locally renowned English abortionist see Andrea Tanner, 'The Threepenny Doctor: Henry Percy Jelley of Hackney', *Journal of Medical Biography*, 10:1 (2002): 28–39. See also, Family Planning Association, *Abortion in Britain: Proceedings of a Conference Held by the Family Planning Association at the University of London Union on 22 April 1966* (London: Pitman Medical Publishing, 1966). Many of the various stereotypes surrounding the lay abortionist were replicated in the papers presented at this conference, but Moya Woodside's contribution, 'The Woman Abortionist' (pp. 35–38), based on interviews with 44 female offenders, challenged many of the prevailing views.

2. Held at The National Archives (TNA), Kew, London, these records were created by the Central Criminal Court (CRIM), the Assize courts (ASSI), the Metropolitan Police (MEPO), the Director of Public Prosecutions (DPP), and the Home Office (HO).

3. The first statutory prohibition of abortion was in 1803. Before this, abortion was permitted under English common law provided it was done before the act of quickening. On the evolution of abortion legislation in England, see John Keown,

Abortion, Doctors and the Law: Some Aspects of the Legal Regulation of Abortion in England from 1803 to 1982 (Cambridge: Cambridge University Press, 1988).

4. This term significantly implied that abortion could under certain conditions be lawfully procured, a loophole exploited by the medical profession in cases of therapeutic abortion; see Keown, *Abortion, Doctors and the Law*, Chapter 3; Barbara Brookes and Paul Roth, 'R. v. Bourne and the Medicalisation of Abortion', in *Legal Medicine in History*, ed. Michael Clark and Catherine Crawford (Cambridge: Cambridge University Press, 1993), pp. 314–43 (p. 314).

5. See Emma L. Jones, 'Abortion in England, 1861–1967' (University of London PhD Thesis, 2007), Chapters 4 and 5.

6. Examples include Rosamond Lehmann, *The Weather in the Streets* (London: Collins, 1936); Archibald Joseph Cronin, *The Citadel* (London: Victor Gallancz, 1937); Penelope Mortimer, *Daddy's Gone A-Hunting* (London: Michael Joseph, 1958); Jane Dunn, *Antonia White: A Life* (London: Jonathan Cape, 1998); Elizabeth Jane Howard, *Slipstream: A Memoir* (London: Macmillan, 2002); Selina Hastings, *Rosamond Lehmann* (London: Chatto and Windus, 2003).

7. Keown, *Abortion, Doctors and the Law*, p. 78.

8. In 1928 there were 1,000 members of the Medical Women's Federation in the UK, the largest number being in general practice. By 1944, women made up just less than 20 per cent of the entire medical profession in the UK; see Lesley A. Hall, 'Women in the Medical Profession: Some Figures', available at http://homepages.primex.co.uk/~lesleyah/wmdrsts.htm (accessed 4 June 2009).

9. See, for example, TNA: CRIM1/177/3; CRIM1/2629; CRIM1/3825; CRIM1/4271; CRIM1/4426; MEPO3/2578; MEPO2/10945; ASSI52/312.

10. TNA: ASSI52/312; MEPO3/856; CRIM1/774.

11. TNA: MEPO3/1015.

12. TNA: CRIM1/3350.

13. On the use of Utus paste, see Satya V. Sood, 'Termination of Pregnancy by the Intrauterine Insertion of Utus Paste', *The British Medical Journal*, 2 (8 May 1971): 315–17; Malcolm Potts, Peter Diggory and John Peel, *Abortion* (Cambridge: Cambridge University Press, 1977), p. 202.

14. TNA: ASSI52/312; TNA: MEPO3/1016. One of the female prisoners interviewed by Moya Woodside claimed that 60 per cent of married women used the Higginson Syringe regularly every month just to be sure they brought on their period; Woodside, 'The Woman Abortionist', in Family Planning Association, *Abortion in Britain*, p. 33.

15. TNA: CRIM1/40/7; CRIM1/162/4; MEPO2/10945; the latter was as late as 1967.

16. TNA: MEPO3/1020; CRIM1/1709; CRIM1/998; CRIM1/2139. Leading medical jurisprudence textbooks refer to the limited use of slippery elm bark in procuring abortion by the second half of the twentieth century; Alfred Swaine Taylor, *Taylor's Principles and Practice of Medical Jurisprudence*, 12th edition, ed. Keith Simpson (London: J. and A. Churchill, 1965), vol. 2, p. 94.

17. TNA: CRIM1/1537; MEPO3/1014; ASSI52/312; DPP2/647.

18. For popular fiction see Ménie Muriel Dowie, *Gallia* (London: Everyman, 1995; first published London: Methuen and Co., 1895), pp. 135–39; Jean Rhys, *Voyage in the Dark* (London: Penguin, 2000; first published London: Constable, 1934), p. 143; and Alan Sillitoe, *Saturday Night and Sunday Morning* (London: Flamingo, 1994; first published London: W. H. Allen, 1958), pp. 77–78, 85–91. The National

Birth-rate Commission (1916) reported on the use of knitting needles, crochet hooks, the boiling down of copper coins and drinking of the resultant liquor, quinine crystals, gin, and salts; see evidence of Miss Martin and Mrs Ring in National Birth Rate Commission (NBRC), *The Declining Birth-rate: Its Causes and Effects* (London: Chapman and Hall, 1916), pp. 274–27, 279–81. For memoirs, see Robert Roberts, *The Classic Slum: Salford Life in the First Quarter of the Century* (Manchester: Manchester University Press, 1971), pp. 99–100. For oral histories, see City of Liverpool Community College, Second Chance to Learn Group, *Women's History – Women's Lives, Can You Hear the Heart Beat? Childbirth and Birth Control 1920s–1980s* (Liverpool: City of Liverpool Community College, 1988), pp. 26, 39; Kate Fisher, '"Didn't Stop to Think, I Just Didn't Want Another One": the Culture of Abortion in Interwar South Wales', in *Sexual Cultures in Europe: Themes in Sexuality*, ed. Franz X. Eder, Lesley A. Hall and Gert Hekma (Manchester: Manchester University Press, 1999), pp. 213–32, (pp. 225, 231 n. 42).

19. TNA: HO45/24782.
20. TNA: HO45/24782.
21. Experiments with electricity to induce abortion had been carried out in America since 1901, as part of attempts to find a method to replace the D and C; see Tanfer Emin-Tunc, 'Technologies of Choice: A History of Abortion Techniques in the United States, 1850–1980' (Stony Brook University PhD Thesis, 2005).
22. TNA: HO45/24782.
23. Amelia Edith Huddleston Barr, *The Measure of a Man* (New York and London: D. Appleton and Co., 1915); Arthur Stuart Menteth Hutchinson, *This Freedom* (London: Hodder and Stoughton, 1922).
24. Iwan Rhys Morus, 'Bodily Disciplines and Disciplined Bodies: Instruments, Skills and Victorian Electrotherapeutics', *Social History of Medicine*, 19:2 (2006): 241–59.
25. See n. 20 above.
26. *The News of the World*, 29 January 1928, p. 4.
27. TNA: CRIM1/420; see also report of 'Medico-Legal: Conviction of a "Medical Electrician: Rex v. Palmer"', *The British Medical Journal*, 1 (4 February 1927): 202.
28. TNA: CRIM1/420. In 1965, Horace Jarvis, an 'osteopath, physiotherapist and naturopath', was alleged to have used the 'electrical method'. Medical evidence at the trial revealed the use of a syringe; see TNA: CRIM1/4426.
29. On moral panics, see Richard Davenport-Hines, *Sex, Death and Punishment: Attitudes to Sex and Sexuality in Britain since the Renaissance* (London: Collins, 1990); *Behaving Badly: Social Panic and Moral Outrage – Victorian and Modern Parallels*, ed. Judith Rowbotham and Kim Stevenson (Aldershot and Burlington, VT: Ashgate, 2003).
30. See, for example, Margaret L. Arnot 'Infant Death, Child Care and the State: the Baby–Farming Scandal and the First Infant Life Protection Legislation of 1872', *Continuity and Change*, 9.2 (1994): 271–311; R. v. Neil Walker and Gerald Norman (1930), TNA: MEPO3/1014; R. v. Thomas Mills (1954), TNA: CRIM1/2510.
31. TNA: MEPO3/1014.
32. Neil Walker was ordered to pay 20 shillings a week for the maintenance of the child; see TNA: MEPO1/1014.
33. *The Evening Standard*, 22 September 1930, in TNA: MEPO3/1014.
34. This 'shock' was most likely 'vaginal inhibition', in which the touching of the sensitive cervix and lower uterine segment initiates reflexes that could prove

instantly fatal when a patient is already taut and nervous; see Taylor, *Principles and Practice*, vol. 2. pp. 96–97.

35. Deposition of pathologist Francis Edward Camps in 1943; see TNA: CRIM1/1497.

36. Deposition of pathologist Donald Teare in 1961; see TNA: CRIM1/3745.

37. William A. Brend, *A Handbook of Medical Jurisprudence and Toxicology: For the Use of Students and Practitioners*, 3rd edition (London: C. Griffin and Co., 1919), p. 117.

38. Leslie Reagan shows this very clearly in the case of doctors and midwives in the US; see Leslie J. Reagan, *When Abortion Was a Crime: Women, Medicine, and Law in the United States, 1867–1973* (Berkeley: University of California Press, 1997), p. 79.

39. Taylor, *Principles and Practice*, vol. 2, p. 152.

40. Taylor, *Principles and Practice*, vol. 2, p. 153.

41. Deposition of pathologist Henry Bright Weir in 1921; see TNA: CRIM1/189/1.

42. Deposition of pathologist Bernard Henry Spilsbury in 1916; see TNA: CRIM1/162/4.

43. Deposition of pathologist Bernard Henry Spilsbury in 1927; see TNA: CRIM1/420. See also, TNA: CRIM1/152/1.

44. NBRC, *The Declining Birth-Rate*, p. 280.

45. The British Medical Association (BMA), *Report of Committee on Medical Aspects of Abortion* (London: British Medical Association, 1936), p. 21.

46. Ministry of Health, *Report of the Inter-Departmental Committee on Abortion* (London: H.M.S.O., 1939), p. 117.

47. Between 1900 and 1933, an average of 609 offences of abortion were known to the police, while an average of only 379 persons were brought to trial; see TNA: HO144/21168.

48. For a comprehensive discussion of the difficulties in measuring maternal mortality, see Irvine Loudon, *Death in Childbirth: An International Study of Maternal Care and Maternal Mortality, 1800–1950* (Oxford: Clarendon Press, 1992), Chapter 2.

49. To give an example, the number of patients treated for 'abortion' at the Bradford Municipal General Hospital in 1937 was 277, rising to 471 in 1947, but no indication is given as to the nature of these abortions; see Bradford City Council Medical Officer of Health Reports, 1937 and 1947.

50. We know this from the evidence of the individual women, and from the findings of post-mortem examinations.

51. Even with more advanced methods of medical termination, this is still the case; see Pro-Choice Forum, 'Late Abortion: A Review of the Evidence. A Briefing Compiled by the Pro-Choice Forum', pp. 3, 11–12; available online at http://www. prochoiceforum.org.uk/pdf/PCF_late_abortion08.pdf (accessed 4 June 2009).

52. TNA: CRIM1/3052; CRIM1/1068; CRIM1/3281.

53. On handywomen, see Nicky Leap and Billie Hunter, *The Midwife's Tale: An Oral History from Handywoman to Professional Midwife* (London: Scarlet Press, 1993). In her interviews with convicted female abortionists, Moya Woodside concluded that these women were seen as 'public benefactors' in their communities, where news spread of their services among friends and neighbours; see Woodside, 'The Woman Abortionist', in Family Planning Association, *Abortion in Britain*, pp. 36–37.

54. TNA: CRIM1/1652.

55. TNA: CRIM1/1652.

56. Naomi Pfeffer, 'Fertility Counts: From Equity to Outcome', in *Medicine, Health*

and the Public Sphere in Britain, 1600–2000, ed. Steve Sturdy (London: Routledge, 2002), pp. 260–78.

57. For this reason, Constable Publishing persuaded Jean Rhys to change the original ending of *Voyage in the Dark*, in which the protagonist dies as a result of an abortion; see 'Introduction', in Jean Rhys, *Voyage in the Dark* (Harmondsworth: Penguin, 2000), p. vii.

58. Hutchinson, *This Freedom*, p. 314; Elizabeth Robins, *The Convert* (London: Women's Press, 1980; first published London: Methuen and Co., 1907), p. 228.

59. Keown, *Abortion, Doctors and the Law*, Chapter 7.

60. On the use of the 1929 Act in abortion trials see Brookes and Roth, 'R. v. Bourne', in *Legal Medicine*, ed. Clark and Crawford, pp. 323–25.

61. On the significance of the Bourne case see Brookes and Roth, 'R. v. Bourne', in *Legal Medicine*, ed. Clark and Crawford, p. 315.

62. TNA: CRIM1/184/1.

63. TNA: CRIM1/184/1.

64. TNA: MEPO3/1007.

65. Tanner, 'The Threepenny Doctor', p. 32; R. v. Henry Percy Jelley, TNA: CRIM1/162/3.

66. TNA: CRIM1/152/1; CRIM1/162/3; CRIM1/177/3; CRIM1/184/1; MEPO3/1015; CRIM1/1600; CRIM1/2503; CRIM1/3350; CRIM1/3492; MEPO2/10945.

67. On maverick doctors and abortion see Angus McLaren, 'Illegal Operations: Women, Doctors, and Abortion, 1886–1939', *Journal of Social History*, 26:4 (1993): 797–816 (810).

68. Carol A. G. Jones, *Expert Witnesses: Science, Medicine and the Practice of Law* (Oxford: Clarendon Press, 1994), p. 5. See also Ian A. Burney, *Bodies of Evidence: Medicine and the Politics of the English Inquest, 1830–1926* (Baltimore and London: Johns Hopkins University Press, 2000); Katherine Denise Watson, 'Medical and Chemical Expertise in English Trials for Criminal Poisoning, 1750–1914', *Medical History*, 50.3 (2006): 373–90.

69. TNA: DPP2/856. See also TNA: CRIM1/1046; DPP2/1342; CRIM1/1472.

70. BMA, *Medical Aspects of Abortion*, p. 20.

71. Joan Mottram, 'State Control in Local Context: Public Health and Midwife Regulation in Manchester, 1900–1914', in *Midwives, Society and Childbirth: Debates and Controversies in the Modern Period*, ed. Hilary Marland and Anne Marie Rafferty (London: Routledge, 1997), pp. 134–52.

72. See, for example, the case of Nottingham midwife Annie Belshaw, who was convicted of abortion offences in 1917 and 1939. Shortly before her first conviction, the Central Midwives Board investigated Belshaw's practice and standards of hygiene. Describing Belshaw as 'dirty and untidy', inspectors found no nail brush or washable skirts among her kit; see TNA: DV5/120, and DPP2/647.

73. Barbara Brookes, *Abortion in England, 1900–1967* (London: Croom Helm, 1988), p. 42.

74. Before 1945, rates of infection and death among women giving birth under medical care in some institutions (for example, private nursing homes and hospitals) were significantly higher than for those giving birth at home; see Susan A. Williams, *Women and Childbirth in the Twentieth Century: A History of the National Birthday Trust Fund 1928–93* (Stroud: Sutton, 1997), p. 199.

75. Fisher, 'Didn't Stop to Think', in *Sexual Cultures*, ed. Eder, Hall and Hekma, p. 216.

76. 'Personal Predicament Letters', Abortion Law Reform Association Archive, Archives and Manuscripts (A&M), Wellcome Trust Library, London, A&M: SA/ALR/A.4/3/1–397; see items 2; 48; 96; 132; 141; 203; 251; 259; 296; 339; 356; 358.

77. A&M: SA/ALR/A.4/3/7; 57; 132; 134; 160; 167; 222; 279; 343; 387.

78. On antibiotics see Robert Bud, *Penicillin: Triumph and Tragedy* (Oxford: Oxford University Press, 2007). On home hygiene see Judy Giles, *The Parlour and the Suburb: Domestic Identities, Class, Femininity and Modernity* (Oxford: Berg, 2004), pp. 19–20, 117–18, 132, 159–61.

79. Nell Dunn, *Up the Junction* (London: Pan Books, 1968; first published London: MacGibbon and Kee, 1963), pp. 68–69.

80. Fryniwyd Tennyson Jesse, *A Pin to See the Peepshow* (London: Virago Press, 1994; first published London: William Heinemann, 1934), p. 286. The 'medical pranktitioner' in Bill Naughton's *Alfie* also displays an impeccable respect for hygiene, 'scrubbing and scrubbing his nails and his hands' and sterilizing the syringes 'like he was boiling lobsters for lunch'; see Bill Naughton, *Alfie* (London: MacGibbon and Kee, 1966), pp. 145–46; see also Sean Hignett, *A Picture to Hang on the Wall* (London: Joseph, 1966), p. 250.

81. Jesse, *A Pin to See the Peepshow*, p. 287.

82. Jesse, *A Pin to See the Peepshow*, pp. 285–88.

83. TNA: CRIM1/1612.

84. Extracted from the Liverpool Instruction Book, TNA: MH71/21, Paper 8, Appendix I.

85. TNA: MH71/21, Paper 8, Appendix II.

86. See also instructions for the investigation of domestic surroundings issued in the late 1960s, in Keith Simpson, 'Abortion Risks', in Family Planning Association, *Abortion in Britain*, pp. 51–53, 52; and the Association of Police Surgeons of Great Britain, *The Practical Police Surgeon* (London: Sweet and Maxwell, 1969), p. 169.

87. Cornelie Usborne, 'Wise Women, Wise Men and Abortion in the Weimar Republic: Gender, Class and Medicine', in *Gender Relations in German History: Power, Agency and Experience from the Sixteenth to the Twentieth Century*, ed. Lynn Abrams and Elizabeth Harvey (London: University College London Press, 1997), pp. 143–76 (p. 167).

88. For beliefs on the unseemliness and danger of menstrual blood and menstruating women, see Sophie Laws, *Issues of Blood: The Politics of Menstruation* (Basingstoke: Macmillan, 1990); on the perceived dangers of postnatal blood in the early twentieth century, see Mottram, 'State Control in Local Context', *Midwives, Society and Childbirth*, ed. Marland and Rafferty, pp. 142–43.

89. Mary Douglas, *Purity and Danger: An Analysis of Concepts of Pollution and Taboo* (London: Routledge and Kegan Paul, 1966), p. 35.

90. *Vera Drake* (directed by Mike Leigh; Alan Sarde and the UK Film Council, 2004). The film grossed a respectable $12,941,817 at the box office worldwide within eighteen months. It was nominated for three Oscars, and won thirty-three other awards, including three Baftas. Information taken from the International Movie Database, available online at http://www.imdb.com/title/tt0383694/business (accessed 4 June 2009).

91. Ryan Gilby, 'Reviews: "Vera Drake"', *Sight and Sound*, 15:1 (2005): 71–72.

92. Jennifer Worth, 'A Deadly Trade', *The Guardian* (6 January 2005), available online at

http://www.guardian.co.uk/film/2005/jan/06/health.healthandwellbeing (accessed 4 June 2009).

93. Since 1967, the illegal abortion era has continued to be a theme in British fiction; Graham Swift, *Waterland* (London: Heinemann, 1983), Elizabeth Jane Howard's *Cazalets* saga, including *The Light Years* (London: Macmillan, 1990) and *Marking Time* (London: Macmillan, 1991), and Sarah Waters, *The Night Watch* (London: Virago, 2006), are some prominent examples.

14

Afterword:
Reading History and/as Vision

KARÍN LESNIK-OBERSTEIN

Having read the fascinating collection of essays in this volume, I am struck afresh by two fundamental and enmeshed questions: how 'history' is produced and what that production may be seen to offer us. For what immediately became clear to me in considering these essays together is that the constitutions of the female bodies in the texts under consideration here, from early modern to twentieth century, on the one hand provide a reading of pasts which, seen retrospectively, may often seem unscientific, ignorant, or sexist compared to our present in terms of their claims to knowledge of female reproduction and sexuality; while on the other hand those problematic aspects may seem at once entirely current and pertinent to our present. I would suggest that this double effect may be attributed both, or either, to reading history as a production of the past in, and as, the present (as many thinkers have famously argued[1]), and/or to seeing the fundamental issues around female sexuality and reproduction that are further illuminated in the essays in this volume as remaining as pressing and relevant in our present as in the pasts examined here.

For across the essays two related issues recur insistently, to my reading: first, the positions of male authority, knowledge, and professionalism in relation to female authenticity, experience, and knowledge; and second, the crucial role of vision in securing male authority over female experience. The essays vary in their claims to locate the most significant historical period in terms of the development of male medical dominance over the female body from the early sixteenth to the late nineteenth centuries, but they are unanimous in diagnosing and charting this development. The essays differ, too, in terms of their theoretical formulations and premises, sometimes overtly but more often implicitly. Some seem more certain that this is, after all, a *progressivist* history, in which whatever ideological doubts may still be brought to bear upon current views of female sexuality and reproduction, past ignorance, superstition and sexism have nevertheless been superseded by scientific and medical, clinical, and factual knowledge. Other essays, on the other hand, seem to ally themselves with the view that, anyway, *all* ideas of female sexuality and reproduction, past and present, and whether or not they are claimed to be scientific and clinical, are necessarily constructed. These two parameters are by now a well-known feature of theorizing about the body, as Judith Butler, who is perhaps the most famous theorist of the body (although she is not explicitly referenced in the essays in this volume), has repeatedly discussed when clarifying her own arguments about the body as entirely constructed (where 'construction' does not refer to a secondary 'invention' on top of an established and knowable real or materiality; nor does it constitute an irrationalist refutation of science, many mistaken critiques to the contrary[2]).

In any case, the issues of history and vision are themselves also enmeshed with the body seen as – at least in some respects – transhistorical in its factuality (sometimes called 'anatomy' or 'biology' or 'materiality'), or as entirely constructed (where 'anatomy', 'biology' or 'materiality' are constructed, too). Both positions leave questions to wrestle with in terms of the production of history and/as vision. In the first case, the difficulty is that history is transcended willy-nilly by those aspects of the body – however residual – that are claimed to be knowable no matter what. Here, the retrospective vision must also necessarily claim for itself, overtly or implicitly, the final achievement of knowledge of these truths about the body. In the second case, the problem arises of how the body – or gender, or sexuality, or reproduction – can be read as such at all, not only in pasts but even across presents, for what, then, can be recognized as such, and how?

All the essays in this volume are in some way implicated in these issues while they retrieve and reconsider texts and contexts. In this sense, they may indeed all cause us to review whether these histories are about pasts that are *different* from each other and/or from our present, or whether they are about *similarity* to each other and/or our present. One way to consider this further is to suggest that where opposition is read between a masculine authority imposed on female bodily experience, the question must be raised (again as, indeed, it has been in much prior writing about the body) whether this dichotomy is not itself a product of reigning epistemes (past and/or present). In other words, whether the idea that the female body is a body of 'experience' rather than of authority is not itself a particular and specific construction.

In any case, such a position allows us to read the ongoing, current pertinence of the two uniting concerns of all of these essays. For we may consider how it can be argued that medical obstetrics and gynaecology continue to be the preserve of claims to authority over female sexuality and reproduction (despite now being practised by individual male and female medical professionals), and that vision continues to play a central role in securing that authority. These continuities may still be traced with respect to contraception, abortion, masturbation, pregnancy, and labour, as is mentioned in the essays in this volume and also in what may seem to be the related but 'newer',[3] (even) more 'scientific', areas of reproductive technologies, genetics, and evolutionary psychology. For in these fields not only are female sexuality and reproduction still often subjected to a masculine authority, knowledge, and vision (again, even when they are also practised by female medical professionals) but also the female body is still often constructed as the source of an authentic, self-speaking 'experience'.

One crucial problem that continues to proliferate on the basis of this underpinning dichotomy (as several writers have analysed[4]) is, for instance, the discussion, which is endlessly recycled not just in the popular press, but also in many academic (including medical) publications, around 'medical' labour versus 'natural' labour and, as a parallel, 'scientific' bottle-feeding versus 'natural' breastfeeding.[5] As long as the first are seen as the scientifically sophisticated saviours of victim-women (and babies) who are not just powerless to save themselves, but have no possible knowledge on which to draw to do so; and the second are seen as happening through instinctive, 'earth mother', powers that are situated authentically and spontaneously in the female body, this discussion can only have one outcome. Where the 'natural' option is preferred, or even passionately defended, it has, by definition, no means of implementing itself. It is either 'naturally' successful, by itself (albeit with perhaps some advice or support from a sympathetic midwife or health visitor), or it fails without recourse to any other possibility than to turn to the scientific saviours. Therefore, the very construction of this 'naturalness' makes it by definition the 'lesser' or 'vulnerable' option, *even when* it is advocated. The 'scientific' option has all the knowledge, options, interventions and procedures on its side, whereas the 'natural' option has only that: its 'naturalness'. As Rayna Rapp writes of Brigitte Jordan's classic 'closely grounded ethnographic account of how medical authority is socially constructed and maintained through the messiness of birth in a North American hospital',[6]

> second stages of labour are recorded [by the nurses] in compliance with ritual exigencies, not rational measurements; doctors' entrances are staged in a manner as grand as the entrada of Aida. [...] authoritative knowledge isn't produced simply by access to complex technology, or an abstract will to hierarchy. It is a way of organizing power relations in a room that makes them literally unthinkable in any other way. [...] Jordan's method, [...] makes visible the enormous work required to impose a consensual reality across power differences.[7]

The arguments and analyses here of Jordan, Davis-Floyd, Sargent, and Rapp are not, then, about proselytizing for a return to 'natural' childbirth, but about analysing for our present, in exactly the same way as the essays in this volume do for pasts, how, as Carol MacCormack argues, 'The concepts of "natural childbirth" and "natural fertility" are *cultural* constructs', too.[8]

This continuity between pasts and presents, which again may be considered as being about something more, or other, than simply continuity, is also clearly visible – in, for instance, the recent development (2008) in the Netherlands of a 'birthing machine', which bears an uncanny resemblance to those described in this volume, particularly in Pam Lieske's chapter on obstetrical machines in eighteenth-century Britain. This new 'patient simulator' is, exactly as Lieske describes those in the eighteenth century, 'a torso with the legs amputated above the knees',[9] and is described as 'true to life' and as 'making it possible to practice emergency situations in birth in a true-to-life manner. By developing materials and sensors further, we have been able to approach reality extremely closely'.[10]

New reproductive technologies also demonstrate how vision, too, has, if anything, only expanded further as the underpinning of the claim of science as authority in the areas of female reproduction and sexuality. Anthropologist Marilyn Strathern writes, '[i]n traditional Euro-American thinking, the mother's identity is created by her offspring in the act of her (visibly) giving birth [...] to see a mother is thus to recognise a natural connection'.[11] Anthropologist Sarah Franklin traces the development of this 'traditional' visuality into the present:

> Visualizing and imaging technologies are critical to the technical and discursive apparatus of assisted reproduction. The development of a light source to enhance laparoscopic technique, for example, was a critical achievement in the realization of successful IVF. Scanning, screening, laparoscopy, x-rays, and powerful microscopic techniques are essential for both research and clinical technique in reproductive medicine. Hence the importance of feminist understandings of the patriarchal nature of clinical gaze.[12]

This vision which, as I have argued extensively elsewhere,[13] is the guarantor for the production of the 'own child' that reproductive technologies were invented for, can also be traced further, into the present, in, for instance, the roles of obstetrical ultrasound. Janelle S. Taylor is one of several researchers who argue that one role attributed to these images (specifically in American culture in this case) is that of promoting and regulating 'bonding' between mother and baby, and that

> The notion of ultrasound 'bonding' equates pregnancy with the relationship

between a woman and her newborn child. In this regard, it presumes a view of pregnancy as absolute, a relationship of unconditional maternal love for the developing fetus. At the same time, however, the ultrasound 'bonding' theory suggests that this relationship forms through techno-logically and professionally mediated spectatorship, and even implies that it is the technology itself that in some sense 'gives birth', to the fetus, construed as a child.[14]

As Taylor suggests, reproduction, labour and birth can under these conditions be conceived of not just as under male control, but as a male production *tout court*.

These issues pose the well-known paradox that the more technology is developed around female reproduction and sexuality, the more it may allocate a central role not to women, but to the technology *of* and *as* the masculine. To clarify, I do not mean to suggest, as some feminist criticism has, that technology is inherently an imposition on the feminine – an alien force to an 'organic' femininity, or a necessarily oppressive mechanism – but instead, as I wrote above in relation to the female body constructed as 'experience', that technology, too, can be analysed for its construction, and use, as masculine or feminine. Indeed, the achievement of the essays in this collection seems to me to be that they demonstrate across a range of periods, texts, and contexts, exactly how such constructions can be analysed from various perspectives.

It is in the senses explored above, then, that I have wondered through my reading of this volume how histories and literatures of the past can be read as being simultaneously narratives of our present. The anthropologists I have drawn on can in this sense, then, indeed be read as the historians of our present, and the historians and literary critics writing in this volume as the anthropologists of the past. In all cases, it seems to me, they demonstrate powerfully how much there is to say, and remains to be said, about the female body, and how, and why.

NOTES

1. There are, of course, many examples, but one might mention some as diverse as Freud's thinking on memory as a production of the past in and as the present, the work of the historians Philippe Ariès, Hayden White and Michel Foucault, or of the literary theorist Roland Barthes. See, in particular, Sigmund Freud, *Introductory Lectures on Psychoanalysis*, trans. James Strachey and Angela Richards (Harmondsworth: Penguin, 1991); Philippe Ariès, *Centuries of Childhood*, trans. Robert Baldick (London: Penguin, 1973); Hayden White, *Metahistory* (Baltimore, MD: Johns Hopkins University Press, 1973); Roland Barthes, 'The Discourse of History', in *The Postmodern History Reader*, ed. Keith Jenkins (London: Routledge, 1997), pp. 120–39.

2. I have extensively discussed these problematic understandings of Judith Butler's work elsewhere as being about a secondary 'constructedness', as well as misunderstandings of such (de)constructive theorizing as necessarily constituting an irrationalist refutation of science. See Karín Lesnik-Oberstein, *On Having an Own Child. Reproductive Technologies and the Cultural Construction of Childhood* (London: Karnac Books, 2008); Judith Butler, *Bodies That Matter: On The Discursive Limits of 'Sex'* (London: Routledge, 1993).

3. For an excellent argument that reproductive technologies need not be seen merely as recent technical innovations, as well as for a thorough consideration of the role of vision with respect to reproduction, see Susan Merrill Squier, *Babies in Bottles. Twentieth-Century Visions of Reproductive Technologies* (New Brunswick, NJ: Rutgers University Press, 1994).

4. See, for instance, Robbie E. Davis Floyd and Caroline F. Sargent (eds.), *Childbirth and Authoritative Knowledge. Cross-Cultural Perspectives* (Berkeley, CA: University of California Press, 1997).

5. For a classic analysis of cultural images of bottle-feeding (as good because commercial and 'scientific') versus breastfeeding (as 'natural' but *therefore* undesirably sexual, unmeasurable and uncontrollable), see Jack Newman and Teresa Pitman, *The Ultimate Breastfeeding Book of Answers. The Most Comprehensive Problem-Solving Guide to Breastfeeding from the Foremost Expert in North America* (New York: Three Rivers Press, 2006).

6. Rayna Rapp, 'Foreword', in Robbie E. Davis Floyd and Caroline F. Sargent (eds.), *Childbirth and Authoritative Knowledge. Cross-Cultural Perspectives* (Berkeley, CA: University of California Press, 1997), pp. xi–xii (p. xii).

7. Rapp, 'Foreword' in Floyd and Sargent (eds.), *Childbirth and Authoritative Knowledge.*

8. Quoted in Robbie E. Davis Floyd and Caroline F. Sargent, 'Introduction. The Anthropology of Birth', in Floyd and Sargent (eds.), *Childbirth and Authoritative Knowledge.* pp. 1–55 (p. 5) (author's emphasis).

9. Pam Lieske, '"Made in Imitation of Real Women and Children": Obstetrical Machines in Eighteenth-Century Britain', see Chapter 5 in this volume. For a photograph of the recent machine, where its close similarity to the eighteenth century models may be noted, visit http://www.trotsemoeders. nl/2008/06/26/robot-verkleint-sterfkans-bij-bevalling.

10. The simulator was designed by the Technical University of Eindhoven in the Netherlands, in cooperation with the European Design Centre (EDC). Information from: http://www.nursing.nl/home/nieuw/1772/nieuwe-simulator-verkleint-sterfkans-bij-bevalling (translation from the original Dutch my own).

11. Marilyn Strathern, *Reproducing the Future. Essays on Anthropology, Kinship and the New Reproductive Technologies* (Manchester: Manchester University Press, 1992), p. 149.

12. Sarah Franklin, 'Postmodern Procreation: A Cultural Account of Assisted Reproduction', in *Conceiving the New World Order. The Global Politics of Reproduction*, ed. F. D. Ginsburg and R. Rapp (Berkeley, CA and Los Angeles, CA: University of California Press, 1995), pp. 323–45, available at http://www. hsph.harvard.edu/rt21/globalism/FRANKLIN_Postmodern.html.

13. See Lesnik-Oberstein, *On Having an Own Child.*

14. Janelle S. Taylor, 'Image of Contradiction: Obstetrical Ultrasound in American

Culture', in Sarah Franklin and Helena Ragoné (eds.), *Reproducing Reproduction: Kinship, Power, and Technological Innovation* (Philadelphia, PA: University of Pennsylvania Press, 1998), pp. 15–45 (p. 23).

Index

The letter n indicates an endnote

gazing
  in anatomy theatres 42–3
  in Brontë's *Villette* 128, 129–30
  in du Maurier's *Rebecca* 190
  penetrative 180n41
  in Pygmalion myth 127
  scientific 43, 53
  specula as 175
Gélis, Jacques 38
General Lying-in Hospital (London) 76
General Medical Council 176
generation theories 16–21
The Gentleman's Magazine 22, 24
Gibbons, Ethel 207
Gilbert, Pamela K.: *Disease, Desire, and the Body in Victorian Women's Popular Novels* 166n7
Gilroy, Amanda 104n30
Goldsmith, Elsie 199
Gowing, Laura 52, 57
Green, Monica 38
Greene, Anne 51–4, 59, 60, 61–2, 63–4
Greenslade, William: *Degeneration, Culture, and the Novel* 140
Grew, Nehemiah 69–70
Groneman, Carol: *Nymphomania* 123
Guillemeau, Jacques: *Child-Birth, or The Happy Deliverie of Women* 40
guilt, sexual 123–4
gynaecologists 7, 120, 124, 130, 141
gynaecology
  definition 6
  knowledge of 46–7
  and masturbation 119
  as a medical specialty 38
  and midwifery 120
  and morality 120
  and obstetrics 120, 141
  Victorian era 115, 120–1

Haighton, John 28–9
Hamilton, William 112
handywomen 202
Harley, David 25
Harris, Ruth 8
Harrison, Barbara 7
Harvey, William: *Exercitationes de Generatione Animalium* 17

Harvie, John 80–1
herbal remedies 24
Higgins, Godfrey 112–13
Hill, Susan: *Mrs de Winter* 192, 195n19
Hippocrates 17
Hirsch, E. Seth 144
Hirst, Barton Cooke: 'The Newer Gynaecology' 141
The Historical Review of British Obstetrics and Gynaecology: 1800–1950 144
Hitchcock, Alfred: *Rebecca* (film) 186
homosexuality
  in du Maurier's *Rebecca* 184
  and heterosexuality 168n35
  see also lesbianism
Horsley, Dr 79
hospitals 76, 114
  abortions 202
  childbirth 213n74, 218
Hunt, Alan 168n35
Hunter, William 81
  The Anatomy of the Gravid Uterus Exhibited in Figures 69
hydrocephalus 26
hygiene
  abortionists 205, 206, 208
  obstetric instruments 28
hysterectomies 141
hysteria 3

illegitimacy 24
Infant Life (Preservation) Act (1929) 204
infanticide 24–5, 51, 52
  law 53–4, 56
Interdepartmental Committee on Abortion 201
Irwin, Joyce 20

Jackson, Mark 65n10
James, Robert 18
Jarcho, Julius 139, 140, 145
Jarvis, Horace 211n28
Jesse, F. Tennyson: *A Pin to see the Peepshow* 206
Jesus Christ 19, 112
Johnson, Samuel 21
Jonson, Ben 35
Jordan, Brigitte 218, 219